The Recommender Revolution

The Recommender Revolution

WHY GOOD
REVIEWS ARE
THE BEST ADS FOR
YOUR BRAND

Jan Van den Bergh

LANNOO
CAMPUS

PUBLISHING HOUSE LANNOOCAMPUS
Erasme Ruelensvest 179 bus 101
B-3001 Leuven (Belgium)
www.lannoocampus.com

Original title: IK BEN EEN AANRADER
Design: PASCAL VAN HOOREBEKE

© JAN VAN DEN BERGH & UITGEVERIJ LANNOO NV,
TIELT, 2013
LannooCampus is part of the Lannoo Group.

D/2012/45/355
ISBN 978 94 014 0357 3
NUR 802, 803

Recommenders are certainly not some kind of modern-day Don
Quixotes, fighting the forces of evil with their egos and their self-proclaimed omniscience. Nor are they virally operating super-influentials
or a human form of the advertising bacteria that has infected the entire
world. No, as already mentioned recommenders are a very large group
of ordinary people who collectively dump their personal experiences of
a product or service into a gigantic database, with the aim of sharing
those experiences with other consumers via various different platforms.

If you can recognise yourself in this description, then you are
probably a recommender, too! You are the person we are talking
about! And if you don't quite see yourself in this light, there will
almost certainly be other people in your immediate environment
who match the profile perfectly. Possibly quite a few. In fact, you
can safely assume that some 15% of your circle of family, friends,
neighbours and colleagues are recommenders.

WHERE DOES THIS 15% COME FROM?

In one sense, this is a purely arbitrary figure. It might just as easily be 12%
or 17%. You can compare the figure with the 1% or 0.1% that the Occupy
Movement is constantly referring to, in its attempt to define the world's
group of mega-rich people. Likewise, back in 1906 Pareto developed
his famous 80/20 rule simply because at that time 80% of land in Italy
was owned by just 20% of the population. In other words, you can draw
your own dividing lines to decide who is a recommender and who is not.
My 15% have lots more friends and acquaintances than the others.
But just how many must a recommender have?
My 15% talk a lot more with these friends and acquaintances about brands.
But how often should this be?
And these friends and acquaintances allow themselves to be more
influenced by my 15% than by other people.
But to what extent?

A recommender is not by definition, nor by nature, someone who
actively seeks to influence others. He is not a preacher, looking to
convert the world. Nor is he a salesman in disguise. In fact, he is not
even per se an efficient influencer. In terms of direct influence, it takes
two to tango: there needs to be someone to do the recommending and
someone to take on board what is being recommended. But this is not
how a recommender works. Recommenders work alone, although
they understand that they are also part of a much larger group.

John the Baptist was a preacher – an extreme form of recommender – who not only appears in the Christian Bible, but also in the Koran. In the Muslim tradition, he is known as Yahya – but they are one and the same person.

If no one from the recommender's immediate circle of family and friends allows themselves to be persuaded by his recommendations, he has no direct influence. He is then like a lonely preacher, wandering in the desert and proclaiming his message to the unresponsive rocks and stones. This is not a lot of fun. What's more, it can even be dangerous. Just ask John the Baptist: it cost him his head! Nobody wanted to hear what he had to say, and so they found a way to keep him quiet – permanently. Knowingly or unknowingly, operating as part of a larger group therefore has its advantages. Fortunately for John, Caravaggio decided to immortalise the unsung prophet in one of his greatest works, painted in 1608.[1] And so the Baptist's message lives on, even if only in oils and canvas.

In this book we will not be discussing John the Baptist-type figures, nor will we be looking at individual recommenders. Instead, I will be focusing on recommenders *as a group*; on the complex interplay between the recommenders themselves and on the relationship between the recommenders and the non-recommenders. Particular attention will be paid to the unpredictable attitudes, movements and balances within the recommender group, which often foreshadow the future reactions of the other 85%.

There have always been recommenders and there always will be: at all times and in all places. However, since the advent of the internet, they have been given – or have taken – a much more important role than in the past. How did this happen? What is their current status? Why are they more important than you probably think? Read on, and you will discover the answers to these and many other relevant questions.

THE RECOMMENDER IN THE INTERNET ERA

Recommenders give their opinion about something, whether people ask them to or not. In fact, they give opinions about almost every-

THE FOUR CONSUMER SEGMENTS	THE QUIET ONES	THE DOUBTERS	THE WHISPERERS	THE 15% OF RECOM- MENDERS
EXAMPLE 1				
Number of times per year that they talk about brands via Twitter, blogs, Facebook,...	10	20	40	80
The number of people in their online and offline circle of acquaintances, who might hear their opinions	20	40	80	120
The total number of brand-related messages that the four segments transmit	200	800	3.200	9.600
The total number of transmitted messages.				13.800
The share of voice of each of the four segments	1,45%	5,80%	23,2%	69,6%

EXAMPLE 2				
Number of times per year that they talk about brands via Twitter, blogs, Facebook,...	20	40	80	260
The number of people in their online and offline circle of acquaintances, who might hear their opinions	40	80	120	240
The total number of brand-related messages that the four segments transmit	800	3.200	9.600	62.400
The total number of transmitted messages.				62.900
The share of voice of each of the four segments	1,1%	4,2%	12,6%	82,1%

thing. Also about brands. Sometimes diplomatically. Sometimes with brutal frankness. In the tables on the previous page you will find two examples of a purely hypothetical division of the consumer community into four segments. [2] The segmentation has been made on the basis of the number of times they talk about a brand, the number of brands they talk about, the number of people who might be able to hear their opinions and the total number of messages they transmit.

The first example is minimalist and assumes the people talk relatively little about relatively few brands. Which, in my humble opinion, probably reflects reality.

The second example is more optimistic, and is based on an assumption that more people talk about more brands.

At the bottom of each table, you will find the 'share of voice' (SOV) for each of the four segments: this quantifies the relative weight of each group within the totality of what can be described as word-of-mouth (WOM) advertising.

If you play with these figures realistically (and not surrealistically), you will notice that the 15% of recommenders account for between 70 and 80% of the brand messages transmitted to consumers. And, as we have already mentioned, this transmission – the pushing of information in the direction of the listener – is not even the essence of the matter. The real essence is the amount of information they make available to others, the pool of searchable data they create via a blog, in a portal or on a review site, which allows the consumer, armed with his Google search robot, to find an answer to the questions: What should I choose? What should I buy?

They manage to chat and type their way to this high share of voice by virtue of the fact that they communicate their opinions about brands to other people several times or more each month. They are also fans of a larger number of brands, which they like to talk about or write about with enthusiasm. And perhaps most important of all: they have more friends and followers than the other three consumer segments.

The crux of this book is not concerned with the question of whether the hundred consumers in the table transmit 13,800 messages or 76,000 messages to the waiting world. This, in itself, is not relevant. The key issue is the value of the famous 15% within the total communication mix. I like to refer to them as the 'human media', in contrast to what I call other 'non-human media': a reflection of the analogue and digital media that we all consume each day.

Yet there is more to it than that. Equally important is the 'purifying' role that the 15% play in respect of brands, both in terms of the market and in terms of society as a whole. For this reason, I also like to call them the '*guerrilla consumers*'.

A word of warning, however. Don't allow yourself to be overwhelmed or disappointed by the above hypotheses and the figures in the tables. The group of your most intimate acquaintances – the people that you most trust and with whom you communicate most frequently, at least once per week by mail, internet, phone or in person – will be fairly small; perhaps ten people at most.[3]

This group probably contains one and a half recommenders. Someone that you can approach to ask questions about the best diet, the best running shoes, the best wine for less than €15 euros per bottle. But no more than this. No one is a self-proclaimed expert in everything. In other words, you need more recommenders than the people you know personally.

If you are planning to buy a new television (or camera, or frying pan or depilator), you will need to find information from a wider circle of people, perhaps thirty or forty in number, who you know less well but whose taste and knowledge is more in keeping with the things that currently interest you. But this is also where things usually tend to stop.

If you want to go a stage further, you can always post your question about the best place to buy a frying pan on Twitter, but it is doubtful if you will get sufficient reaction to make a well-considered decision. (Personally, I would recommend Greenpan.)

The safest way to make your decision about a choice of product (unless you are a member of a consumer association) is to consult one of the many review sites: Tripadvisor, IMDB, Powerreviews, Kurkdroog, Yelp or one of literally hundreds of others. Perhaps also my site Holaba in China (see chapter 2). These are the places where you can find the recommendations of the recommenders. I now even use Amazon as a review site and then buy on iTunes. Amazon will not be amused!

The collective impact of digital 'user generated evaluations' (UGE), in many cases based on personal experiences, give modern consumers a power that they never had during the pre-internet era. During this era, offline conversations were the most important aspect of inter-

**THE MANY PEOPLE
I NEED TO THANK**

I have included in the following list the names of all the people who helped me with this project during the first half of 2012. In particular, the people whose names are annotated with a 'P' for proof-reader have ensured – by repeatedly pointing out the shortcomings in both my reasoning and my writing style – that this book (hopefully) can also be 'recommended': Alain Thys (P), Arlette De Pauw, Ben Caudron (P), Berrie Pelser, Bram Van den Bergh (P), Clo Willaerts (P), Coenraad de Vos Steenwijk, David Leyssens, Dirk Rodriguez, Frank Bekkers, Fred Reichheld, Geert Debecker (P), Gemme van Hasselt (P), Hans Similon, Hedwig Bogaerts (P), Ilse Godts (P), Iris Dochy (P), Jan Rezab, Jan-Willem Van Beek, Jelle Van den Bergh, Jess Huang, John Kearon, Liesbeth Theeuws (P), Louis Ingelaere (P), Karen Nelson-Field, Marc Roisin, Mark Schaefer, Menno Lanting, Michael de Kruijf, Nico Schoonderwoerd, Nicole Berx (P), Peter Saerens, Rob Markey, Roland Van der hoff, Sinan Aral, Stefan Kolle (P), Ted Rubin, Thomas Marzano, Wenli Liao, Zlatan Menkovic, Viralheat, Klout, Peerreach, Engagor, Metavana, Kred, The Gem, KLM, Trader Joe's, Holaba Dataotuan, Futurelab & Wonderful Alice.

---

consumer communication. These good, old-fashioned 'chin-wags' (in bed, in the pub, in the sports club, on the telephone) are still the decisive factor today, but the effect of everything that the recommenders say has been immeasurably strengthened by the internet. A consumer no longer hears just one voice (the voice of someone from his intimate circle of family and friends), but instead hears a thousand and one different voices, sometimes in agreement but just as often in disagreement. And this dissonance is precisely what the consumer is looking for: he wants to hear the pros and cons before he decides – in the delusion that his decision will then be a rational one.

The recommenders and the platforms on which they operate have a healthy and purifying effect from two different perspectives. Because the various platforms allow people to distinguish good from bad, not only do consumers know what they should buy but the companies can also identify the strong and weak elements in their product portfolios. Brands that are more frequently recommended than other brands will grow more quickly than those other brands. Brands that are less frequently recommended, or are even criticised, will shrink or perhaps disappear altogether. The evidence for this is clear – although we hesitate to use the word 'scientific'.

If marketing can be described as the attuning of products and services to the needs of their market, then the 15% of recommenders are worth their weight in gold. Also for the companies. All the more so because they automatically support the good products – which can drastically reduce communications costs.

IS THIS BOOK WORTH 'RECOMMENDING'?

As far as the credibility of this book is concerned, you can already assume that you will be confronted with a number of suppositions, hypotheses and unanswered questions. It would, of course, be nonsense to say that I know nothing about my subject – but I certainty don't know everything. And I don't believe in selling hot air. Even so, I have been actively studying this phenomenon since day 1 of the internet back in 1994 and in recent years my investigations have been continued within the context of my operations in China. But many things are still unclear to me – as they are to everyone in this field of specialisation. In part, the reason for this is that we are yet to feel the full effect of the data and network tsunami that will soon sweep over all of us, inextricably linking everyone and everything, whether we like it or not.

As you read, you will gradually learn to sense the difference between the matters where I am almost arrogantly certain of my ground (until the contrary has been proven) and the many developments that are still shrouded in doubt, even for an insider like myself. Please forgive me for these momentary shortcomings; after all, I am only human!

Remember also that you don't need to read this book from cover to cover. You can start it at the end or in the middle. In fact, just dip in anywhere you like. It is not a novel and I have few 'scientific' pretensions. Likewise, it is neither a 'do' book nor a 'how to' book. Desperate marketeers will need to search for their instant remedies elsewhere. It is simply a plea that you should devote greater attention – hopefully much more than is currently the case – to the people who have an opinion about your brand. I repeat: they are worth their weight in gold. And not just for you. But for everyone.

For further inquiries contact me at: jevedebe@gmail.com

For further information on our research methodology at Holaba China: www.holaba.com.cn

1 Recommenders: viewing matters from a personal perspective

- 'Should I recommend something' is just as tricky and introspective a question as: 'Should I follow that advice'.
- What a recommender writes or says is never objective. It is always relative and only becomes a recommendation if someone follows the advice.
- A positive recommendation for something is, by definition, also a negative recommendation for something else. This might seem to be a problem for the seller whose products are not positively recommended, but it may prompt him to organise a big clean-out – something that every company needs to do every once in a while.
- Recommenders are not happier than ordinary people. They are simply more prepared to share with others the intense moments of happiness they occasionally experience as a result of a brand that pleasantly surprises them. And their recommendation of that brand makes them even happier.
- In the Net Promotion System (NPS) surveys carried out in the United States, JetBlue often comes out on top. Not American Airlines. JetBlue has initiated its own NPS programme and they calculate the ROI (return on investment) on this programme – and the figures are compelling. For every five promoters (positive recommenders who give them a score of 9 or 10), they win on average an additional two customers. However, it takes sixteen detractors (negative recommenders who give a score between 0 and 6) before they lose a single client.

A few weeks before I flew to America to make a study visit in preparation for this book, I read a short recommendatory piece in the *De Standaard* newspaper about a hotel in New York. I immediately booked a room, without stopping to consult Tripadvisor, the hotel and restaurant review site. This is something that in other circumstances I never fail to do. Normally, I like to be well-informed about the bed that is waiting for me on arrival and I always try to imagine what my room is going to look like. But on this occasion, I made a conscious decision to arrive in a state of virginal ignorance. As a kind of test for myself. Here is the newspaper article that persuaded me.[4]

THE GEM:
BUDGET-
FRIENDLY

The three recently opened Gem hotels in New York offer modern comfort at a very modest price. The hotel in Chelsea has integrated itself comfortably into this arty part of town and is ideally situated for people who want to try out the bars and restaurants in the Meatpacking district in the evening. The compact rooms contain a comfortable bed, a functionally equipped bathroom and free wifi. In addition to Chelsea, there are also Gem hotels in Midtown West and Soho. A fourth hotel will be opened in Union Square in 2012. The Gem Hotel, 300 W 22nd Street, New York, www.thegemhotel.com, from $143 dollars/night.

I slept in this hotel for four nights.
And what do you think: will I be prepared to recommend this hotel to others, or not?

First read my initial reactions to my experience and then draw your own conclusions. Make a guess: will I give the Gem Hotel 0 points or 10 points on the scale of Reichheld[5] (the man who surprised the marketing world in 2003 by putting forward a completely new question in the field of loyalty research)?[6]

1 If you like a large room with a metre and a half of walking space on the three sides of your bed, then the Gem Hotel is not for you. The room is small. Very small. So small, in fact, that there was hardly space to open my suitcase. I could almost turn the gigantic television screen on the other side of the room on and off from my bed with my big toe. I thought that the room was tiny, even for someone travelling alone. For a couple it must be almost impossible, unless they share a suitcase.

2 The room had fitted carpet – something that I am allergic to. Fortunately, the air conditioning didn't make too much noise and I was

able to sleep warmly and in comfort throughout the night.

3   If you like a decent-sized table and easy chair in your room, you won't find either of these things in the Gem Hotel. The work 'table' was actually more like a shelf (on which my laptop hardly fitted) and the 'chair' was just a three-legged stool. When I wanted to work on my book, I preferred to lay stretched out on the bed, my back supported by cushions, while Bloomberg TV kept me informed about the latest ups and downs of the Nasdaq and the soaring price of Apple shares.

4   The fire alarm was in excellent working order. I know this, because on the second day of my stay it woke me with a start at five-thirty in the morning. I pulled on my trousers, grabbed my iPad and a few other essentials, and rushed out into the hall (all within 30 seconds!). Then the alarm stopped – and so I went back to bed. When I asked the receptionist a few hours later precisely what had gone wrong, it seems that a drunken guest had forgotten about the smoking prohibition and had accidentally set off one of the smoke detectors. So now I know that the smoke detectors work just as well as the alarms. Which is very reassuring – but not at five-thirty in the morning.

5   I was on the fourth floor of the hotel, where the wifi signal – one of the plus-points mentioned in *De Standaard* – was so weak that I could scarcely get on Skype and was unable to download YouTube at all. It was almost as if my room was isolated by a Chinese internet wall, an aspect of life in the Far East (I live and work for part of the year in Shanghai) with which I am all too familiar!

6   Are you a lover of long, lazy baths, soaking away all the aches and pains of the day? Not much chance of that here. There was, at least, a spacious, 'ecologically responsible' shower, which produced a fine and regular flow of warm water – but hardly a jetstream.

7   You almost needed to be contortionist to fill the coffee machine next to the bed and the resulting fluid was weak and tepid. I hate people using cheap coffee pads. Even when I put two pads on top of each other, the only effect was to turn the murky water in my cup a slightly darker shade of brown. The taste remained just the same: bloody awful. There were also tea-bags, but I didn't think it was worth taking the risk.

8   There was no mini-bar. But with my experience of hotels, I probably wouldn't have used it, even if there was one.

9   If you are a fan of extensive breakfast buffets, complete with fresh mango, English bacon, chocolate buns (75% cacao!) and eggs 'sunny

side up', you had better stay somewhere else. This hotel didn't even have a restaurant and there is no room-service option. Fortunately, there are a number of good breakfast bars and eating houses nearby.

10 It was in one of these nearby restaurants – where all the diners were male couples and there was a suspicious absence of women – that I came to understand why Chelsea is known as one of New York's leading LGBT[7] districts. Back in my hotel room I was curious to learn more, and my surfing soon revealed that my hotel was an active participant in and supporter of the local (sexual) community. Hence the preponderance of males guests, who I constantly saw whipping in and out of my Gem Hotel (pun intended!).

11 The reception (perhaps not surprisingly) was also staffed by men. As a rule, they were friendly, helpful and mild-mannered, usually migrant workers of one kind or another. So, too, were all the Americans whom I met during my two-week research tour (friendly and helpful, I mean, not migrants). One of them even had his family roots in Surinam, and was proud of the fact that he could pronounce my family name with a near-perfect Dutch accent.

12 It was very quiet in the hotel. There was seldom more than a single couple checking in or out of the small reception area at any one time and the guests were generally calm and well-behaved. Moreover, my room was not on the street side. The only view I had from my window was the brick wall of the building next door – and while walls might have ears, they don't make any noise. Of course, this meant that there wasn't much natural light in my room, but since I was out all day this didn't really matter. In short, it is not the most romantic place to spend the night (or perhaps an even briefer period) with your partner, whatever sex he or she might be.

WHAT DO YOU THINK? RECOMMENDED OR NOT?

Did I give the room a score of 0 or 10? Or something in between? Notwithstanding my subsidiary (and often tongue-in-cheek) remarks, I actually gave the Gem Hotel a generous score of 9 points. You can read a shorter, more business-like version of my comments on Tripadvisor.[8] There you will discover that it is not, in fact, possible to give a score of 9, since their ratings are based on stars – and it is not possible to give half a star. And so I settled for four: ****.

How is this possible, you might ask? Bearing in mind all my sarcastic remarks, how could I give such a good score? The short answer is: I don't really know. In spite of all the things I wrote, I just felt comfortable in the place. The hotel exuded an atmosphere of honesty, authenticity, good taste and simplicity. There was no question of a 'take the money and run' approach. The people there were doing their best to provide a good if basic service – and they did it well. It was this indefinable 'good feeling' that finally determined my score.

Could it be that I am just sick and tired of the pretentious hustle and bustle that I associate with Chinese hotels? Or is it simply that I am no longer prepared to pay more money for the luxury of a swimming pool and a huge breakfast buffet that I don't really need? I repeat: I don't really know. All I can say is that I was 'satisfied'. On this occasion, less was indeed more. And I know that plenty of my other friends and acquaintances will feel exactly the same way about The Gem. Like me, they will regard it as 'highly recommended' – and recommendable.

Which people from my immediate circle and my wider Twitter and Facebook circles am I likely to influence with my Tripadvisor review? Once again, I have no idea. And that is not really important.

Are you
a recommender?

- Recommenders are a very large group of ordinary people who collectively dump their personal experiences of a product or service into a gigantic database, with the aim of sharing those experiences with other consumers via various different platforms.
- The essence of what recommenders do is not to convince you of the merits (or otherwise) of this, that or the other product or service. The real essence is the information they make available to others, the pool of searchable data they create via a blog, in a portal, on a review site, which allows the consumer, armed with his Google search robot, to find an answer to the questions: What should I choose? What should I buy?
- This 15% of recommenders might seem like a small group, but they account for between 70 and 85% of all brand conversations. And that's a lot of conversations. And those conversations have much more influence than you might think.

WHAT IS 'RECOMMENDED' – AND WHAT IS A 'RECOMMENDER'?
Something becomes 'recommended', or even 'highly recommended', if lots of people simultaneously say something positive about that thing: a new novel, a chic hotel, Belgian beer (or chocolate!), an expensive wristwatch, a new brand of baby's nappy... In other words, a 'recommended' product or service first needs its own group of 'recommenders'.

In this book we will be looking at both these dimensions. Not only will we look at what is recommended, but also at who is doing the recommending – and how. This latter aspect – the human aspect – is crucial. We will focus on the recommender as a person. A person, for example, who praises the virtues of a particular brand. A person who searches, reads, listens and thinks more than other people. Above all, a person who talks and writes, and who, as a result of all this talking and writing, influences the people around him. To a greater or lesser degree. Consciously or unconsciously.

I have said what I wanted to say – it is now up to others to do what they want with this information. I know for certain that my comments will be read by more people who don't know me than by people who do know me. And I also know that I am not the only person to have given the hotel a good score (just look at the site, if you don't believe me). The point is that I have made my contribution. I have provided others with additional data that will help them to make their own choice of hotel in accordance with their own tastes, opinions and conscience. Because this is the way consumer decisions are taken.

If friends of mine are travelling to New York in the months ahead and if they ask me whether I know of a good place to stay, then I will not hesitate to recommend The Gem. And if they ask me why, I will attempt to explain to them the unexplainable: the story behind the score.

With this account of my experiences in The Gem, I want to make clear just how complex the issues relating to recommenders and recommendations really are. It is these complexities that I will seek to unravel in the later pages of this book. For example:

> Who are these people that recommend brands? What makes a recommender?
> Why do they do this? Are they in any way special?
> Do others allow themselves to be influenced by them? How does this work?
> Is this influence measurable? If so, in what manner?
> How large is this group that is capable of influencing others? Is their number also measurable?
> Are these men and women capable of replacing advertising campaigns?
> Are they paid? Do they want to be paid?
> What will be the role of these 'activists' in the future?
> How should brands react to their existence?
> What are the potential traps and pitfalls?

This is not so much about the one or two recommenders that you might know personally, but rather about the numerous recommenders who give their opinions collectively, thereby helping us all on our way.

But let's continue briefly with the story of The Gem.

The presence of the Tripadvisor link in the above photograph of a board displayed in The Gem is worth noting. I am being asked explicitly to say what I think about the hotel. Moreover, this board is not hidden away in some dusty corner of the lobby, but occupies a prominent position near the lift. The Gem is almost challenging us to give our comments. They are telling us that they want to listen. And perhaps they even mean it.

Do they actually do anything with all these opinions, including my own? How should I know? Perhaps I am the first person who has ever commented is such great (some might say exhaustive) detail. Will they take my comments to heart? Or will they file them away as the ravings of a know-it-all busybody? Time will tell. Maybe the coffee will have improved when I next visit.

And what if people are no longer willing to share their opinions online or if other people no longer go in search of such opinions? Surely the 15% of recommenders only have any meaning if they are able to reach and influence the remaining 85%?

Correct. If people don't visit review sites (like Tripadvisor), the reviewers have no readers and so their story comes to an end. Their influence fades and dies – and so they stop. When this happens, however, things start to move in the opposite direction. Apart from the one or two recommenders that every consumer knows personally, the remaining commentators on sites of this kind then become the most important and most reliable source of information on which to base purchasing decisions. As a result, their influence cannot fail to increase – and keep on increasing.

Now take a look at another of the photographs I made during my American trip. It shows a miniature model of a JetBlue plane, standing behind the reception desk in The Gem, not far from a glowing Tripadvisor recommendation. The plane is there for a good reason. It symbolises a mystic marriage between The Gem and JetBlue. In one way or another, they both attract the same type of customer. For now, just remember that JetBlue scores very highly in its annual net promoter survey[9] of its customers, making it America's most successful airline.

After I had checked out of The Gem and was waiting in the lobby for the taxi that would take me back to the airport, I overheard the conversation of a new arrival, who was staying at the hotel for the fourth time. Not, I admit, very polite of me (I hate people eavesdropping on my conversations!), but even so I found myself asking the following questions:

> What is his brand profile (I would have loved to ask him!)?
> Does he fly with JetBlue?
> What make of car does he drive?
> Which shampoo does he use? His own? His wife's? His girlfriends?
> What coffee does he like drinking? Nespresso, Illy or the lukewarm dishwater that they serve up in The Gem?
> What kind of suit does he wear (if he ever wears one)?
> Which make of suitcase is he carrying? A battered old leather affair (probably inherited from his grandfather) or a shiny new Samsonite on wheels?
> Is he a 'typical' Gem customer?

This last question is a good question. Just how homogeneous or heterogeneous is the group of people that comes to The Gem? Are they, for example, all fans of the same ten brands, which they are prepared to praise to the heavens? Or are they all haters of ten other brands, which they would like to see damned to hell and beyond? How conscious are the members of such an informal brand community that they actually all belong to the same small, unstructured club? A club, moreover, which sometimes passes on brand recommendations almost without knowing it, like people passing on flu to each other in a crowded winter train. Is the gay community in Chelsea such a tight-knit little community and is this how The Gem achieves its success, by spreading its reputation like a 'virus', both online and offline? Is the recommending of a brand nothing short of the launching of an all-conquering, all-destroying epidemic? Or is it a phenomenon that can be quantified and contained within the responsible scientific discipline of memetics?[10] Perhaps, instead, brand recommendation is a mild form of peer pressure, with social influence being applied by the people with whom you live, play and work. Or do recommendations need to be more obviously explicit, before they can actually be considered as 'real' recommendations? Probably not. But these are just some of the issues that we will examine along the way in this book. Patience, dear reader, patience.

ARE THE RECOMMENDERS
APPLYING THEIR PRESSURE ON ME?

When considering a purchase, people are always inclined to look at themselves through the eyes of others. They also do the same if they are planning to recommend or rubbish a product. What will friend X think of me if I buy product A instead of product B? Or if I advise someone in favour of product C and against product D? Will he cringe with shame in my place, embarrassed by my crassness and stupidity? Will he cry out in outrage and amazement? Will he applaud me or admonish me? Perhaps most importantly, will he follow my advice when he comes to make his own choice between product C and product D? What I think about what others think of me is one of the strongest forms of self-recommendation. And self-recommendation is a positive form of self-censure: no product C for me, it has to be product D! Indeed, you do have to make a choice. After all, you can't stay the same night in two different hotels.

Having said this, I experienced no such peer pressure when I gave my score of 9 out of 10. I assessed The Gem independently and in isolation, with no outside influence exerted by my immediate environment.

So the question is therefore this: what does my 9 really mean? To begin with, it needs to be said that 9 is a very good score. But what score can I then give when I next stay in a four-star or even a six-star hotel? 10? 11? Of course not, that's not possible. 10 is the highest score you can give. In fact, it is perfectly possible that some 'better' (i.e., more expensive) hotels will actually get a much lower score, simply because that is all they deserve – if they fail to live up to their reputation. Their price and their number of stars mean that they have set the bar very high. As a result, my expectations are also very high. I have paid a lot of money and I expect to get a lot for it. I am going to be more critical, less willing to make allowances. Faults that seem minor in The Gem will seem huge in a Sheraton or a Hilton – and I will make sure that everybody knows it. In other words, recommenders colour the facts of the situation in accordance with their own personal perspective, on the basis of their own experience.

A RECOMMENDATION IS ALWAYS RELATIVE: IN FACT, VERY RELATIVE

You must always compare a pinot gris with a pinot gris – and not with a shiraz. There is no point in comparing a grand cru from a great chateau with a cheap bottle of plonk from the village wine cooperative. And it is the same with your recommendations. They must always be viewed from the perspective of the receiver. If someone asks me to make a recommendation for something, I will adjust my list of criteria in function of the person making the request.

This means registering the objective and measurable parameters on each separate occasion, and then reshaping them into a very subjective final balance.

The room is small, but does it really need to be any bigger?

There is no bath, but what's wrong with a shower?

There is no breath-taking sea view, but who cares, if I am never in the room during the day to enjoy it?

The recommender will always play the logical game of 'if not this... then that'.

'Either... or'.

'On the one hand... on the other hand'.

I would probably not recommend The Gem to conservative, homo-phobic sixty-plussers or to families with young children. For them, I would find something else, something 'more suitable'.

Of course, it is impossible to include all this in my comments on Tripadvisor. But there are more than 200 other travellers who have also detailed their experiences of The Gem. As a result, the type of person who wants to know everything about a place before they make a reser-vation will soon find out what sort of neighbourhood Chelsea really is.

By now, it should be clear that a true recommender is not some kind of human advertisement; is more than just the mouthpiece for a brand. Nobody listens to someone who always gives the 'thumbs up' to everything. People who are deciding where to spend their $100 dol-lars (or more) per night will look for the arguments that allow them to make a balanced choice. Unless, of course, they consider $100 dol-lars to be just loose change. At Holaba, we have noticed that it is not the human megaphones who are most listened to, but rather the con-sumers who set out all the pros and cons in a clear and concise man-ner. This allows the reader of the comments to pick out the things that are important for him. He distils the essence from the mass of available information, without there being any need for a single rec-ommender to write tailor-made comments specific to his situation. This is *the wisdom of crowds*.

CAN A COMPUTER DISTINGUISH BETWEEN A POSITIVE RECOMMENDER AND A NEGATIVE RECOMMENDER?

Not yet – but then it is no easy matter.
On the basis of my initial comments about The Gem, a sentiment-analysis tool would probably conclude that my overall assessment would be negative. In reality, the very opposite was true.

But is this how the computer really reads the situation? We will be looking at this more extensively in chapter 8. For the time being, let me just say that automated text analysis is still a very imperfect way to assess whether or not someone is giving a positive or negative rec-ommendation. And this is without consideration of the fact that the greatest number and the most effective recommendations are still given offline. On the reverse side of the coin, it is also true that the crowd sourcing of user-generated evaluations is improving all the time, but there is still a long way to go before they are wholly reliable.

Having said this, I have no doubt that one day I will no longer be required to physically give a score for anything, but that my points and recommendations will be transferred automatically from my thought-patterns direct to the Holaba server. The pleasure zone in the brain is distinct from the pain zone and the indifference zone," and in the future it will be possible to distinguish and transmit the different signals emitted by the different zones. So what score will the brain scanner give to the following story of my experiences with Canon?

I have always been a big fan of Canon cameras. I purchased my first model back in 1977, when my daughter was born. Canon was the first company on the market with an electronic reflex camera. I just had to have one – so I bought an AE-I. I used it for more than 20 years, but when I lent it to my son Bram for a full year in Senegal, it finally gave up the ghost. Too much desert sand was fatal! In the following years I bought a couple of IXUS models, until in 2007 I decided that what I really wanted was a new reflex. I again opted for Canon, this time with a monster lens that looked more like a cannon than a Canon. When Bram later had a son of his own – our first grandchild – I decided to move away from my favourite brand, and settled instead for an Olympus. Big mistake. I didn't have a clue how it worked. It's still in the cupboard. My youngest son, Jelle, had also begun by buying himself an expensive Canon, but a few weeks before he went off to climb Mount Kilimanjaro he switched to a Sony Nex5. My Canon-lovers heart was torn in two, but I had to admit that he was right: at that time, Canon had no real comparable alternative in the higher price range. Jelle lent me the Sony to take on my book research trip to the United States and (to my surprise) I was very happy with it. Does this mean that I am now going to buy one for myself? I'm still not sure. I am rather hoping that the Canon R&D people will get a move on and develop a Canon equivalent (or better) that will be on the market before too long. As a true Canon recommender, I am prepared to remain faithful to my first love – and so, for the time being at least, I will postpone my new purchase. But it isn't easy!

Let us take a brief step back in time. Before I could arrive at The Gem, I first had to take a Sunday afternoon flight from San Francisco to New York with American Airlines.

Even though they had a low NPS score, at first glance there seemed to be nothing wrong with the American Airlines operation. Everything went smoothly enough. The staff were courteous, the check-in procedures were efficient, the plane left on time and we even had wifi!

It was the first time that I had been able to surf in the Mile High Club! The flying web came into operation above 10,000 metres and worked perfectly for 30 minutes. Exactly 30 minutes. There then appeared an interrupter message on my screen that informed me that I would have to pay $14 dollars if I wished to keep my wifi connection for the remainder of the flight.

At first, I was just surprised. I didn't know that I was restricted to just half an hour of free wifi time. Perhaps I had not been paying attention, but as far as I can remember I had not seen, heard or read anything about a 30 minute cut-off. True, before I logged on there was something about long-term subscription arrangements for regular airline users in the U.S., but since I normally only fly between Shanghai and Amsterdam, this was of no interest to me. And so I didn't take up the offer. Why should I?

And so, as I said, when my screen went blank, my first reaction was one of surprise. 'My iPad must be on the blink.' I considered the possibilities of technical failure or even an altitude bug, but when the real reason for my problem finally dawned on me, I first became angry and then stoically indifferent. I spent the rest of the flight muttering to myself about the reasons why some brands are defended to the death by their supporters, while others are hardly worth wasting your breath on. Was this small incident just one of many small symptoms of the wider problem at American Airlines?[13]

Another one of these symptoms was soon to appear. When the charming stewardess passed along the aisle during her first free coffee-water-wine tour, she asked me whether or not I would like to buy some extra nibbles to eat. McEnroe-like, I thought to myself: 'You cannot be serious!' This was more akin to the tactics of a bucket airline à la Ryan Air than to a supposedly 'reputable' American carrier.

As was mentioned in the introduction to this chapter, JetBlue always scores somewhere near the top of the NPS surveys and American Airlines somewhere near the bottom. JetBlue is a fanatical enthusiast of NPS systems and they even calculate an ROI (return on investment) on these systems – and the figures are compelling. For every five promoters (positive recommenders who give them a score of 9 or 10), they win on average an additional two customers. However, it takes sixteen detractors (negative recommenders who give a score between 0 and 6) before they lose a single client. In comparison with an average customer, a promoter brings JetBlue an additional $33 dollars of income; a detractor some $114 dollars less. (There is even a correlation between what the pilot tells the passengers during the flight and the NPS score).[12]

They'd probably be asking me to pay for the toilet next! I declined politely and decided to wait for her next tour, when I hoped some freebies might be on offer. No such luck. And it was precisely the same on the third tour. By this time I was starving but I adamantly refused to pay for something that you get for free on any half-decent airline. $200 dollars for a five-and-a-half hour flight and nothing to eat! And this for a first time customer who didn't know any better and hadn't been warned in advance! I didn't expect a free three course meal, but I did at least expect something. Even on the short 25 minute hop between Amsterdam and Brussels you get something to eat with your free orange juice. Nice one, KLM! Up yours, American Airlines!

DO UNEXPECTED AND IRRITATING MISTAKES LEAD TO A LOW RECOMMENDER SCORE?

And vice versa: do small acts of kindness and attention to detail result in more positive brand approval? My first reaction is to think that such matters cannot be decisive. Even so, it cannot be denied that they play an important – if largely symbolic – role.

Most of the thousands of things that go wrong could probably be avoided. But there is a silver lining: every time something does go wrong (and your customer explodes) it gives you the chance to put things right – and reattach him to your brand more strongly than ever before.

Research should be able to show the importance of these 'incidents' and also assess how the service procedures of companies deal with them when they arise. Just exactly how do after-sales personnel react when faced with their company's failure and their customer's anger? Do they take a hard or soft approach to conflict resolution? Do the proposed solutions work or are they not really interested in finding a solution?

Do the smaller 'cute and cuddly' companies, which are by nature friendlier and more generous, respond differently to customer problems than their large rivals? If so, how should the Big Brands respond to this situation? Precisely! They must identify their points for improvement using NPS and then take the necessary steps to initiate corrective action.

Or does the concerned approach of the smaller companies (genuine or not) allow them to attract more tolerant customers, who will be more inclined to overlook minor irritations and errors? People who know that 'to err is human' and are consequently prepared to forgive and forget. If people (and brands?) have been kind and helpful towards you over a long period, are you going to suddenly drop them like a hot potato if something relatively unimportant goes wrong? ('Yes madam, it's true that the battery in the iPhone is not very good, but Apple is working on it and we expect an improved version in the near future.')

And is it possible for a brand to artificially create this attitude in its customers? Is this the 'loop' that Reichheld refers to: the continual reinforcement and strengthening of the positive human values that (hopefully already) exist within the DNA of the company? I am convinced of it!

Are these the companies that have the highest recommender score: the companies that are not arrogant, always listen, are always helpful, give answers, admit their mistakes, ask forgiveness? Because

we do all make mistakes, of course. But perhaps it is easier to forgive a company of this kind, which adopts a 'vulnerable' position. It's a bit like in a marriage: from time to time you argue and disappoint each other, but this is no reason to immediately rush out and get a divorce! You should judge the process rather than the end result; the journey rather than the final destination.

Do more 'human' companies attract more 'human' people? Do they have more honest, genuine and enthusiastic humanity amongst their workforce and can they 'infect' their customers with this value-based approach? In the United States, are companies such as Amazon, Apple, Zappos, USAA and Trader Joe's examples of this phenomenon?[14]

And is this good score in some way related to 'small' and 'niche'? Trader Joe's seeks to attract fanatical organic price-hoppers and tries to make everything more attractive by dressing its staff in Hawaiian beach shirts! In this manner, are they also trying to consciously build a sense of community? Or is this just so deeply ingrained in their DNA that it simply allows them to be what they are, naturally and effortlessly?

I once sent them an e-mail: you need to read the humorous small print to understand their mentality.

In reality, however, their reply to my mail was not so humorous – or helpful: they didn't want to answer my question.

Alison Mochizuki   Feb 10
to me

Thank you for your email. I'm sorry I missed your call yesterday as I was out ill. Unfortunately, Trader Joe's does not participate in books. Hence, we have to decline participation. Thank you for the opportunity and I wish you all the best.

Alison

-----Original Message-----
From: jevedebe@gmail.com [mailto:jevedebe@gmail.com]
Sent: Wednesday, February 08, 2012 12:22 PM
To: Web Customer Relations
Subject: Trader Joe's General Feedback Form

Name:Jan Van den Bergh
Phone Number:0032475427882
Email Address:jevedebe@gmail.com
Your Trader Joe's:Belgium

Comments:For a book I am writing on the phenomenon of recommenders I'd love to talk to mrs Alison Mochizuki and ask her 1 question:" What's the reason why so many customers recommend TJ's?". Jan Van den Bergh. Chairman Holaba and writing his first book

When I finally came to the end of my research tour in the U.S., I took another American Airline flight; this time from New York to Brussels. I had the good fortune to be sitting next to a beautiful Polish woman of about forty, who was travelling with her ten-year-old daughter. She told me that she had lived in New York for the past decade and earned between $120 and $150 dollars per hour as a physical coach. Her customers were either rich, fat or both. In spite of her good income, she did not live in fashionable downtown Manhattan, but across the river in Queens. I asked her if there was a Trader Joe's near her home. She replied with a certain pride that she went to do her shopping there every week. When I enquired why, she replied with the familiar answers. Low price. Great quality. Unbelievably friendly staff.

I DO NOT RECOMMEND THE THINGS THAT MAKE ME 'ANGRY'

People are always able to justify the things they recommend with (what seem to them) rational arguments. Why is a free snack not included in the price of an American Airlines ticket? How come that JetBlue can do this? And Virgin? And Southwest? These are all air carriers that have a high NPS score.

One of the problems that I have with KLM is that they are not very good at solving their own problems. True, I must admit that they don't have many problems, but when something unexpected happens it is almost impossible to get it put right. I have never managed to change flights on the occasions it has been necessary. I have tried three times in recent years, but always with the same negative result. The last time I decided to pay the supplement that would allow my flight to be postponed. Curiously enough, this time everything worked perfectly!

But first back to the bad news about KLM. During the preparations for my book trip, I was confronted with the following situation.

On the KLM website I found full details of their flights to the U.S. at what seemed like a very reasonable price. I filled in the necessary online form, but when the moment came to pay my €800 euros a message appeared on the screen, informing me that 'unfortunately, the selected tickets are no longer available for sale; there are still seats

24-HOUR CUSTOMER CARE

To **promote** its new efforts to provide customer service on Twitter and Facebook, KLM created a living alphabet to **respond to social media inquiries.**

450 KLM employees

held up letters to **spell answers to the questions** on Twitter, Facebook, and Hyves (a Dutch site).

The living alphabet was videoed and sent out as responses on *social media.*

KLM also **invites customers**

SUBMIT IDEAS

for **improvement** via Facebook on its Bright Ideas page.

http://wallblog.co. uk/2012/03/05/five-compa- nies-rocking-social-media- infographic/

available on your selected flight, but in a different price category.' A different price category? A higher price category is what they should have said. In fact, €2,669 euros: more than three times as much.

Once again, my first reaction was: 'this can't be right!' It must be a bug, I thought. And so I began to make my reservation all over again. To my amazement, I received the same 'apology' message and this time an even higher price: €3,723 euros! I could hardly believe what I was seeing!

I picked up the telephone and dialled the KLM information line. All I got was a confused explanation, which only served to strengthen my rapidly growing latent distrust of the airline. Apparently, the problem was the result of the slowness with which Delta updated reserved flights on the KLM server. This meant that what I saw on the KLM website was not the actual position, but an outdated position. The young lady on the phone said that it might be a good idea to contact Delta directly! Which I promptly did. And hard though it is to believe, there were still plenty of seats available on the flight that I wanted at the original €800 euro price! I was no longer interested in finding which of the two companies was messing me about in this ridiculous manner. For me, it was over and out. The result: I now have nagging doubts about the honesty and/or competence of both Delta and KLM. Fortunately, however, KLM flights are famed for their 'dedicated' team of stewardesses, who quickly help one to forget irritations of this kind!

This is illustrative of the fact that it is sometimes very difficult even for good companies to make their customers happy. And it is doubly difficult to keep them happy year after year. And it is even more difficult to pick out the real recommenders: the customers who are prepared to defend your brand, come what may.

IT SEEMS TO BE EASIER FOR A CONSUMER TO SUPPORT A COMPANY THAT HE IS CLOSE TO (FOR WHATEVER REASON)

A company with premises in your neighbourhood. Or one that is based in the province or county or state where you come from. This is a not unnatural reaction. It is obviously easier for Chinese people to support a Chinese company than its European competitor.

For who else is it also easier? For companies that can project a 'feel good' factor. Positive stories about their founder. Or their roots. Stories that are full of humanity, compassion and authenticity.

Stories of this kind are often based on the extreme things that happen to people. What is 'extreme' in your company? What might be able to convince the doubters of your honesty and sincerity? What are the defects on which you detractors repeatedly focus? Where are your weak points? As a company, you usually tell your story through very expensive advertising campaigns. But recommenders (and non-recommenders) also need to be able to tell their story. And if you listen to them carefully, you will soon find yourself on the right track. Because the more passionately your promoters and detractors tell their stories, the more heavily they will score with their own willing public. And the more easily they will be believed – to the advantage or disadvantage of your reputation and your market position.

The decision to recommend or not to recommend seems to be an almost unconscious one that can be completed in a few short steps. If there is nothing extreme about these steps, then there will be no story. Everything will flow naturally, in an unemotional, business-like manner. No doubts and no come-back. The steps are as follows:

1 First, there needs to be an 'Olympic minimum'. The things that are measurable (and can therefore be compared with the competition) must be accurate and correct. If you fail at this first hurdle, you can forget it. Your customers will be gone.

2 Next follows the implementation of the process: the moment of service delivery. Does everything work smoothly? Is everything transparent? If there are no problems here, then once again there is no story to tell.

3 Then there are your people, the staff who work their butts off on your behalf (or not, as the case may be). Are they alert, friendly and helpful or do they do their jobs without enthusiasm? Are they content with just the bare minimum or do they try to go the extra mile?

4 Superimposed on these three basic layers comes the key question: do these things make me intensely happy? Is their enthusiasm infectious? Do they give me an unforgettable experience?

5 Or is the ultimate moment of recommender truth to be found in conflicts and the manner in which they are resolved? You'd better believe it!

If these five steps are completed successfully, there is a good chance that you will become a recommender. After all, it is the poorly resolved conflicts that linger longest in the memory and are therefore most crucial for determining your story.

The higher the level of customer involvement and the greater the number of service aspects in the different steps, the more important the 'human factor' becomes. A car is not just a car, but also the garage that maintains it. A computer is a product, but it is also a shop where you bought it.

In contrast, the last four steps play very little role for a manufacturer of disposable nappies for sale in a supermarket. Step one is the only place where he can get himself into unnecessary difficulties.

It is also open to question to what extent a recommender can influence people with a very positive or very negative story about one or more of the five steps. If he is a convincing storyteller, he might have some success in his immediate circle of family and friends. But not every recommender is an influencer. To be an influencer, you need to 'sell' your story, often by using sales tricks. This is not something that every recommender is able to do.

Having said this, it is of course true that many recommenders can exercise influence. Even intense influence. Here is a piece by one of the many Trader Joe's recommenders; a piece drawn from life and read by literally thousands of people on Yelp:

TJ's seems to be everything I hate, and I did hate it, at first. The gimmicks like the 'crewmembers' and their Hawaiian shirts, the cute little names for the food, the strange artwork in the store and the flyer. It didn't take long for me to come to love the place. If big corporations have to take over the world, they should at least model themselves on TJ's. Nothing cold and impersonal here. The employees are actually pleasant and helpful. When they call me by my name, it is because they really do know me, not because they read it off the credit card slip. The scale of the store is just right. Much smaller than a supermarket but still manages to hold nearly everything I could want.

The prices are another reason to shop at TJ's. I have seen the very same chocolate truffles that TJ's sells for $4, sold for $12 elsewhere, as just one example.

Yes, it can be hit or miss with some products, but you can always ask the employees for their recommendations, and the other shoppers are helpful as well. The friendly atmosphere pays off. My must trys: Tarte d'Alsace, carrot cake, peanut butter cups, frozen cherries, Mandarin orange chicken, Valrhona 71% chocolate bar, Niman Ranch BBQ ribs, chocolate ice cream bars, Manchego cheese.[15]

I RECOMMEND THE THINGS THAT MAKE ME INTENSELY HAPPY

This is not what I originally thought, but I am forced to yield to the incontestable fact: you will only recommend a brand if it makes you intensely happy.

This sounds like Hollywood-fake, but the real recommenders are just ordinary people who occasionally experience the deepest happiness (a brand orgasm) as a result of their contact with a particular product and who like to write or talk about it. They – and their numerous 'happy endings' – are the central theme of this book.

Even so, I must admit that some recommenders do occasionally misrepresent the truth. It can sometimes happen, for example, that if someone on holiday visits all the five-star hotels in his resort, he might write rave reviews about every hotel where he stays, whereas in reality he was deeply unhappy in one of them. In this case, the man is writing about himself, and not the hotels. So much is clear. He wants to let his readers know that he has 'been there, done that', and feels obliged to be exclusively positive about it. In chapter 5 we will be returning to the question of what makes a real recommender. For now, I will content myself with the following quotation: 'And among Cialdini's weapons of influence is Consistency and Commitment, the socialized desire to be trustworthy and consistent in one's actions and statements. No one wants to be labelled a "fake" or 'braggart", or a liar, so we're programmed to demand consistency in our behaviours and actions. We're socially programmed to follow through on our commitments. Programming that is often exploited by compliance professionals.'[16]

In other words, just because someone says that he is happy, it ain't necessarily so.

Fortunately for this book, things don't always work out for the recommenders the way they had hoped. Sometimes they are plagued by bad luck, almost like they are temporarily jinxed. Tarred and feathered. Furious. Disgusted at what is being done to them. They twitter their unhappiness to anyone who will listen. Warning others not to fall into the same trap as themselves. Recommenders (who can also sometimes be non-recommenders) are an open book: they just blurt out whatever they want to get off their chest – and the more people who hear them, the better.

HAPPINESS, DISGUST AND EVERYTHING IN BETWEEN. SO WHAT'S IT ALL ABOUT?

BrainJuicer[17] launched an interesting pilot study to identify the crucial role that strong emotions (such as happiness, anger and disgust) play in relation to the processes of recommendation and non-recommendation. Their conclusion? Brands only need to concentrate on one single thing: making their customers as happy as possible. The happier they are, the greater the chance that they will make a positive recommendation. Other more negative basic emotions, or even the absence of an emotional response, reduce the likelihood of a recommendation significantly. If anger and disgust are the dominant emotions, then the situation can easily switch to the opposite extreme. You can see this in the following table of results:

Satisfied customers will give recommendations more easily than others
% of change in recommender scores for each emotional % change
Gain/loss in net recommender score per % change in emotions

A Happiness / B Surprise / C Fear / D Neutral / E Contempt /
F Sadness / G Anger / H Disgust

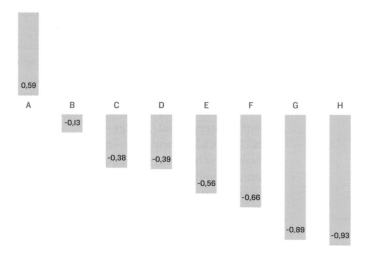

The manner in which the basic emotions should be classified in relation to the 0 to 10 scores in the NPS system is as follows:
> For people who give a score of 10, 9 or 8, deep happiness is the dominant emotion.
> For people who give a score of 7, 6 or 5, the share of neutral emotion is doubled and the overall emotional intensity is significantly lower.
> For people who give a score of 4, 3 or 2 on the Reichheld scale, nega-

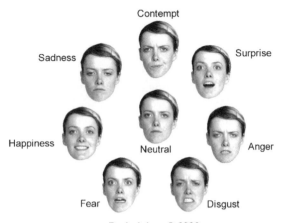

BrainJuicer © 2006

tive emotions (namely, anger and contempt) are gaining the upper hand at the expense of happiness. This process is intensified still further for people who give a score of 1 or 0. A strong sense of disgust, combined with anger, now expunge any residual feelings of happiness completely.

BrainJuicer used a model based on facial expressions to allow people to indicate the emotions they were feeling in relation to a particular brand, experience or advertisement. The seven emotions used are in turn based on the work of Paul Ekman (www.paulekman.com.). The emotions are: (1) happiness; (2) surprise; (3) sadness; (4) fear; (5) anger; (6) contempt; and (7) disgust.

BrainJuicer added neutrality – or the absence of emotion – to this list. BrainJuicer believes that emotions are of primary importance in obtaining an understanding of human behaviour. For example, in March 2012 they used their emotional model to predict the extent to which certain advertisements were capable of being spread widely on the internet (in other words, to establish their viral potential).[18] Following in their footsteps, Satmetrix also adopted a system based on facial expressions.

IF RECOMMENDERS ARE GAINING IN IMPORTANCE, DOES THIS MEAN THAT ADVERTISING IS LOSING GROUND? YES, IT DOES!

We have hardly started our book, but the harsh reality of this statement should already be evident. Having said this, the following pages will be full of references to adverts. And every time you see a new graphic, you should ask yourself (with me): what role does advertising still have to play? Some might say: 'To create a presence of the brand, when the brand itself is absent.' But this seems to me a very humble role. A brand needs to remain present in the hearts and minds of its users, and this is not possible relying exclusively on the product itself and the shouts or whispers of its recommenders. 'Traditional' advertising therefore still has its 'traditional' role to play, but its relative importance in the necessary mix of measures will be significantly reduced.

If between 20 and 50% of purchasing decisions are taken on the basis of direct influence exercised by people in your immediate environment (as McKinsey claims[19]), then the role of advertising in the ultimate decision-making process must indeed be less decisive than in the past. This, in turn, will reduce the influence of advertising agencies and spin doctors – which is no bad thing. The self-created and self-glorifying 'wind' generated by these 'influence gurus' will henceforth only have a very limited and temporary impact on the hot-cold feelings that consumers have for a particular product. From now on, it will be a very weak – and very expensive – wind.

The corresponding ground gained in the influencing process by the hyper-active consumers (because this is what recommenders are) conclusively proves their newly won importance. In the communication mix, the consumers now stand head and shoulders above all the other component elements. They are a crucial and reliable source of information.

Every forward-thinking marketer now pays lip service to this new role. Even in China. My Chinese business partners often tell me: 'My dear Jan, we know that they are important.' But it is often another matter when it comes to the action and investment necessary to transform recommender marketing into a truly effective instrument.
And this is a missed opportunity – twice over.

ı The average consumer (the 85%) either consciously ignores advertising or suffers from advertising blindness, preferring instead to be guided by the recommenders.

2 The brand promoters (the 15%) are becoming less inclined to allow themselves to be influenced by campaigns for their favourite brand, preferring to rely instead on their personal experience of the brand.

SUBSTANCE – NOT SHAM

This is what both these consumer groups want: a true and accurate picture of the brand, not a photo-shopped image, where it is difficult to distinguish between fantasy and reality.

The only problem is that recommenders also tend to be information junkies, which means that they are still sometimes susceptible to the propaganda put out by their brand companies. They soak up everything that they see, hear or read – but don't always stop to ask whether or not it is 100 percent reliable. Yet in the final analysis, it is their own experience of the product (whether past and extensive or recent and cursory) that continues to be crucial in the forming of their opinions. And the assessment process of a recommender is a continuous one – because that's the way they are.

The average consumer now listens more to the recommenders and less to the advertising windbags. Every recent research study has confirmed this. And the recommenders don't need the advertisers to maintain their key position. This is the new 'double dip' for paid advertising, which flourished unchallenged for almost a century.

The judgements of the recommenders about their brands are often clear, simple and honest: good product, bad product, mediocre product. They know what they are talking about. They use the media in which their favourite products are discussed to justify and sometimes modify their opinions. But they will not fall into the trap of keeping up appearances and will never talk up a product that is essentially weak: a bad experience remains a bad experience. End of story.

In view of the position they occupy in the 'to-buy-or-not-to-buy' decision-making process, it is difficult to overestimate the importance that the recommenders now have for the manufacturers of goods and their brands. Instead of thinking about which media to use for the transmission of their marketing message, the brand strategists and planners could better spend their time by trying to find out who these fanatics are and how they might best be influenced, bearing in mind that self-experience is always their final touchstone. This means that they must primarily be convinced by tangible, visible and measurable improvements in the product or service they love, and much less by the classic tactics of perception influence.

A media plan always begins with the identification of the most appropriate media from the thousands of available options. And it is much the same with recommender marketing. Everything starts with the correct identification and understanding of the most appropriate recommenders. Someone who knows everything about fish is not necessarily an expert in cooking fish. He will have his followers on the riverbank and lakeside, but not in the kitchen.

In part, the brand holders should be able to identify at least some of their recommenders from their own databases, painstakingly built up over a number of years. This is useful, but must be quickly followed by a segmentation exercise: who are the positive recommenders, who are the neutral ones, whose name is in the database only because he once mailed us for information about product X or service Y?

Of course, not all the people you are looking for will already be included in your database. For example, you will not find the people who don't recommend your products – and they too can be of interest to you, since they are the ones you are ultimately trying to reach. This means that there is also a need to explore the possibilities offered by different platforms (blogs, review sites, consumer associations), where recommenders can make themselves known (whether invited or uninvited), so that they can build up a brand public. In one sense, each of these persons is a 'medium', which needs to be charted and mapped, just like any other media. This does not relate to the very small 0.01% of consumers who actively tweet about their favourite brands. Nor does it relate to the slightly larger 0.1% of consumers who actively blog about their favourite brands. And it certainly has nothing to do with the Justin Biebers of the world, who have millions of followers. No, it relates to the vast majority of consumers, the ones who have a real life in addition to their online life.

One of the consequences of this development (which will torpedo another of the marketing sector's current hypes) is that it is no longer sufficient to monitor conversations digitally and measure who is saying what about your brand (see chapter 7). It should not be forgotten that 90% of conversations about brands still take place offline or IRL (In Real Life).[20]

It would be nice to think that what is being said online is a faithful reflection of what is being said offline. Unfortunately, that is not the case. Moreover, the crucial offline influencing cannot be steered by the brands (even though many advertisers still like to claim that it can!). The blind fanatics amongst the recommenders (a minority) recommend their favourite brand simply because they are 100 percent convinced that their choice is the right one. In contrast, the moderate majority is less inclined to 'spread the word' at every available opportunity, whether appropriate or not. They are certainly happy to spread, but prefer to wait for the right moment; perhaps when they are asked or during a discussion. They will then come forward and say what they feel needs to be said; no more and no less. This relevant and focused engagement is something very different from the 'click-like-share' engagement more common to social media, which often forms the basis for much of today's marketing and advertising.

The massive switch away from the lunacy of advertising towards the disconcerting realisation that 'people influence people' has scarcely begun. Of course, people have been influencing other people for a long time. But only on a small scale. Modern communication techniques have increased that scale exponentially. At the same time (how can it be otherwise?), there is a renewed focus on the relationship between the consumer and the product. It is only when the product, on the basis of its own merits, can prove in real life that it is useful for the consumer that the product will have any chance of success. This shifts the emphasis away from 'push' mass marketing and towards product development, listening and sincerity. Nowadays, you have to earn a good reputation; you can't just buy one.

Before closing this chapter, I would again like to underline that this book is about the possibility of capitalising on a trend that is much more than just another hype; a trend that reflects the beginning of a slowly changing reality. Platforms such as Tripadvisor, Powerreviews, Yelp and Holaba are the first answer to the question that everyone in marketing is asking: 'what can we do if the consumer is no longer capable of being influenced by the classic push model?' Further answers are bound to follow.

The more we understand that 'recommendation' really works in real life, the quicker we will be able to improve our measuring systems, so that we know what we can measure, where and when we can measure it, and how we can meaningfully analyse the resulting mass of data. This task of trying to put a quantifiable number on a person has only just begun and is destined to continue for some time. Perhaps we will never reach full agreement about a definitive scoring method. A runner is better than another runner if he wins more races. A politician is better than another politician if he wins more elections (in theory, at least). A businessman is better than another businessman if he earns more money (also in theory, at least). But what is the yardstick for measuring whether or not someone recommends more brands more efficiently than someone else? Not easy, is it? But nonetheless necessary, when viewed from a marketing standpoint. Brands, political parties and NGOs (Non-Governmental Organisations) all want to know where they should invest their marketing budgets. That is the million dollar question. In fact, hundreds of millions of dollars.

In 'Arousal Increases Social Transmission of Information' Berger suggests that feeling fearful, angry, or amused drives people to share news and information. These types of emotions are characterised by high arousal and action, as opposed to emotions like sadness or contentment, which are characterised by low arousal or inaction. 'If something makes you angry as opposed to sad, for example, you're more likely to share it with your family and friends because you're fired up', continues Berger. When people are physiologically aroused, whether due to emotional stimuli or otherwise, the autonomic nervous is activated, which then boosts social transmission.[21]

How do you find brand recommenders? A short introduction to a complex story. In China!

– NPS and the One Question ('How likely is it that you will recommend this brand?') were a turning point for me, but were neither the beginning nor the end of my story.

– Identifying the recommenders of your brand (and your competitors' brands) is a non-stop process. Hour after hour. Everywhere. How else do you expect to find them and get to know them?

– Everything begins with the One Question, but it is also advisable to ask a few other questions as well.

– Don't become fixated on RFM data (Recency, Frequency, Monetary Value). If you do this, one day soon you may find yourself running into a brick wall!

– China is not yet the reference. But it offers an interesting example of the results that can be achieved with the One Question and its correlation with sales.

– 20% of the people who tell you that they are satisfied will desert your brand. While 28% of 'dissatisfied' customers will remain loyal. So make sure you ask something more than 'are you satisfied'.

I have already mentioned NPS a number of times in passing. NPS originally stood for Net Promoter Score, but is now more commonly known as the Net Promoter System. And I have likewise mentioned that I operate a platform in China under the name of Holaba. Perhaps I should begin this chapter by clarifying what NPS and Holaba have in common with each other – and what they do not.

My basic reasoning is simplicity itself:

1   A growing market share is the result of more people spending more money more often on your products in comparison with the products of your competitors. Your products therefore have a greater share of wallet.

2   The key question is: why do customers behave in this manner? Why do they prefer you to your neighbour? Unfortunately, there is no single, all-inclusive explanation for this phenomenon.

3   If we did have to choose a single reason, it would almost certainly be related to the quality of the product or service. Pure and simple. But if there are a number of top products in the market, the competitive battle has to be fought with other weapons.

4   The list of secondary influencing factors is usually very long. In fact, there are libraries full of examples. But one thing is certain: marketing plays an important role. This role is overestimated by some companies and underestimated by others.

5   One of the largest marketing costs – and here there is almost universal agreement – is the marketing communication budget. During crisis periods, this is the first budget to be cut. A big mistake, but one that is repeated time after time. In order to capture a larger share of the market than its competitors, a company must first build up a larger share of voice.[22] The more frequently you are noticed in more places, the greater the chance that the consumer will also notice your product when he is out shopping.

6   To a large extent, it is the share of voice that determines a company's ultimate share of wallet. You can try to beat your rivals with creative fireworks, but marketing history shows us that in the end it is always the 'big spender' who wins. And a company with a larger share of wallet will also have a larger share of the market.
I hope that we are all in agreement so far.

The greatest change in respect of these principles in recent years has occurred with regard to the costly share of voice element. During the last decade and a half, the traditional push and mass media techniques have become increasingly less effective. Marketers have not been blind to these developments. They now talk more and more about the role played by the discerning customer, who pulls instead of being pushed, and about the role played by the people who we have called the recommenders. The share of voice of the unsolicited 'push' is losing ground every day, while 'pull' is very clearly on the way up. Non-human media are being banished to the margins by human media. In other words, by the recommenders and their reviews.

SHIFTS IN THE SOURCES
THAT THE CONSUMER SEES AND HEARS

Halfway through the 1990s we saw and felt (in our first year as an interactive agency) that the people who were active on the web and on the sites of our customers were playing an important and positive role for the brands. But it was difficult to quantify just how important. We could see that they came more frequently to their brand sites, were quicker to download coupons and were quicker to use them. We could also see that they brought more friends to the site, played more games and requested more samples. Most importantly, we recognised that not only did these activities all work for the brand, but also that this work was done for free. Gradually, we began to think more about this group: its value, its size, its composition.

What we didn't know then – because a team of researchers only discovered it in 2011 – is that the value of mouth-to-mouth advertising increases if people actually feel rewarded for doing it. Not only is the positive advice well received by the receiver, but the giving of that advice also has a positive effect on the recommender. Companies that encourage their satisfied customers to recommend their brands more frequently therefore yield a double benefit: they make these satisfied customers even more satisfied and they attract new customers at a relatively low cost. 'By conducting experiments in two different service settings, it is demonstrated that providing a recommendation influences the senders' attitudinal and behavioural loyalty. The effect is found to be stronger for customers with low expertise in the service category and little experience with the provider. This means that encouraging customers in the early stages of their customer life cycle to give recommendations is specifically effective in increasing loyalty to the provider. Managers should consider using positive WOM (word-of-mouth) as a loyalty-enhancing instrument and take additional value from the increased loyalty of their customer base into account for return-on-marketing calculations regarding WOM marketing campaigns, as well as customer equity calculations.'[23]

FRED REICHHELD

At a time (2003) when we had already been experimenting for a few years with these ideas, an article by Fred Reichheld was published in the *Harvard Business Review*. Its title was: 'The one number you need to grow'.

I was familiar with Reichheld as a great evangelist for loyalty marketing, but his article made clear that he had now taken things a stage further. He had spent two and a half years investigating which question about satisfaction and loyalty showed the greatest correlation with growth figures. When he had found that question, he spent another year fine-tuning and testing it.

The magic question turned out to be one that made no direct reference to satisfaction and loyalty, but inquired instead about the recommender behaviour of the person being questioned. The answer to this now famous question corresponded far more closely to growth figures than any of the other questions asked by Reichheld's team.

Reichheld worked over a long period with a panel of 4,000 consumers, whose purchase and recommendation behaviour he monitored closely. The data was compared with the results of the twenty questions in the Loyalty Acid Test, which Bain had already been using for four years.

Data was collected for six different sectors: financial institutions, telecom, personal computers, e-commerce, car insurance and internet service providers. On this basis, they developed fourteen detailed case studies, in eleven of which the One Question correlated most closely (first or second place) with the growth figures. Reichheld was surprised by the results. He had thought that the best correlation would be for a question like: 'How strongly do you feel that company X deserves your loyalty?' But he was wrong.

It was only when the One Question had been clearly identified and defined (around 2001) that Bain and Satmetrix began to pose it systematically to thousands of people in relation to more than four hundred companies in twelve sectors. In this way, they were able to collect between 12,000 and 15,000 scores each quarter. They plotted these scores against the companies and sectors for which they had reliable growth figures. In his 2003 *Harvard Business Review* article, Reichheld commented: 'The results were striking.' The correlation with the One Question was not the highest in every sector, but it was a clear winner when the scores were averaged out over all the sectors. You want to know more? Why not check out the Reichheld article for yourself.

THE ANTI-REICHHELDIANS

Wiemer Snijders is one of these. But what he writes about the start period seems to me to be incorrect. 'Reichheld collected data during a period of three years. At the end of that three years he had a nice set of companies (about 400), which all had relatively high NPS scores. Next, he checked the growth development of these companies over the previous three years! But companies that now score high on NPS have obviously grown in the previous years. Little wonder that he found a strong correlation – but it explains nothing. (In fact, correlations seldom explain anything.)'[24]

Snijders will have to fight it out with Reichheld to decide whether or not the start period was 'falsified' in this manner. But the One Question now exists, whether some people like it or not. And the facts are indisputable: nearly a decade after its launching more than a third of all American companies are using Reichheld's magic formula.

Perhaps it is worth looking a little more closely at Snijders' second contention, namely that the correlation between the One Question and growth explains nothing: '… it offers marketers insight into the extent to which customers value your brand. But to say that this leads to growth is to take matters a step too far. As is the idea that the word-of-mouth of promoters is of great value for the brand (as a consequence of its supposed advertising effect).' Here, he is wrong on two accounts.

I   It is self-evident that the question itself does not create growth. Nor does the NPS score or the Holaba score that results from the posing of the question. These are purely measuring instruments that not only allow you to determine what the current situation is, but also – providing you ask two crucial additional questions[25] – to understand how this current situation has come about. NPS gives you an immediate idea about whether you are likely to move forwards or backwards from where you are now. If you limit yourself to this knowledge and do nothing about it, then that is precisely what will happen: nothing. But if you use this information as a basis for further action, you can achieve a great deal. There are several excellent examples of this – as detailed in Reichheld's second book, which was published at the end of 2011.[26]

2 Snijders' second error is to reduce the group of brand enthusiasts and promoters to proportions that he describes as 'small', without actually providing figures to support this claim. Whereas statistics show that the recommenders actually represent a significant group of some 15% of consumers. Moreover, Snijders not only underestimates the size of the group, but similarly underestimates their reach. Once again, there is firm evidence to show that the recommenders have a larger than average circle of friends, both online and offline, and also talk with these friends about brands with an above average level of frequency. Snijders says with more justification (after all, we must give the man some credit) that there is often not all that much that a recommender can say about a brand, since the product may remain stable for long periods, so that there is no fresh news. As a result, it is primarily customers who have only recently discovered the brand who do the online and offline talking. It is also true that only 0.5% of the Facebook fans pass on information about brands. True, but it misses the point. We all know how easy it is to become the fan of a brand.

If, like Snijders, you go in search of a permanently preaching evangelist, pumping out non-stop information about brands, then it is indeed very unlikely that you will find one – because they simply don't exist. But if you take as the starting point for your search the consumer who seeks information because he wants (or needs) to buy something, then he will automatically find his way to the recom-mender, who will be happy to provide him with information, if he feels that there is a valid question to be answered. This will give the consumer access to an Aladdin's cave of marketing information, in the form of literally millions of product reviews. And so you tap into two sources that the modern consumer regards as being important and trustworthy. All the rest – classic advertising work – is irrelevant and unreliable.

Let us return briefly to where we started. Reichheld is a notorious propagandist in favour of 'loyalty-related growth'. Nobody would dispute that loyal customers are important to every company. But the level of importance of these customers in terms of the total customer base has not yet been accurately quantified. This applies equally to the level of resources (both human, financial and material) that need to be committed to retain profitable customers. Reichheld is a fanatic in these matters. I have a more circumspect view: 'A company must continually seek to provide the best service and the best product, but should not exhaust its reserves in an attempt to save a failing relationship that is already beyond economic saving.'

Most relationships reach a terminal phase, sooner or later. I try to be realistic about such things. And I am not the only one. Customers also want a satisfactory solution. They do not necessarily need a marketing orgasm. 89% of companies want to be 'exceptional', but on the other side of the equation 84% of consumers say that their expectations of a product are seldom exceeded. Even the very positive customers are only marginally more loyal.[27]

Working on the basis of his loyalty philosophy, Reichheld prefers to conduct 'his' inquiries with loyal customers. I see the matter in broader terms and am therefore less inclined to take a company's desire to retain customers as my starting point, but prefer instead the consumer's desire to go in search of purchasing information. The cacophony of voices that bombards the searching consumer is a mixture of the opinions of current customers, ex-customers and people who are thinking about becoming customers. The searching consumer then weighs each of these opinions and makes a decision.

In other words, it is the searching consumer who picks out of this uncoordinated, unharmonic din the notes and sounds that are relevant to him, and it is on this basis that he decides which information he will allow himself to be influenced by. Consequently, this is also a pull process initiated by the consumer-questioner and not a push process governed by the teller of the story.

As a result, at Holaba we also pose Reichheld's One Question to everyone who thinks that they have something meaningful to say. We try to explore and define the boundaries of the real environment of the searching buyer. And that environment, as we have said, is a mass

of conflicting noises, like a very bad case of static on your radio!
And it is precisely for this reason that we are able to arrive at a more
accurate measurement of the entire market: because we not only ask
questions of the people standing at a single stall in the marketplace,
but also listen to all the passers-by, who voluntarily offer their
own opinions.

That is the great thing about the One Question: it can be answered
by everyone who knows something about the subject under consideration. In contrast, a question about satisfaction, loyalty and repur-
chasing intentions can only be answered by customers. A question
like 'would you recommend this?' can be answered by anyone.

Because let's be honest: someone who recommends or advises
against a particular product has (in many cases) already acquired the
information on which he bases that opinion from others. For example, I became a recommender of Jaguar, simply because a month or
two ago someone arrived at my Shanghai office in that make of car
and offered to take me for a spin (I was very impressed!). The fact
that I do not yet have a Jaguar myself has nothing to do with it: I am
a fan, and so I recommend.

Consequently, you must make every effort to identify the recommenders – whether they be a force for evil or good. And you must
do it even if you are convinced that you are already the very best in
the market.

If, like McKinsey and I, you accept that recommenders are directly
responsible for between 20 and 50% of the purchases made by non-
recommenders, then you will already understand why it is so important to trace these people. These are the people you must reach and
influence. There are lots of them, but they are not always easy to find.
Some of them may already be in your database. But they are not the
kind of people who hand out folders all day at traffic lights or chat
endlessly about how wonderful your products are. Not even on Twitter. No, they are the guerrilla consumers: you know that they are
there but you can't always see them and you don't always know
what they are doing.

So how do you track them down? Simply by asking them a very
precise question on one or more occasions. And the question is not
just a blunt: 'Are you a recommender?' In that case, nobody would
understand what you mean. What is the alternative? To ask a very

concrete question about a specific product at a relevant moment (for example, immediately after purchase).

In a few days (or perhaps even hours, if you are really enthusiastic) you will have read this book and I would be interested to hear if you plan to recommend it to everyone you know. In this case, there is no option but to ask you straight off: 'How likely is it that you will recommend my book? Give a 10 if you think it is very likely or a zero if there is not a snowball's chance in hell.'

If you give a score of 9 or 10, all I can conclude is that you are a recommender of my book. But perhaps you recommend things other than books to your family and friends. I can only discover this if I ask further questions. And if I ask you to list the brands you recommend (or don't recommend) in ten other sectors and if you give a series of scores that are consistently high or low, then I can conclude that there is a good chance that you are a very well-informed and aware consumer, who also likes to share his opinion. In fact, I can say that you have a recommender profile – and that you are the core subject of this book.

And it is always about the same question. A question that you must ask all your customers, whenever and wherever you can. Remember: one-third of American companies are already doing it. It is not difficult. So begin now – and begin at the beginning: with identification.

It was for this reason that we have 5,000 brands and 50,000 products recorded in our Chinese database. And every Chinese internet-user can give a score on each one of these products, if he wants to.

HOW THE PROCESS WORKS -
A CHRONOLOGICAL SUMMARY
The consumer can choose a number of brands for which he would like to give a score

First we organise a market research survey, either on our own initiative or on behalf of a particular brand. Public. Transparent. Open to everyone who wants to take part. It might be about airline companies. Or shavers. Or digital cameras. Or fast-food restaurants. There are no limits. We show the logos of 12, 14 or 18 popular brands from the relevant sector on our Holaba website and then invite people to give scores for they brands the know or of which they have experience.

You might even call it Tripadvisor for brands. The public make their own choice of brands. We only want people who are interested in brands and are prepared to talk about them.

Below you can see a webpage from our site in Chinese. The logos are for the best daily deal sites in China: the Groupon-like clones. (On the website linked to this book you can find more details about this case.)

Scores only count if the score-givers are registered

In order to give a score, you first need to register: name, age, sex, place of residence and an e-mail address are sufficient. People are free to give more information, if they so choose. At the end of the summary, they can play a mini-lottery game, for which the prizes are a number of free call minutes for your cell phone. This means that if you want to play the game to win, you first need to give us your cell phone number. For us, this is an extra way to check that the players/participants really exist. But you can never be 100 percent sure.

Click on a brand and answer the One Question.

If they are certain that they will recommend the brand, they give a score of 9 or 10.

If they have doubts and ultimately think that they will say nothing about the brand, either good or bad, they usually give a score of 7 or 8.

If they know that they wouldn't recommend the brand for all the tea in China, they invariably give a score between 0 and 6. Not surprisingly, a zero is interpreted as an ultra-negative score (equivalent to a non-recommendation), with a 6 indicating a less radical but still ultimately negative opinion.

User? Ex-user? Future user?

We ask whether the score-giver is actually a current user of the product in question. If that is not the case, we inquire whether they have ever used the product in the past. If the answer is again negative, we ask whether they have the intention to use the product in the near future. There is even a fourth alternative: have they been considering a purchase of the product, but have not yet made a final decision. In contrast to an NPS survey – which is usually conducted with your own (good) customers – everyone has access to the Holaba website: permanent customers, one-off customers, old customers, prospective customers, etc. The more the merrier.

Recommenders are not just to be found amongst your current customers

Holaba records score in four different customer experience segments

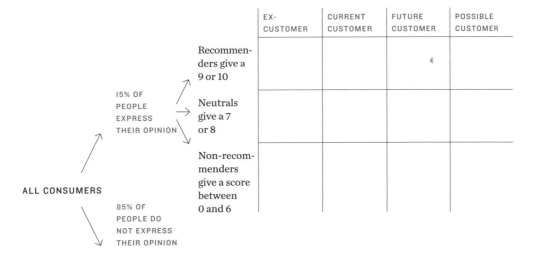

The scores differ in relation to the level and type of experience
The table below shows the extent to which the scores for the four groups can differ. It is true that the current customers are the most credible, but the recommenders in other groups are also capable of influencing potential buyers. The Holaba score is calculated by deducting the total of the low scores (0-6) from the total of the high scores (9-10). The very high positive score for Nike indicates that in China there are many more Nike recommenders than non-recommenders. In contrast, the situation for Erke (a Chinese sports brand) is less rose-coloured.

The value of the Holaba score (HS) at four different levels of experience

AVERAGE HS	NIKE 26,2	LI-NING 19,1	ANTA -5,7	ERKE -36,2
HS current user	40,3	32,7	12,9	-9,5
HS ex-customer	1,3	-3,9	-42,9	-59
HS almost customer	30,7	-8,6	-16,4	-21,3
HS interested consumers	-39,2	-47,2	-59,9	-86,9
Men	23,7	16,2	-7,2	-41,6
Women	30,1	23,5	-3	-25,6
Age 14-22	28,4	7,8	11	-35,2
Age 22-35	24,1	14,3	-5	-38,4
Age 35-50	25,5	22,2	-24	-36
Beijing	31,4	6,8	-25,8	-68
Shanghai	37,8	5,4	-36,6	-63
Guangxi	20	27,8	14	3,1

People who have time enough and interest enough can also make small comments to clarify their scores. This is most frequently done to justify an exceptionally high or low score. These comments give potential customers and the brand holders a first impression of the things that are of greatest concern to the respondents.

After giving a score and comments for one brand, you do the same for five others. It takes just two or three minutes in all. That's not very much to ask from someone who is interested in brands and in helping his fellow consumers!

When you are finished, you can also give scores to a number of randomly selected brands. In other words, you can carry on rummaging through our lists – or you can just sign off immediately. People who are not interested in buying something have nothing further to look for. And let's also be clear on this point: it is not actually possible to buy anything on the Holaba website. That is not its purpose. It simply helps you to decide what you might want to buy elsewhere. But there is nothing to stop you from returning to the site after your purchase to give new scores – or change old ones – on the basis of your resulting purchasing experiences.

Everyone gradually builds up their own brand profile

By returning occasionally to the site and giving new scores, everyone gradually builds up their own highly personal brand profile. This is worth its weight in gold to the other site users. Everyone can see who is recommending what brands or is rubbishing others. This is a useful indicator for deciding which people you want to follow.

It is also worth its weight in gold for the brand holders, since it is an equally useful indicator of the exact profile of their current, former and future customers.

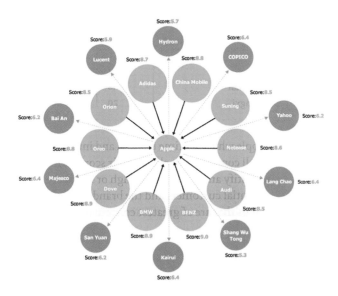

How do you read the graphic on the previous page, which appears on the dashboard of Holaba customers for every brand? The 'netizens' (internet-citizens) who have given Apple a high Holaba score are in the centre. The orange planets orbiting around this centre show the other brands that have also received a high Holaba score. The blue circles indicate the brands that are not recommended by the people who recommend Apple. In this manner, we generate thousands of different profiles and gradually gain a very clear picture of each micro-segment of the market.

The Holaba score in various segments for various brands of shavers

A Average HS / B HS men aged 20-30 / C HS men aged 30-40 / D HS women, all ages / E HS men, current users / F HS men, former users / G HS men, almost users / H HS Beijing / I HS Shanghai / J HS North-East

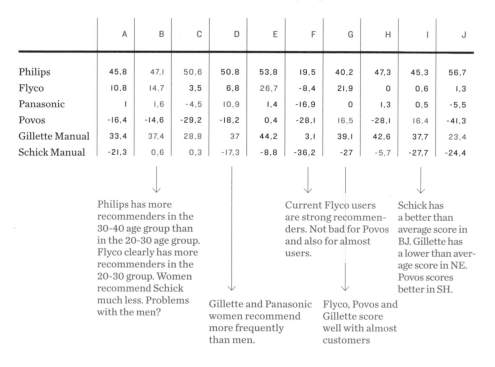

	A	B	C	D	E	F	G	H	I	J
Philips	45,8	47,1	50,6	50,8	53,8	19,5	40,2	47,3	45,3	56,7
Flyco	10,8	14,7	3,5	6,8	26,7	-8,4	21,9	0	0,6	1,3
Panasonic	I	1,6	-4,5	10,9	1,4	-16,9	0	1,3	0,5	-5,5
Povos	-16,4	-14,6	-29,2	-18,2	0,4	-28,1	16,5	-28,1	16,4	-41,3
Gillette Manual	33,4	37,4	28,8	37	44,2	3,1	39,1	42,6	37,7	23,4
Schick Manual	-21,3	0,6	0,3	-17,3	-8,8	-36,2	-27	-5,7	-27,7	-24,4

Philips has more recommenders in the 30-40 age group than in the 20-30 age group. Flyco clearly has more recommenders in the 20-30 group. Women recommend Schick much less. Problems with the men?

Gillette and Panasonic women recommend more frequently than men.

Current Flyco users are strong recommenders. Not bad for Povos and also for almost users.

Flyco, Povos and Gillette score well with almost customers

Schick has a better than average score in BJ. Gillette has a lower than average score in NE. Povos scores better in SH.

All the relevant data is entered into our database and people who buy access to this data can learn a huge amount about brands, consumers and the relationship between the two. In fact, they can learn just about everything – apart, of course, from their identities!

The manner in which things develop after the initial phase is really dependent on what you want to know about a brand. If you prefer, you can bring matters to a close at this point. You will already as a minimum have a good SWOT (strength-weakness-opportunity-threat) analysis of your own company and your competitors. The same data will also give a good indication of the way in which your share of market is likely to develop in the future. The predictive accuracy of the figures has been proven repeatedly during the past five to seven years.

What if we want to investigate a brand more deeply?

The process can be taken a significant stage further, until in some cases we have collected 40-60,000 scores in a particular branch for a particular brand. In this case, the brand in question – let's call it brand A – will be our paying customer.

For example, for brand A we may be asked to continue until we have scores from a sufficient number of people in a sufficient number of locations, all of whom have purchased brand A during, say, the past 12 months.

We might then ask these people further questions (all online!), because we want to focus primarily on customers who have also been in a shop where brand A is on sale during the last two months. Similarly, we might want to know whether they made an actual purchase or left without buying.

And so the process continues. Concentrating on the people who have been in one of the hundreds of shops countrywide where brand A is on sale and have made an actual purchase during the last two months, we might be interested to know how great the likelihood is that they will be prepared to recommend that shop to others. In other words, we want individual scores for hundreds of different shops provided by many thousands of different customers.

In some cases, the scores given by the customers will be the same as the scores they have given previously for the same brand or shop. In some cases, they will not – so that we may need to investigate the reasons for any differences. (This reminds me of JetBlue, which asks all its customers the One Question on each occasion they fly, so that the company can conduct a continuous assessment of all aspects of its service before, during and after the flight.)

Of course, we also ask many of the same questions (again, all online!) that you might find in a traditional market research survey of the kind carried out in shopping malls around the world. What did the shop window look like? Was everything in the store clean and tidy? Were the sales staff helpful? Disinterested? Pushy? Did they have the right (technical) information about the product they were trying to sell? Was the product actually in stock?

And each question can lead on to another question. For example, the last question about product availability can be supplemented by a further question inquiring about the customer's response to this situation. What did he do if the product was out of stock? Wait patiently for a new delivery? Buy it elsewhere? Buy a different brand that was immediately available? The answers to these questions can say much about brand reputation and customer loyalty.

The results at shop level

The results of these deeper investigations often confirm what we expected; for example, that shops with a high Holaba score also score better across the board than shops with a low Holaba score. This is evident from the following five graphics.

Shops that recorded a high Holaba score (top 30%) showed an average growth of 8%. Shops that recorded a low Holaba score (bottom 30%) showed an average growth of just 0.5%.

Sales increase in comparison with the previous year
Sales in relation to annual budget
A Holaba score top 30% of shops: 8.0%
B Holaba score bottom 30% of shops: 0.5%
C average for all shops: 4.2%

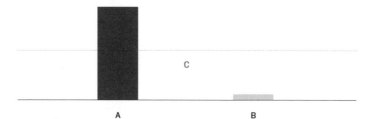

Shops that recorded a high Holaba score (top 30%) achieved results that on average were 3.7% better than their budget projection. Shops that recorded a low Holaba score (bottom 30%) achieved results that on average were 7.2% worse than their budget projection.

Sales in relation to objectives

Sales in relation to annual budget
A Holaba score top 30% of shops: 3.7%
B Holaba score bottom 30% of shops: -7.2%
C average for all shops: -2.8%

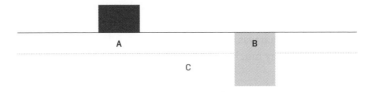

Shops with an HHS (high Holaba Score) also had a higher average amount per sales invoice.

Value per sales invoice

A Holaba score top 30% of shops: 572
B Holaba score bottom 30% of shops: 462
C average for all shops: 505

Shops with an HHS also had a higher average number of items per sales invoice.

Number of items per sales invoice

A Holaba score top 30% of shops: 2.1
B Holaba score bottom 30% of shops: 1.8
C average for all shops: 1.9

Shops with an HHS had an average turnover of ¥3,215 RMB (Chinese unit of currency) per square metre. The turnover per square metre for shops with a LHS (low Holaba Score) was almost 30% lower.

Productivity per M²month

A Holaba score top 30% of shops: 3,215
B Holaba score bottom 30% of shops: 2,400
C average for all shops: 2,528

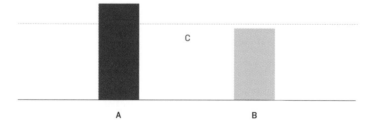

These five sales parameters do not explain per se why one shop scores better than another. The reasons why someone gives a high score or a low score to a shop are many and varied: the quality of the staff (helpful, friendly, arrogant, ill-informed, etc.), the availability of products, the layout and decoration of the store, the attractiveness of its displays, etc.

The figures do confirm, however, that it also possible to speak of a clear loop effect for shops. Good shopping experiences are passed on by word of mouth to others, resulting in yet more new customers, who in turn attract even more new customers, and so on. This is the work of the recommenders. At least in part. Let's not forget that it is also the result (first and foremost, in fact) of the many thousands of Chinese who give the best of themselves every day in the high-scoring shops and stores where they work.

What do we do with the RFM data?

The first and most important conclusion for brands is that they need to move away from the hyped RFM nonsense of recent years. People who buy regularly and in large quantities are not all equally important. They might be important today, but may not necessarily be important tomorrow.

The old one-dimensional RFM model takes no account of the recommender dimension

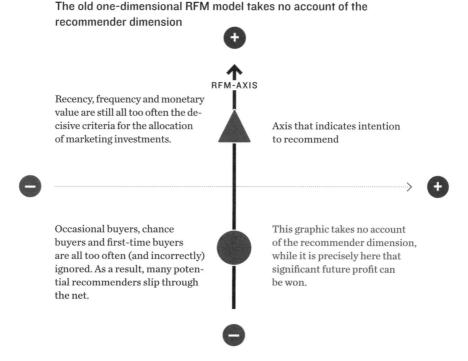

Recency, frequency and monetary value are still all too often the decisive criteria for the allocation of marketing investments.

RFM-AXIS

Axis that indicates intention to recommend

Occasional buyers, chance buyers and first-time buyers are all too often (and incorrectly) ignored. As a result, many potential recommenders slip through the net.

This graphic takes no account of the recommender dimension, while it is precisely here that significant future profit can be won.

Where exactly are the recommenders?
The various customer groups

	A	B	C	D
Size of group	37%	23%	30%	10%
Holaba score	9.67	8.43	8.85	5.26
Holaba score for shops	9.63	7.81	8.64	5.30
Number of products in possession	5.48	5.20	1.86	3.06

A Heavy user & recommender / B Heavy user /
C Light user & recommender / D Light user

In this respect, it is curious that these important consumer insights are still to an important extent extrapolated from purchase data (see the table below), whereas in reality there are always more people who (for whatever reason) do not make a purchase. Their stories could be real mind-openers for the brand owners. Unless, of course, you already know why people are not buying your products.

RFM (recency, frequency and monetary value) is still the most important data source for 64.1% of respondents in a recent survey. Customer lifetime value occupied second place with 51.1%. And the 'young' NPS (net promoter score) took third spot with just more than a third of the votes.[28]

Which data do you consider to be important for the gaining of valuable insights into customer behaviour?[29]

Select a maximum of three answers
% of respondents

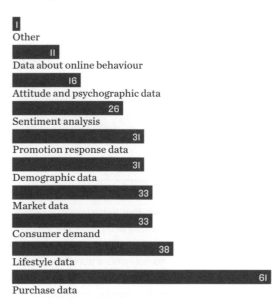

Other	1
Data about online behaviour	11
Attitude and psychographic data	16
Sentiment analysis	26
Promotion response data	31
Demographic data	31
Market data	33
Consumer demand	33
Lifestyle data	38
Purchase data	61

The people who recommend you are, of course, much more important for the future of your brand than the people who do not recommend you. This applies equally for the large and important group of light users, who are often ardent recommenders, notwithstanding the fact that they have not purchased very much of your product. These are people who are nearly always overlooked in a 'classic' marketing approach. Mass advertising and direct marketing is usually targeted at buyers, and not at recommenders. In the past, this was 'normal'. Not any more.

How can you distinguish recommenders from non-recommenders unless you ask them? And if you do ask them, you will soon know who is for and who is against your products. Every brand can pose this question to the people who are already in their databases. Broader platforms can bring a much wider range of new people into the picture, people who have not yet found their way to the brand website.

AFAQS   'With talk of digital media growing ferociously in Asia, does mass media still rule in China?'

DOCTOROFF   'Oh yes! China is a mass media market. Television is critical to reach the Chinese consumer. Digital, too, is becoming fundamental in a media plan and presently constitutes about 10-12 per cent of it. While this figure will of course increase, it will always play an incremental role to television and print. The centre of gravity isn't shifting anytime soon!'[30]

HOW IMPORTANT ARE THE RECOMMENDERS IN CHINA, IF YOU KNOW THAT THEY INFLUENCE THE PURCHASE BEHAVIOUR OF 1.4 BILLION CHINESE?

- 1.4 billion people should be easy to segment: so why aren't they?
- It is noteworthy that only half of Chinese internet users still give credence to internet advertisements, and that this number is decreasing all the time. Are the Chinese simply more suspicious of advertising than the Americans?
- Just 27% of Chinese consumers say that advertising is a useful source of information for the making of purchasing decisions. This puts advertising in last place on the list of influencing factors.

China is a mass market and it is precisely for this reason that the belief still persists that you need mass media to penetrate the market. It is by no means easy for new concepts such as 'segmenting' and 'targeting' to gain ground. The old ideas are still defended staunchly by some of the market's biggest players.

If you ask consumers in America how important it is to be supplied with product information that is tailor-made to their own requirements, almost 50% say that it is important or very important. In China the figure is just 15%. So where does this discrepancy come from?

Fortunately, in the larger cities (Beijing, Shanghai, Guangzhou) the figure amongst 18 to 24 year-olds is already above 20%. And the more people earn, the more likely they are to place emphasis on the new trends. These facts offer hope for a brighter future for all concerned. Including Holaba, which ultimately provides its customers and users with the benefits of super-segmentation and super-targeting.

Make it more relevant

'It is important to be supplied with product information that is tailor-made to my own requirements.'
% of respondents who agree

A China / B USA / C China level 1 cities / D China 18-24 years old /
E China income 8,500-12,300 RMB / F China income above 12,300 RMB

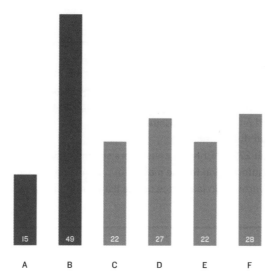

| A | B | C | D | E | F |
| 15 | 49 | 22 | 27 | 22 | 28 |

Source: McKinsey Insights China – Annual Chinese Consumer Studies (2011), Online Benchmark Survey (2011)

The following table relating to the reach and credibility of online media (for consumer electronics), published by McKinsey, indicates clearly the differences between China and the United States. All online media have a wider reach in the U.S. than in China. Similarly, the percentage of consumers who visit brand or retailer websites and who are reached by internet advertising is almost twice as high. But in matters relating to the penetration levels of online fora and social networks, the difference between the two countries becomes much smaller. Moreover, the growth figures for China in 2011 (in comparison with 2010) seem set to narrow the gap still further. Equally significant, this Chinese growth is likely to be bigger than the growth in the American market.

The differences between China and the USA are less marked in matters relating to credibility. The Chinese consumers are more inclined to regard the information they obtain from the websites of brands and retailers as 'credible' than their American counterparts. However, they are less inclined than the Americans (for the time being, at least) to believe what they hear and read in internet fora and on social network sites. Having said this, the level of credibility of these sites in China is increasing – and at a spectacular rate. Another remarkable trend is that the credibility of internet advertising is moving in the opposite direction: only 50% of Chinese internet users still believe the content of internet-ads, and that figure is falling all the time. Does this mean that the Chinese are just more suspicious by nature than the Americans? Or is there some other reason?

A China 2011 / B China % change v 2010 / C USA 2011 /
D China 2011 / E China % change v 2010 / F USA 2011

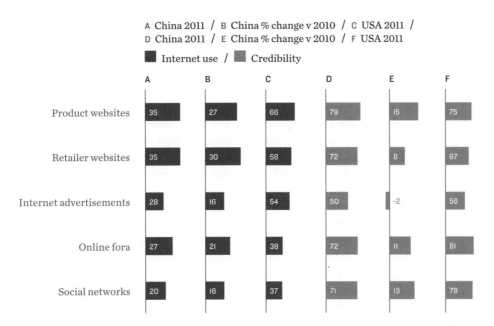

Source: McKinsey Insights China – Annual Chinese Consumer Studies (2011),
Online Benchmark Survey (2011)

I found another research investigation that appears to confirm distrust of advertisements. It seems that this distrust starts to grow as early as the building-up phase of brand recognition (see Table 1).

Jack Morton interviewed more than 10,000 people online, with an even coverage in terms of age and geographical distribution. One of his many conclusions is that the decisive factor in developing brand trust or distrust is played by family and friends who – *unasked* – begin to talk about products and services. This is true even in the early phases of the brand cycle, when brand recognition is still being built up (see the first line in Table 1).

No other source of information is valued more highly than family and friends for the discovery of products with which you are not familiar personally. This is remarkable, since the evangelists of mass media and mass advertising are constantly claiming that it is essential to use these channels of communication if you want to obtain the required reach with your customer base. They argue that the development of the ultimate fast moving consumer goods (FMCGs) from P&G, Unilever and other Johnson & Johnson's is impossible without the use of the time-honoured, tried-and-tested awareness builder. Or this is what they would like us to believe. But is this still the case? Or are the times, to quote Mr. Dylan, a-changing?

A quick glance at the second line in the table shows that the value of advertising during this 'key' first phase of development is most seriously called into question by... the Chinese! In the United States, Brazil and India, all forms of advertising still come after 'family and friends' in terms of product awareness and familiarisation. But in China second place is occupied by 'observing people using the product'. Third spot is taken by 'the explicit questioning of family and friends'. Advertising is down at a lowly number four! Remarkable – and a sign of hope for the future.

TABLE I   Top 10 ways that consumers come into contact with the brands
that they buy

A Friends and family who give their unsolicited opinions / B Advertising by
the brand itself / C Observing people using the product / D Family and friends
whose opinions I specifically request / E Brand websites / F Information at
the point of sale / G Promotions / H Research on internet / I Expert product
reviews / J Experience at the point of sale

	GLOBAL AVERAGE	US	BRAZIL	CHINA	INDIA
A	51	49	53	50	53
B	45	41	50	38	50
C	43	36	47	44	46
D	37	29	38	40	41
E	29	26	28	30	32
F	28	22	33	26	29
G	27	29	27	26	25
H	27	27	31	22	26
I	22	17	21	19	30
J	20	16	21	21	22

ADVERTISING SCARCELY PLAYS A ROLE AT THE MOMENT WHEN THE DECISION TO PURCHASE IS MADE

During the subsequent pre-purchase phase – the phase in which the decision to buy is made – the value of advertising becomes even more minimal. And this loss of importance is again most marked in China. When asked, only 27% of Chinese consumers said that they regarded advertising as a useful source of information when deciding what products to buy (see Table 2). Worse (or better?) still, this places advertising in tenth and last place of all the influencing factors.

Advertising is likewise regarded as the least important factor by American consumers, but in their case the difference between ninth place and tenth place is just 12% points. In China, the difference is a massive 34% points. The figures show that the Chinese are equally as willing to listen to the unsolicited advice of family and friends as their American counterparts (61%), even though these people, however well intentioned, are effectively poking their nose into someone else's business. In America consumers are more inclined to ask explicitly for advice from people they know and the Americans are also more likely to search for second opinions on the internet.

A Family and friends whose opinions I specifically request / B Friends and family who give their unsolicited opinions / C Self-research online / D Expert product reviews / E Experience at the point of sale / F Advertising by the brand itself / G Peer group product reviews / H Promotions / I Brand website / J Offline research

	GLOBAL AVERAGE	US	BRAZIL	CHINA	INDIA
A	56	65	55	58	44
B	55	61	53	61	43
C	47	61	41	48	37
D	47	55	45	45	43
E	44	55	46	41	35
F	43	53	51	27	41
G	43	57	41	40	35
H	42	57	40	40	31
I	42	57	39	35	35
J	42	56	34	46	32

In America it is predominantly older people who still believe what the advertisers tell them. Just 44% of the 18 to 25 year-olds still find advertising 'useful' in helping them to make purchase decisions. This figure rises to 53% amongst the 26 to 42 year-olds, and climbs to 63% for the over 42-age group (see Table 3).

It is also noticeable that women have slightly more belief in advertising than men – although it must be pointed out (if only to avoid claims of sexist discrimination) that women tend to give higher scores for almost every influencing factor. Men seem more inclined to rely on their own opinions when making their decisions. Does this mean that we men are bigger gamblers? Or just unthinking machos?

The highest result in the entire list was recorded for women: a score of 69% for the advice given by family and friends. And in this respect it is perhaps important to remember that women account for two-thirds of all purchases – equivalent to $12 of the $18 trillion dollars of purchases each year! 'Overall, it is safe to conclude that women have the last word in spending decisions pertaining to most of the product categories. So it makes sense for marketers to keep the ladies happy to stay in the family's consideration set.'[31]

TABLE 3 Top 10 most valuable sources of information for making purchase decisions (US consumers only)

A Family and friends whose opinions I specifically request / B Friends and family who give their unsolicited opinions / C Self-research online / D Peer group product reviews / E Promotions / F Brand website / G Offline research / H Expert product reviews / I Experience at the point of sale / J Advertising by the brand itself

	US AVERAGE	18-25 YEARS	26-42 YEARS	OVER 42 YEARS	MEN	WOMEN
A	65	64	63	68	61	69
B	61	61	59	64	57	65
C	61	59	61	63	60	63
D	57	59	57	56	56	59
E	57	51	54	66	52	62
F	57	55	56	60	55	59
G	56	52	55	61	55	56
H	55	55	55	56	54	56
I	55	52	50	63	53	56
J	53	44	53	63	51	56

THE BATTLE BETWEEN THE CREDIBILITY OF PEOPLE
AND THE LACK OF CREDIBILITY OF ADVERTISING HAS
BEEN DECIDED – AND ADVERTISING HAS LOST

What is interesting about the final table in this section on China is the fact that the Chinese still get much more advertising rammed down their throats via their television screens than most other nations: in China 91% are afflicted in this manner, in comparison with just 80% in the U.S. Even more interesting, perhaps, and certainly a source of future hope for everyone who believes in the power of recommenders and their recommendations, are the results detailed in the second line: 71% of Chinese consumers reported that in the two months before the survey was conducted they had received recommendations from family and friends (a growth of 14% in comparison with 2010!). And while the results in the U.S. are lower, 'recommendations' still occupy a very respectable second place. If in both cases we compare the 'believability' of family and friends with the 'un-believability' of television advertising, then it is very clear which way the wind is blowing – on both sides of the Pacific Ocean, and probably on both sides of the Atlantic as well!

TABLE 4   Media reach

% of respondents who had received product information in the two months prior to the survey

A China (2011) / B China change v 2010 / C USA (2011)

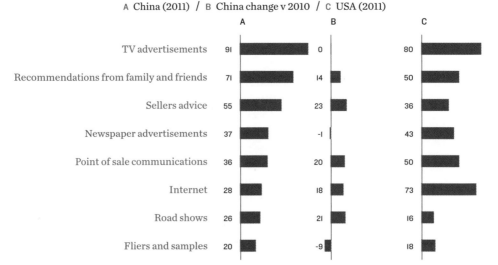

	A	B	C
TV advertisements	91	0	80
Recommendations from family and friends	71	14	50
Sellers advice	55	23	36
Newspaper advertisements	37	-1	43
Point of sale communications	36	20	50
Internet	28	18	73
Road shows	26	21	16
Fliers and samples	20	-9	18

Source: McKinsey Insights China – Annual Chinese Consumer Studies (2009, 2011), Online Benchmark Survey (2011)

3 Brands, recommenders and consumers: We fight the same battle!

- Recommenders fight against bad products and dishonest PR practices. This works to everyone's benefit. Even to the benefit of the companies that for the time being still think differently.
- Sooner or later there will be a recommenders' manifesto. This will no doubt contain words such as 'honesty', 'reliability', 'proven experience' and 'openness'. Plus a whole heap of other wishes and demands from all three parties.
- Recommenders must inevitably be prepared to sacrifice a little bit more of their privacy than the average consumer. Fortunately, most of them don't seem to mind.
- Recommenders don't need to scream and shout to make themselves heard. They can also be introvert non-networkers, providing they have meaningful things to say that others are prepared to spread. Above all, each recommender is a part of the whole.

Because this book is about the guerrilla consumer, I have deliberately chosen a provocative title for this chapter, based on the language used by protesters and occupiers throughout the ages. Because make no mistake: it is a battle. A battle between incompatible interests projected on both companies and consumers. Companies try to produce their goods at the lowest possible cost, often in low wage countries, and then try to sell these same goods at the highest possible price, usually in high wage countries.

In recent years, we have discovered to our cost that this economic paradox has caused us great harm. The drive to maximise profits has damaged – if not destroyed – everything that we worked so hard to build up in the days when profits were normal. Various religions, mass media and the permanent 'feel-good' communications of the advertising industry have brainwashed us into accepting that the maximisation of profit is the only way. And we simply didn't know any better.

However, the realisation is gradually beginning to dawn that we need to do things differently. And there is also a parallel realisation amongst some people that this is perfectly possible. Some companies are already trying to save on their huge, almost crushingly high PR and advertising budgets (that are yielding ever smaller economic returns) and more and more consumers are learning to ignore (or even fight back against) the non-stop bombardment of the advertising industry. Nowadays, advertising only exists to keep the advertisers in work.

THE EIGHT RECOMMENDER COMMANDMENTS

It is in the interests of both brand builders and brand consumers to cherish, purify, inform, activate and animate the 15% of people who are actually recommenders, or who pretend to be, or who are accorded this status by those around them. Both the brands and the consumers quite rightly make a number of demands of this 15%. For this reason, in this chapter I will be looking closely at the following eight recommender commandments.

1 Recommenders exist.
2 Recommenders act in good faith.
   a) Recommenders must be honest. As far as possible.
   b) Recommenders must be trustworthy.
   c) Recommenders must not be in the pay of the brands.
   d) Recommenders must never become advertising in human form.
3 Recommenders must know something about something.
   a) Recommenders must have a degree of knowledge about the subjects they discuss and the products they recommend.
   b) Recommenders must – preferably – have relevant experience.
4 Recommenders must dare to open their mouths and say what they think. After all, that is their raison d'etre!
5 Recommenders do not necessarily want to or need to influence others.
6 Recommenders must also be open to the influence of others, to prevent them from becoming too set in their ways.
7 Recommenders of a particular brand must continue to monitor other brands.
8 Recommenders will already have their own network.

When I first entered the Chinese market with my Holaba project, the most pertinent question that my potential customers kept on asking me was: 'Do these people really exist?' I could hardly believe what I was hearing. I already knew that the research data could be used in many different ways for many different purposes, but that the actual existence of the source of this data should still be doubted? I was flabbergasted.

Of course, by this time The Netherlands had already had its own Stapel affair and we had all become wiser as a result. This once respected professor first formulated his conclusions and then fabricated the data to prove that he was right. The people from whom he had supposedly obtained this data simply did not exist. He had made it all up. In short, dozens of academic articles and fourteen doctoral theses were written on the basis of data that had been obtained from people who were nothing more than a figment of the professor's vivid imagination.[32]

In this respect, it is important that people should operate under their own real identities on the internet. Particularly on review sites. This gives brands and consumers more confidence in the recommender in question. In China, there was initially a good deal of commotion about this need for transparency, because it was the custom there for people to say things on the web without revealing who they are. Suspicion and distrust (of others, of the state) made people believe that this was the only 'safe' thing to do.[33]

Fortunately, privacy issues are less important in relation to brands (even though I have a number of good friends who would still disagree entirely with this contention). Recommenders tend to be extrovert people who are less concerned about being identified as the maker or breaker of a brand than, say, a dissident in China or an opponent of the regime in the Middle East.

On the Holaba website, we ask for a cell phone number. This does not exclude the possibility of fraud completely, but at least allows it to be localised. As a rule, the person who gives the number can be called and therefore traced. People have the option to allow their number to be made public – or not. But we always insist on having a number.

When we launched Holaba in China, we explained to our fraudulent members that we would scrap them from the site if they failed to put a stop to their dishonest practices. And sometimes this sanction was applied. If you receive a number of unidentifiable web names from the same IP address within the space of a few hours, all telling more or less the same story, then you can be reasonably sure that something fishy is going on. When this happens, it is better to act quickly to clear up the mess – before the stench of corruption becomes too great.

RECOMMENDERS ACT IN GOOD FAITH
Recommenders must be honest. As far as possible.

We usually ask people visiting our Holaba site to give a single score to six different brands. We offer them a choice of 14, 16 or 18 brands from a particular sector and they pick the six that most interest them.

They have nothing to gain by giving brand X a deliberately high score and brand Y a deliberately low score. Unless, of course, they are being paid by a brand to do so. We cannot yet prevent this practice, but we at least seek to discourage it by making clear that the giving of a score or the writing of a review on our site is not linked in any way to a financial reward.

It is also easier to choose a couple of brands from our relatively long list, about which you can say something in good faith. We are not forcing people to give opinions on products that they know nothing about. In these circumstances, there is once again nothing to be gained (or lost) by giving a fair and honest score. People only give a score if they feel that they have sufficient experience of the brand to make a valid judgement. If there is a subject about which I know absolutely nothing (for example, fast-food restaurants), I will simply avoid that section of the website. Why should I give my opinion about restaurants I have never even visited? That is just a waste of time and effort – and helps no one.

If I nevertheless insist on choosing a subject about which I know nothing, there is a good chance that my lack of knowledge and experience will quickly be discovered. But not if I remain honest. However, if I deliberately praise one brand to the heavens and deliberately pull a competing brand to pieces, while in reality the quality of both products reflects precisely the opposite of my scores and/or comments, then I am actually undermining my own credibility by allowing my 'expertise' to be misused in this manner. And this is something, as a recommender, that I wish to avoid at all costs. Recommenders are narcissists at heart. They want to be the centre of attention and they want to be believed. And to be believed, you need to be honest. As far as possible.

It is of great importance to both brands and consumers that the majority of the people who put themselves forward as recommenders or who are identified as such by one of the many search engines are actually trustworthy.

If there is one other matter that is difficult to measure accurately (apart from the level of influence exercised by particular individuals), it is this question of trustworthiness. To what extent can a recommender be trusted? It is simply not possible to subject every would-be online recommender to a lie-detector test. And even if we could, it would still not guarantee 100 percent trustworthiness.

In order to trust someone, it is first and foremost necessary to have no real reasons not to trust them. The better you know someone and the more experience you have of his behaviour, the easier it is to judge whether or not he is acting impartially. If you know someone less well, the more you need to rely on the opinions of others who are closer to him.

It is easier to find 'trustable others' online than offline. Unknown persons who have given a score or a review that has been rewarded with numerous followers and 'thumbs up' are much more likely to be trusted by strangers than the occasional score dumpers.

Disclosure can be a part of the solution: admitting right from the start that you are an interested party. If I work for Apple or have shares in Apple, then my recommendation of Apple is less trustworthy than the recommendation of an ordinary member of the public. But turning matters on their head, what is the value of the recommendation of someone who has no Apple shares or – even worse – no Apple products? Disclosure alone must be sufficient to create a degree of trust, since the person considering the recommendation is still assumed to draw up his own final balance of the situation, which can take account of the recommender's vested interest – providing he is aware of it. Disclosure statements of this kind are common practice in investment circles and there is no reason why they should not be introduced at consumer level. A potential conflict of interests is always less likely to cause problems if you know that it exists.

PS. Just so you know: I am an Apple recommender and an Apple shareholder. I wouldn't want you to think that I am hiding anything!

Someone who is on the payroll of the brewers of Johnny Walker whisky is likely to be one of the strongest recommenders of that whisky. Unless, of course, he is a teetotaller. Having said this, there is always a high correlation between the recommender scores of employees and the recommender scores of external parties (the customers).

The immediate circle of friends around a Johnny Walker fan will also know that he is a recommender of that brand. This is not a problem. But he should think twice before getting heavily involved in online discussions about whether Johnny Walker is better than Jack Daniels. Or else he should reveal his identity and his interest.

Ordinary people normally do not consider allowing themselves to be paid for the writing of a positive review. The loss of reputation and the shame of being discovered are simply not worth the few euros that they might otherwise receive for their 'services'. Nevertheless, third party sites like Holaba should, in my opinion, be able to offer various benefits – or perks, to use the jargon – at the basic platform level.

About a decade ago, when I was manager of an interactive advertising agency, we began experimenting for Nivea with the giving away of all kinds of free gifts to the women who communicated regularly and with positive results about the brand. They brought their friends and family to the site, did more forwarding than other women, took part more frequently in surveys, were more likely to request samples of new products, etc. Each month the most active recommenders were 'rewarded'. But everyone knew this and could follow online what was being given and to whom.

This brings us to a question that I am still asked with monotonous regularity: why do people bother to invest their time and energy in the writing of reviews for which they receive little or nothing in terms of financial gain? The answer is simple and is already supported by a considerable body of research evidence. The first article that I read on this subject was published as long ago as 2008 by Roger Dooley.[34]

The part of the brain that is activated when you are paid for what you do is precisely the same part that is activated if someone praises you for what you do. The part in question is known as the striatum, and this aspect of its functioning was first discovered by Japanese researchers during an FMRI-scan (FMRI stands for functional magnetic resonance imaging). In essence, this means that people do 'good

things' for other people because it makes them feel good: they know
that they are appreciated.

Recommenders must never become advertisers in human form

Some time ago I received a mail from an American consultant, who
asked my opinion about the duality of the recommender's role. He
had the feeling that the influence of recommenders (with their followers) continued to grow, almost irrespective of whether they wrote
positive or negative reviews. I found it difficult to disagree with his
position. The frequency, variation and quality of the reviews will all
increase the authority of the recommender. And if some of the reviews
are negative? One man's meat is another man's poison. Someone will
always like what he has to say.

We began to try and quantify this with our Holaba data. The top
500 (T500) in the followers ranking had 146 times more followers
than 500 people (A500) chosen from our database at random:
2043 followers against just 14.

It appeared that the number of reviews written by the T500 was
the key factor in attracting this large number of followers: on average, they wrote 139 times more reviews than the A500. What's more,
for the T500 just 19% of these reviews related to scores of 9 or 10,
whereas this figure rose to 56% for the A500. At the other end of
the spectrum, 30% of the T500 reviews related to a low (0-6) score,
against just 16% for the A500.

So what does this all mean? In China there are more brands with
a negative score than a positive score. In many of the surveys that we
present to our netizens, only 3 to 5 of the 16 or 18 products receive a
positive Holaba score. (NB: a brand gets a negative Holaba score
when more people give a low score than a high one.)

Looking at the figures against this background, we must conclude
that Chinese recommenders are not the type of recommenders who
scream that something is either brilliantly good or appallingly awful.
Instead, they are people who give a well-considered score, which is
something they do regularly, and they back up their score with well-
reasoned argument, which many people are inclined to follow.

RECOMMENDERS MUST KNOW SOMETHING ABOUT SOMETHING
Recommenders must have a degree of knowledge about the subjects they discuss and the products they recommend

Someone who buys his first shaver, his first bottle of whisky or his first hot-water kettle is probably someone who has little knowledge of these things. To acquire such knowledge, it is first necessary to have kept your eyes and ears open for what is happening in the market over a period of time.

Ideally, recommenders should be 'experience experts'. Being aware of what is going on in the market is a good start. I can be aware of the quality of different disposable nappies without being a young mother; perhaps because my three children have all recently had babies and I spent the Easter, Summer and Christmas holidays with one or other of them. In this case, I am an expert in the assimilation and aggregation of stories told to me by others, who are unquestionably each experience experts in their own right.

I have no idea how many recommenders are subscribers to one or more of the various consumer magazines that are now available. Quite a lot of them, I should think. Someone who is looking for something, with the idea of making a purchase, must decide whether he attaches more weight to the opinion of someone who has experience of that thing or someone who has heard a lot about it from others. In general, most of us find the former a more reliable source of information than the latter.

The recommender also confirms to the brand (more readily and more frequently than the average consumer) that he wants to be kept informed about their products. The opinion of his peer group is directly proportional to his level of knowledge. The more he knows, the more highly he is regarded. For this reason alone, it is important for him to keep his knowledge up to scratch.

In this respect, it is difficult to understand (in the following table) how printed matter and television still score so highly with top marketers when they are asked to list in order of importance the media that they use to stimulate and strengthen the brand commitment of their consumers: the so-called channels of engagement. The table shows that they are planning to make greater use of social media during the coming 12 months. But if by this they mean placing adverts or drumming up extra fans for their home page, they will be wasting

Source:
http://www.management-
thinking.eiu.com/sites/
default/files/downloads/
Oracle_.pdf

Which marketing channels were important for you during recent months for stimulating consumer engagement?

Give points on a scale from 1 (very important) to 5 (not at all important)
% of respondents

● 1. Very important ● 2 ● 3 ● 4 ● 5. less important

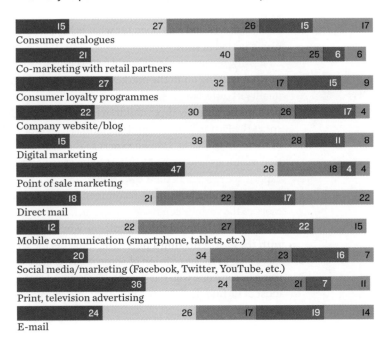

15	27	26	15	17

Consumer catalogues

21	40	25	6	6

Co-marketing with retail partners

27	32	17	15	9

Consumer loyalty programmes

22	30	26	17	4

Company website/blog

15	38	28	11	8

Digital marketing

47	26	18	4	4

Point of sale marketing

18	21	22	17	22

Direct mail

12	22	27	22	15

Mobile communication (smartphone, tablets, etc.)

20	34	23	16	7

Social media/marketing (Facebook, Twitter, YouTube, etc.)

36	24	21	7	11

Print, television advertising

24	26	17	19	14

E-mail

their time – and money. Because these are very definitely not the channels to build up engagement.

One of the proofreaders of this book hit the nail on the head when he said: 'Do you know what? The fundamental problem is that marketers do not have full control over the company. Recommending a company is not only the result of "good" communication and "good" product presentation, but also of the company's service, after sales, logistical organisation, etc. And these are things that the marketer – in most cases – does not have under his control. In other words, he is obliged to limit himself to the "channels" he can influence and control.'

*Source:
http://www.management-
thinking.eiu.com/sites/
default/files/downloads/
Oracle_SalesandMarketing_
120207r1.pdf*

Which marketing channels do you think will be important for you during the coming 12 months for stimulating consumer engagement?

Give points on a scale from 1 (very important) to 5 (not at all important)
% of respondents

● 1. Very important ● 2 ● 3 ● 4 ● 5. less important

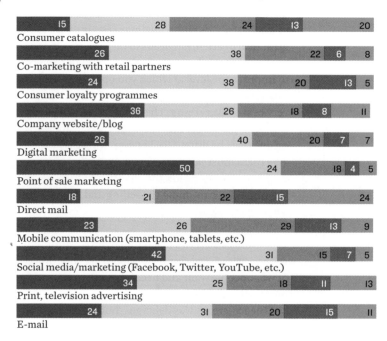

	1	2	3	4	5
Consumer catalogues	15	28	24	13	20
Co-marketing with retail partners	26	38	22	6	8
Consumer loyalty programmes	24	38	20	13	5
Company website/blog	36	26	18	8	11
Digital marketing	26	40	20	7	7
Point of sale marketing	50	24	18	4	5
Direct mail	18	21	22	15	24
Mobile communication (smartphone, tablets, etc.)	23	26	29	13	9
Social media/marketing (Facebook, Twitter, YouTube, etc.)	42	31	15	7	5
Print, television advertising	34	25	18	11	13
E-mail	24	31	20	15	11

Recommenders must – preferably – have relevant experience

We know from research that people who have experience of the relevant sector and a number of the key brands in that sector are more convincing to others than people who have only heard about these brands at second hand.

It is primarily for this reason that experience scores are important. My 90-year-old mother has no experience of digital cameras and so her opinion is not relevant, unless she can talk about the advantages and disadvantages that her children and grandchildren have encountered with their own cameras. In contrast, the experience of a young mother of three bouncing babies is of great value, if you are talking about nappies, shampoo, car seats for kids, etc.

A profile sketch of recommenders will show that they are just ordinary people who are more open for all kinds of experience and feedback than most other ordinary people. They are curious about all different types of input and are willing (and able) to process them.

In view of the fact that the quality of their experience is of decisive importance for the content of what they say to their immediate circle of family, friends and acquaintances, this is an aspect to which a great deal of attention needs to be paid. As a brand guardian, you must constantly be on the lookout for bugs. And constantly seeking to improve the level at which you operate. Consumers are no longer satisfied with the notion that 'good is good enough'. They want the very best of everything. They demand red carpet treatment all the way. And the carpet must be wide enough and without creases! This means that the difference between what they expect and what you give them must not be too great.

If you sell ice-cream, the quality of the ice-cream is more important than the girls doing the selling and the parlour in which it is sold. The same is true for hamburgers. Or for a flight between Beijing and Shanghai.

It is only when you reach the Olympic minimum (of which we spoke earlier – and this means focusing your product on the essence of what people want and need) that other, less important criteria must be considered.

'The ice-cream was delicious, but the girls selling them were not very nice. Not very friendly, either. And the shop was a bit dreary for an ice-cream parlour. What's more, they had no more pistachio, and I was so looking forward to pistachio. Such a long wait and then no pistachio!'

In the past, you might have got away with this. You have the best ice-cream in Siena – and that is the most important thing. Unfortunately, there are now five other ice-cream sellers in Siena making equally delicious ice-cream – and in their parlours everything is pico bello in order! 'It's the total experience, stupid!'

These clever competitors take as their starting point everything that a potential ice-cream buyer might have in his head and are constantly adjusting their business to reflect all these 'needs'. If you fail to do this, you are simply digging your own grave. This is particularly the case in service industries, where people – your staff – are an integral part of the total package that is being assessed. But even with 'ordinary' products it is becoming increasingly easy to identify the manufacturers that have taken the trouble to look at things from the customer's point of view. Why do you think that Apple is so much easier to use?

If someone asks you tomorrow whether you would recommend the pistachio-less ice-cream parlour where you bought your ice-cream yesterday, you would probably say: 'The ice-cream was great but the rest was all a bit so-so. There are better places in Siena. I would give it an 8.'

To discover which things are likely to irritate your consumers in this manner, you not only need to question your loyal customers, who will keep on coming to your parlour every week notwithstanding all these small defects (which they are used to by now). No, you must also ask the occasional customers, who you only see every once in a while, because they also buy ice-creams in the other parlours as well. They are not blind, are not willing to tolerate shortcomings and are prepared to vote with their feet: they either come… or they go. And once they are gone, it is hard to get them back again.

http://www.slideshare.net/jackmortonWW/best-experience-brands-a-global-study-by-jack-morton-worldwide-10365627

Consumer experiences

Relative importance (on a scale from 1 to 7) of the factors that can influence consumer experiences (average scores)

5.8
Product experience
6.1 – Products and services that answer consumer needs
5.6 – Finding new ways to surprise long-standing customers

5.8
Point of sale experience
5.8 – Makes it easy for the consumer to find information and buy products when and where he wants (shop, online, mobile apps.)
5.8 – Ensures an efficient purchasing experience

5.7
Customer experience
5.9 – Understanding of customer needs
5.8 – Repeat customers get continued good service and commitment
5.8 – Exceeding expectations
5.6 – Showing consumers – even repeat customers – how to make best use of their purchases

5.4
Discovery experience
5.6 – The first impression made by the brand
5.5 – What distinguishes the brand from other similar products and services
5.0 – What the brand says about itself in marketing and advertising

4.9
Social experience
5.0 – The brand supports socially worthy causes that are close to the consumer's heart
4.8 – The brand gives the consumer the feeling of belonging to a special group

4.8
Digital experience
5.0 – A series of digital apps to create 'engagement' with the brand
4.8 – Online presence (website, social networks, advertising)
4.5 – Active online follow-up and community

In this sense, internet retailers find it easier to excel. They do not have to physically face the consumer, and their complaints (if there are any) are confined to matters like the user interface, late or wrong delivery, payment problems, etc.

The above table gives details of the criteria most frequently applied by consumers. The only criteria directly linked to a product or service is the first criteria, which receives the highest score of 6.1. All the other criteria help you to understand what else a customer expects when he enters your shop, ice-cream parlour, website, etc. Consumer experience with products and services also helps to steer recommender behaviour. In this respect, petrol stations and supermarkets clearly have plenty of room for improvement, if we are to believe the table on the next page. But it is only online retail that stands head and shoulders above the rest. And that is good news.

Complaints about online purchases in China
Source: China E-commerce Research Centre

Late delivery	18%
Repayment	12%
Other	11%
After sales	9%
Online fraud	9%
Return/exchange of goods	8%
Quality problems	8%
False promotions	7%
Trade fraud with virtual property	7%
Delivery	6%
Order cancellation	5%

Because consumers do not come into contact with other people in the context of online retail, the business transaction is not 'spoilt' by the small human problems that can sometimes arise as a result of this contact. Having said this, when things do go wrong (which, as the above list shows, always happens from time to time), the human element becomes vitally important. This is the point at which the staff of Amazon (or Abe or Ebay) need to step in to solve the mini-crisis and pour oil on troubled waters.

http://www.marketing-charts.com/interactive/tra-ditional-retailers-see-im-proved-customer-satisfac-tion-lag-online-21245/

Customer satisfaction in different retail sectors

Customer satisfaction index 2009-2011
Source: American Customer Satisfaction Index

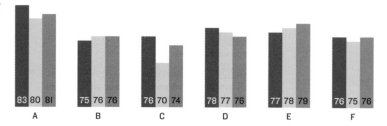

● 2009
○ 2010
● 2011

| 83 80 81 | 75 76 76 | 76 70 74 | 78 77 76 | 77 78 79 | 76 75 76 |
| A | B | C | D | E | F |

A Online stores / B Department and discount stores /
C Petrol stations / D Health stores / E Specialist stores / F Supermarkets

If we are talking about the way customer experiences give inspiration to a recommender, then the role played by women is particularly important. Women are not quickly satisfied. And they are right. Marketing research has also shown that men have difficulty in selling to women: they show too little emotion, offer discounts when it is not necessary, pay inadequate attention to time-saving features, while generally overstating everything else. They try to make things seem better than they really are – and women don't like this.

A man's approach to shopping is goal-oriented. A woman's approach to shopping is process-oriented. That, at least, is what the researchers tell us. Men want to complete the shopping experience as quickly as possible. Women do not. Women always buy for the whole family – and not just for themselves. And they are particularly dissatisfied with investment products, cars and car insurance, banks, life insurance, doctors, work clothing, hospitals and homes![35]

RECOMMENDERS MUST DARE TO OPEN THEIR MOUTHS
AND SAY WHAT THEY THINK. AFTER ALL, THAT IS
THEIR RAISON D'ETRE!

You can compare it with the political balance of power in a democracy. People who remain silent automatically vote with the majority. People who do not agree with what this majority are saying and doing can sometimes be forced into silence through fear. Or they can talk

Web sector / internet retailers

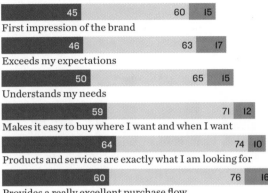

	Performance	Importance	Gap
First impression of the brand	45	60	15
Exceeds my expectations	46	63	17
Understands my needs	50	65	15
Makes it easy to buy where I want and when I want	59	71	12
Products and services are exactly what I am looking for	64	74	10
Provides a really excellent purchase flow	60	76	16

● **Performance**
○ **Importance**
● **Gap**

Product-based sector / mobile devices

	Performance	Importance	Gap
Shows me how to make best use of the product, even if I am already an established customer	41	58	17
Exceeds my expectations	40	59	19
Provides a really excellent purchase flow	43	62	19
Makes it easy to buy where I want and when I want	51	63	12
Understands my needs	43	69	26
Products and services are exactly what I am looking for	53	72	19

Service-based sector / airlines

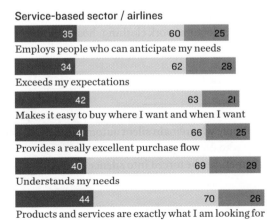

	Performance	Importance	Gap
Employs people who can anticipate my needs	35	60	25
Exceeds my expectations	34	62	28
Makes it easy to buy where I want and when I want	42	63	21
Provides a really excellent purchase flow	41	66	25
Understands my needs	40	69	29
Products and services are exactly what I am looking for	44	70	26

about their political ideas within their inner circle of trusted friends. Or take matters a stage further by writing about their beliefs. Another step further might see these beliefs posted on Facebook. And so the process continues. The greater their determination to air their opinions and the greater the level of adaptation of their listeners, the greater their chances of success become – at the next election.

The process is very similar for the market share of a brand. A bad brand that depends on the inertia of the public for its success ('I buy it because I have always bought it', 'I vote for him because I have always voted for him') will maintain its position as long as nobody raises a voice of protest or offers a viable alternative. As soon as someone begins to talk about his positive experiences with a different brand and as soon as these comments are repeated and spread by others, the situation quickly begins to change. Share of market directly reflects the thoughts and feelings playing around in the heads of many thousands of consumers. If more and more people are ready to switch from brand A to brand B, then the floodgates open and change takes place. But please: let's not call this a Twitter or Facebook revolution! The main role in bringing about this transformation is played by the 15% of recommenders, who dare to open their mouths and then drag the silent majority along with them.

If a brand begins to invest in whatever manner in its recommenders (above all, by trying to be better than its competitors, time after time), it needs to be sure that the recommenders are going to spread the word. And when. And how. Let's be clear on this point: you don't always need to initiate conversations. Broadcasting relevant information and providing relevant links is an ideal way to achieve good reach and secure a growing number of satisfied followers.

How often do the recommenders need to open their mouths? An American study by Zuberance showed that a subgroup of the people surveyed (the people who we refer to as recommenders in this book) recommended more than 15 different brands and talked about one or other of those brands several times a week. This strikes me as being a lot.[36]

Because ours is a young discipline, there is still a degree of confusion with regard to terminology. Zuberance calls 40% of consumers 'brand advocates', with the top 15% that group being 'power advocates'. It is these power advocates who push their brands online and offline several times per week. In other words, just 6% of all consumers. We could perhaps refer to these people as super-recommenders. After all, they have more brands about which they talk more often to more people than the 'ordinary' recommenders. Maybe the time has come for our branch to agree a list of common definitions, linked to specific criteria.

Zuberance	average consumers	60%
	brand advocates	40%
	average brand advocates	34%
	power advocates	6%
Holaba	ordinary consumers	85%
	recommenders	15%
	ordinary recommenders	9%
	super-recommenders	6%

Categories in which brands are often recommended

Most brand advocates make recommendations in different categories
Source: Zuberance

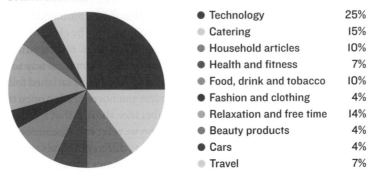

●	Technology	25%
●	Catering	15%
●	Household articles	10%
●	Health and fitness	7%
●	Food, drink and tobacco	10%
●	Fashion and clothing	4%
●	Relaxation and free time	14%
●	Beauty products	4%
●	Cars	4%
●	Travel	7%

In China at least half of all consumers discuss brands on a daily basis, either online or offline.[37]

Chinese consumers who discuss brands online and offline (ordered according to size of city of residence)

Age 13-45: talked about a brand on the day before the survey was conducted
Source: Starcom MediaVest Group, 'China Yangtze Study', October 2011

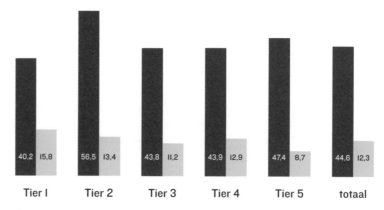

Tier 1	Tier 2	Tier 3	Tier 4	Tier 5	totaal
40,2 15,8	56,5 13,4	43,8 11,2	43,9 12,9	47,4 8,7	44,6 12,3

● Talked OFFLINE with others about a brand they like
◐ Talked ONLINE with others about a brand they like

RECOMMENDERS DO NOT NECESSARILY
WANT TO OR NEED TO INFLUENCE OTHERS

In chapter 4 we will look in detail at the difference between someone who recommends something (our recommenders) and someone who has influence. These are two completely different things. Someone with influence in a certain field can, in the final analysis, recommend three or four different brands relating to that field, leaving the final choice to the consumer. Someone who repeatedly and frequently pushes the same single brand, more or less acting as a live commercial, will often elicit a cool response from many consumers, in particular the ones he is most keen to influence. In the advertising world, it is notoriously difficult to predict the reaction of consumers to TV advertisements or banners. Finding the right key in a one-to-one discussion is even more difficult.

The only way to find out what really works is to launch all your various comments and opinions on the public and measure how they react. If you replace 'dead' media with human media – recommenders are people and not a cog in a machine – the reaction of the 85% of consumers who receive the recommendations (i.e., the non-recommenders) is still unpredictable. But the source of the recommendation – the sender of the message – is much more important than with classic media. There are people who can persuade others to follow them quite far with just a nod and a wink, while there are others who are less verbally gifted and find it hard to persuade anyone of anything. This means that in time profiles can be identified of people with great powers of persuasion and others with none at all.

A very simple method, but one that is difficult to carry out on a large scale, is to ask would-be recommenders which people they have influenced during the past year, and then ask these 'followers' if and by whom they have been influenced (for purchasing decisions) during the same period. In sectors where large amounts of money per transaction are involved, this should be possible. Who influenced your choice of mortgage provider? Who influenced your choice of car? Or television? Or computer? Or insurance policy? Klout has evolved in this direction in recent years: they can now identify people who their server thinks are likely to influence me and people who the server thinks I am likely to influence. But let's not get carried away: this information still relates to broad fields of activity and not to specific brands.

Reply percentage and number of followers

Source: Hubspot

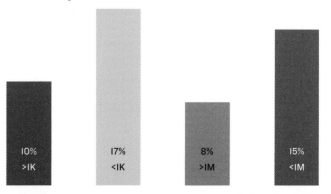

| Someone with less than 1,000 followers replies less than someone with more than 1,000 followers | Someone with less than 1,000,000 followers replies less than someone with more than 1,000,000 followers |

Someone who keeps on going to the same camping site for his holidays, year after year, is clearly someone who never bothers (or feels a need) to check whether the grass might be greener on the other side of the hill. The influencing power of this person is almost zero, precisely because he has no idea what other campings have to offer. People like him are set in their ways: the kind of person who still prefers a horse and cart to all other, more modern means of transport. People who keep on stubbornly following old ideas will one day discover that they have been left far behind the rest of us!

In order to form their judgements about possible purchases, searching customers find the opinions of ultra-loyal customers less useful than previously thought. Opinions from brand-hoppers, who have a wide experience of the world in all its facets and have even fallen flat on their recommender faces more than once, are potentially more interesting and useful than those of a stick-in-the-mud loyal user, who always has the same story to tell. Like me, you probably know plenty of people who waited for years before they could be convinced to try any other wine than French wine!

Of course, I understand that faithful customers are real cash cows for any brand, but their annual litany about 'the best camping in the world' is not going to persuade anybody to follow them. In fact, their inertia actually works against the brand they love so much. They are not credible as ambassadors because they refuse point-blank to try anything else. Their stories have a 'last-century' feel to them: outdated, outmoded and no longer relevant. Most consumers want to change brands from time to time – safely and not too often, but change nonetheless. If all they hear is the same old sad song about Sunshine Camping, they will stop listening straight away. In short, loyal customers do not make the best brand ambassadors: they stay with their brands not because they are the best, but because they are unwilling to experiment with other alternatives. And that is hardly a good recommendation.

The ideal recommender tells lots of different stories to lots of different people in lots of different ways. At the same time, he also wants to receive lots of different stories from others. Brands love the consumers who click on 'Yes, I would like to receive more information', but are less keen on those who shut themselves up in a box. Recommenders are delighted to be deluged with interesting stories, but they will not tolerate spam. They want access to new ideas that they can reprocess and repackage in their own story.

A recommender is also happy (proud, in fact) if a brand reacts to a tweet or a Facebook status-update. This is the ultimate reward from a brand for what the recommender says about that brand. But be careful before you start calling this kind of reaction 'a conversation'. That is taking things too far. Conversations take place between friends and can deal with all manner of different subjects. Sometimes – just sometimes – one of these subjects might be a brand. A brand that interacts with a consumer shows that it is alert, that it listens, that it has respect. But no more than that. That, however, is good enough. If or when the shit hits the fan, the consumer expects the brand to clear up the mess. A brand is not a friend, still less the lover of whom you just can't get enough (until, of course, one day you discover that you can get enough – in fact, have already had enough).

True, the recommender gives up a small part of his privacy, time after time after time. But he regards this as less of a problem than the average consumer might, because he is more reckless and more of an exhibitionist than the average consumer. People who give their opinions are exposing themselves to possible comeback, as a result of the fact that Twitter and Facebook ID's are easier to link to actual addresses and telephone numbers. The likelihood that they are pestered by stalking brands is much greater than with consumers who adopt a 'silence is golden' approach.

That the love between a brand and 'its' customer or between a customer and 'his' brand does not always glow with Romeo-and-Juliette-like passion is also evident from the fact that visits to brand websites are relatively infrequent. Moreover, since 2008 the number of visits has actually been falling. People hang around on social media, where they are supposedly engaged in 'engaging', but where in reality they are simply waiting for a discount, a coupon or some other kind of promotion.

Wave 6[38] followed 40,000 adult internet users in 62 different countries. Only seven out of every hundred netizens had visited a brand website during the previous six months! This is hardly a figure to write home about. And certainly no evidence for a 'passionate' relationship between brands and consumers. Moreover, this coolness is general: it is in no way related to age or gender.

I am not all that impressed by the idea of engaging through social media. Whereas the brand sites were categorised by 25% of the Wave 6 respondents as 'something I can learn from' and by 23% as 'I will come back again', the figures for social media were not all that much higher: 36% and 27% respectively. You also need to take into account that during this study the respondents spent an average of seven hours each week on social media and an additional six hours on microblog-media, such as Twitter. For the 14-16 age group these figures increased to nine hours and seven hours. People who spend 14 to 16 hours per week in a social media environment are clearly busy with other things than brands.[39]

RECOMMENDERS WILL ALREADY
HAVE THEIR OWN NETWORK

With SMMMMS[40] you can now chart how many followers you have and what they do with your posts (do they react, send or delete?). But no one is yet in a position to say whether your tweets about Canon have actually persuaded anyone to buy a single camera. That is still pure guesswork.

To know the answer with certainty, it would be necessary to ask a small fraction of the 1 billion Facebook users whether they were influenced to make a purchase by one or more of the 150,000 recommenders.

At the same time, you would also need to ask the recommenders how their offline network operates. The people who you see most often (face to face) are easier to influence than people who you only see at a distance (Facebook). You are a member of a church, a political party, a sports club, a hobby club, a wine club, etc. and within those clubs there are numerous conversations about brands. How many? God knows!

THIS IS ALL WELL AND GOOD…BUT

Are you the ideal recommender? To know this, we first need to have some facts and figures about you, which then need to be balanced and assessed with care. This is something that Holaba is already working on. Fill in the answers to the following questionnaire with a number and send your results by e-mail to jevedebe@gmail.com: that's me!

1 I have a list of ……. brands that I regularly recommend.
2 I have a list of ……. brands for which I regularly give negative advice.
3 I estimate that my circle of friends consists of ……. people, who I call or mail at least every two to three months.
4 During the past month I have discussed brands with friends, neighbours and colleagues approximately ……. times. And I am certain that on ……. occasions I was able to convince people.
5 Apart from the people in my immediate circle of friends, I belong to one or more social networks, such as Facebook, Netlog, Hyves, Twitter, etc., where I have a total of ……. followers.
6 I post a tweet or do an update about brands roughly ……. times each month. In addition, I write ……. comments each month about products and brands on sites such as Tripadvisor or other subject-specific blogs.

Just how many people a person must have in his network before he can be considered as a recommender is another matter.[41] A recommender who does not operate online must have between 200 and 450 people in his network. If he also operates online, this figure increases to between 300 and 600. At least, this is what Zuberance tells us.[42] An average Facebook user has 245 friends.[43] But the average Facebook user is not a recommender. Moreover, these figures contradict the results from a different survey that concluded that the average American (and therefore not a recommender) has no fewer than 634 social ties, some weak, some strong. If someone frequently uses the internet, this total rises to 732. If they use the internet just once per day, it falls to 616.

4 Not every recommender is recommended

- It is fortunate for the advertisers there is such a thing as recommenders. They still see, hear and read the outpourings of the advertising industry. The other 85% of consumers follow the recommenders.
- I wanted to write that advertising doesn't work anymore. However, I will be correct and restrict myself to: 'advertising is working less and less all the time'.
- Not everyone who claims to be a recommender actually is one. Consumers should really give each other a score. Then they would know for sure. Sucking up to a brand is different from recommending a brand. Sucking up is for creeps.

The last chapter in this book is entitled 'No More War'. There we will be discussing the disgustingly high costs that brands incur in their efforts to charm a few billion consumers. Perhaps you should read that chapter first, and then return here. Or if you prefer, you can just carry on. It's up to you.

Consumers are at saturation level with online advertising messages

Total number of impressions* (in millions)
172 billion impressions in 1996 = 30 ads for every person on the planet.
5 trillion impressions in 2010 = 735 ads per person per year. 66% of adults in the UK and the US say that they see too many promotions and advertisements.

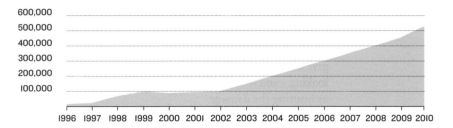

* impression = an advertisement shown on a website; this does not necessarily mean that they are seen by the consumer.

This is where we begin our search for the recommenders: with an analysis of what a fraction of the world's online citizens – namely the online consumers in the UK and the US – experience when they go on the web or pick up the phone or play with their tablets.

If we are talking about advertising, what they experience is not all that much fun.

And what is the consequence of the advertising bombardment to which they are subjected? It simply means that they no longer click on the banners. The graphic below shows how the response rate to such advertising has collapsed between 1996 and 2012. And the end is not yet in sight. What we don't know is how many of the 5 trillion (that's an American trillion – a five with twelve zeros) impressions are actually seen. If they are posted just so they might be seen – but nobody knows if they really are seen – then what in God's name are we playing at! This is self-deception on a huge scale. And we all know that self-deception can sometimes last a very long time. Until everything starts falling around your ears.

The (negative) consequences of the bombardment by CTR

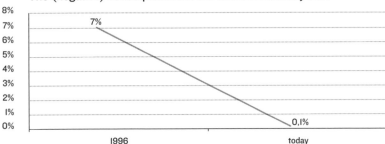

If the current unsatisfactory position continues – with consumers saying: 'there is too much advertising and we are now blind to it' – then the placing of advertisements on the web simply becomes a massively expensive, almost surreal waste of time and resources. We give consumers billions of chances to see us, but they are no longer looking – and so they don't click. The advertisers actually regard this as limiting the damage.

But is that really so? Consider the following figures. The damage for brands that continue their advertising bombardment is significant. Huge, in fact.

If 66% of your customers notify you that they no longer wish to receive your promotional mails and if more than a quarter respond negatively to the mails they have already seen, then surely it is time to change course? And if you don't change course, your customers probably will. Believe me, this possibility should not be underestimated.

Wait a minute! There is even more damage...
● USA ● UK

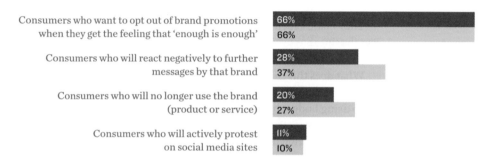

Consumers who want to opt out of brand promotions when they get the feeling that 'enough is enough'	66%	66%
Consumers who will react negatively to further messages by that brand	28%	37%
Consumers who will no longer use the brand (product or service)	20%	27%
Consumers who will actively protest on social media sites	11%	10%

And there aren't all that many solutions available to the brand owners. If you look at the table below, you will see that the situation can be improved slightly if you attune your message better to the needs of your customers. Google has made relevant adverts on search results pages its trademark. If the message bears some kind of relation to the place where it is seen or if it fits within the context where the web-users are currently surfing, it has more chance of being noticed and read. And 7% still allow themselves to be tempted by a catchy slogan (those will no doubt be the literary souls amongst you). Understandably, perhaps. Advertising at its best can indeed be moving, funny, shocking... I should know: I have been in the business long enough.

What does this mean for the impact of your message?

Consumers who are inclined to click on messages that are relevant to the things that interest them	26%
Consumers who are inclined to click on messages that are relevant to the context in which they are currently situated	22%
Consumers who are inclined to click on messages that are relevant to what they are currently doing	21%
Consumers who are inclined to click on messages that are relevant at the moment when they are seen	14%
Consumers who are inclined to click on messages that have a catchy or moving text	7%

And this is just the top of the iceberg. An important piece of work about the continuing devaluation of advertising appeared in 2011, when Gerard J. Tellis (professor/director of the Centre for Global Innovation in the Marshall School of Business at the University of Southern California, writing with Raj Sethuraman and Richard Breisch) published *How Well Does Advertising Work?* In the prestigious *Journal of Marketing Research*.[44]

They made a meta-analysis of 750 short-term and 402 long-term B2B (business to business) cases between 1960 and 2008. The average ST-elasticity of advertising is now 0.12 and no longer 0.22.

What does this mean? It means that twenty to thirty years ago you could win an additional 2.2% of market share if you increased your advertising budget by 10%. To achieve the same effect today, you now need to increase your marketing budget by 20%. A budget that is already melting like a snowman in the sun. I wanted to write that advertising doesn't work anymore. However, I will be correct and restrict myself to: 'advertising is working less and less all the time'.

In chapter 6 you will read that advertising is no longer regarded as an important source for information about brands, a role that has been taken over by your family, friends and acquaintances, together with the review sites. This lack of confidence in advertisements is probably worse for their future in the long run than the short-term effects of their irritation, irrelevance and excess.

Consumers are not worried by the fact that advertising is becoming increasingly useless. All we now need to do is convince the advertisers that the recommenders are not the enemy – and then we might finally be able to make some progress.

You can compare the 15% of hyperactive recommenders to a guerrilla army. You can't see them, but they are there. You only see them when you need them.

The group of recommenders is a sizeable minority. So far, we have been speaking about 15%. They primarily operate offline. During the coffee break in the office. In the pub. In the changing rooms at the gym. At home with friends. In bed. On the phone.

OF ALL THE ACTIVE PEOPLE ON THE WEB, ONLY 15-20% ACTUALLY OPEN THEIR MOUTHS

A Forrester study conducted in 2010 (based on figures for 2009) estimated the number of 'mass influencers'[45] at 16% of active web-users. This 16% generates more than 75% of the word-of-mouth advertising about brands.[46] How did Forresters arrive at their 16% figure?

> 13.4% were mass mavens, who are more likely to be found on YouTube, blogs, fora, rating sites and review sites. This group consists of the original content creators, so that they do not necessarily need a large network.
> 6.2% were mass connectors. They generate a massive 80% of all comments on Twitter and Facebook about brands. They are active on the social networks and pass on the content created by the mavens to their peer group.
> 3.7% are both mavens and connectors. Hence Forresters overall estimate that the group of mass influences amounts to some 16%. This is very probably our group of recommenders.

INTERNET HAS RESULTED IN MASSIVE ACCELERATION

In the pre-internet era it was difficult to check the opinions of third parties during the pre-purchase trajectory. Like me, you probably don't have too many friends who know everything about wet and dry shaving (or pinot noir, or New York hotels) at precisely the moment when you need the information. What a shame, because these are the informants who you are most likely to trust.

In the past, you could always turn to the consumer associations, which regularly tested vacuum cleaners, cameras, washing powders, etc., but the problem was essentially the same: when you wanted to buy a new television you found that their last survey was either out of date or didn't cover the model you were interested in. What's more, the experiences of customers who had a bad experience seldom came to light, unless the dissatisfied customer wrote to the press (and the press chose to publish the letter).

Internet has added a number of new dimensions to this situation.
The consumer associations that were smart enough to recognise the approaching tsunami of digital data were quick to open sites on the web and made their now extensive databases easily available. In addition, in many countries a number of grassroots start-ups have developed, specialising in the comparison of products and prices. A welcome evolution.

But for the real opening up of this gigadata to the public, the sensible, aware consumer (many of whom have since become recommenders, since they were forced to do much self-research during their own pre-purchase trajectories) first needed to wait for the cement of the social networks, which link people with people, instead of people with products and services.

I think that the group of recommenders is likely to get bigger. But those who were already recommenders in the past no longer confine their chatting to the coffee machine or a pint in the pub after work, but are now also active online. As a result, the 15% are going to produce more and publish more.

The social network sites not only brought your friends back into the picture, but also the friends of friends, and the friends of their friends, and so on. Suddenly, everyone had access to a wide circle of previously unknown people, who between them possess a wide range of knowledge in diverse fields of expertise.

Links take the process a stage further, contacting yet another level of people, some of whom may know even more about the specific subjects under consideration. This is an intense activity during the pre-purchase phase. You know how it goes. You get a mail with a question. You don't immediately know the answer. But you know a friend who probably does. And so this friend gets a mail from you. And so it continues. Recommenders are on the side of the listeners (you can always take your questions to them), but also on the side of those who find or give the desired answers: they like being read and they like being asked.[47] They are more than just flattered if their advice is followed. In fact, they will be inspired to write more and more. Some might even become bloggers.

Does this mean that all our problems are solved, now that we have this self-proclaimed army of recommenders at our disposal? Unfortunately not. You need to be on the lookout for fakes. Your network of experts is not 100 percent secure. Most people are not bribable. But some people – and some countries – are more susceptible than others. They lie in wait, but then spring into action when they sense that they can make a killing. In China, for example, there are 300 companies specialising in the writing and publication of completely false reviews about applications. Apparently, 30% of the app-builders are paying them to get a higher ranking.[48] It's just like a protection racket!

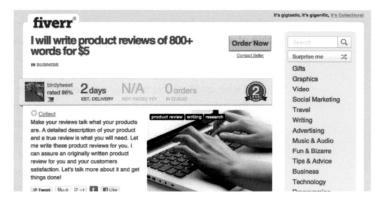

Whichever way you look at it, ordinary people (like you and me) obviously do not know everything we need to know before making many of our purchases. And we seldom know personally the people who can fill these gaps in our knowledge. To this extent, shopping remains something of a gamble. But in contrast to the casino, we can increase our chances of success by following the right recommendations of the right recommenders. But what exactly is 'right'?

Giving scores is something that we all do all the time. However, these informal rankings are seldom collated and made public. Nevertheless, it is an implicit evaluation of the knowledge of others.

Even amongst friends there is usually a pecking order for each field of interest. I have friends who know a lot about wine and others who couldn't tell the difference between a grand cru and a bottle of vinegar. But I don't have any friends who could tell me which Cabernet Sauvignon for the Napa Valley is the best.

The more certain I want to be about a purchase, the more I will need to climb the information ladder by a series of reliable steps, in order to better differentiate between the winners and the losers.

A young father who needs to decide which nappies to buy has a much easier task than a woman faced with a choice between five Cabernets.

Mothers with young children influence each other. Patients with hip replacements also influence each other. So, too, do foreign entrepreneurs in China. And in these small groups, often no bigger than ten or twelve people, there will always be two or three who know more, because they have more experience, or because they have read more, or because they have a bigger network. Usually, these people have the DNA of a recommender in their blood. And they are followed by the others; not slavishly, but at a distance that allows some room for manoeuvre, if necessary.[49]

But who are these two or three people, the ones you need to pick out from the larger group, so that you can follow their advice? Unfortunately, there is not yet a consumer association to rank recommenders, in the way that doctors, plumbers and professors are already ranked.

However, a start is being made on something of this kind. There is a system for the rating of human sources by the people who have consulted those sources. This is a useful step in the right direction; the direction of auto-selection.

FINDING THE RIGHT RECOMMENDER

But first test yourself. Below are two real examples of people who have written reviews for Tripadvisor. Both reviews were described by site users as 'helpful'. The question is: which one do you trust the most? The man (Profegrino) who has written 36 reviews, 16 of which were deemed to be helpful, or the man (smacs77) who has only written 5 reviews, but with an impressive 4 'helpful' references to his name? I have no idea. Nor do you, probably. You will most likely pick the person whose comments feel right. In which case, you will make another of the intuitive, emotional decisions that so often characterise the pre-purchase phase.

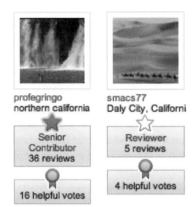

If you scroll further down the page, you will find something more than pure intuition to help you make your decision: because there you can discover more about the people who hide themselves behind their site pseudonyms.

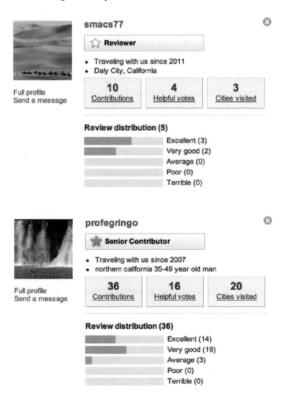

And if you want to know still more, you can read all the reviews they have ever written. For absolute certainty, you can even send them an e-mail.

If you are planning a really expensive holiday or some other expensive purchase (will you go for an iPad or an Android?), then you might take the trouble to do this. But you won't do it if you are standing in the supermarket, trying to decide which type of shampoo to buy (all of which promise to remove your dandruff within days). In this latter case, all you want is a quick click and a rating figure, so that you can make your decision, buy your shampoo and go home (probably to wash your hair). This is currently how I choose my wine in the supermarket (as you will read later in chapter 8): one click on the Kurkdroog wine selection website and the best rated wine on the screen is the one that I put in my shopping basket. And I have never been disappointed. As long as there are enough wine drinkers prepared to contribute their scores to the site, you can follow their recommendations with almost complete confidence. The wisdom of crowds often works.

'WE HAVE ZERO TOLERANCE FOR FAKE REVIEWS' (TRIPADVISOR)

This excellent principle should (in principle) be the basic starting point for every review site. We try to make this clear on our Holaba site in China. Every effort is made to find fraudsters as quickly as possible and remove them to our black list. A brand that writes its own reviews or pays others to do its dirty work is not only deceiving itself, but also its potential future customers. It is actually digging two holes for itself and is guaranteed to fall into one or the other, with disastrous consequences. This is not simply an ethical matter, but also a commercial one: cheating only creates dissatisfied customers, and no company ever built success on dissatisfied customers. Consequently, recommenders must be more than just walking-talking human advertisements, but must instead provide authentic evaluations that hopefully serve the public good. At least, that's the way it should be.

This has not always been easy to explain in China (it still isn't). When we had our first few thousand registered users, I proudly made my tour of the Chinese advertising and media agencies, explaining what we were doing and what we could do for them. When I was actually let in the door (which didn't always happen), the first question I was inevitably asked was: 'But my dear Jan, do these people really exist?' I soon discovered that the survey and review markets had been brought into near total discredit by so-called experts filling in their own spreadsheets with non-existent samples, which they then tried to peddle as 'market research'. In these circumstance, try explaining that you are somehow different!

When our measures to distinguish 'true' from 'false' finally persuaded them of our good intentions, we were immediately confronted with a second, equally unpalatable question: 'Do you pay your reviewers?' When we explained who recommenders are and why they do it, the Chinese marketers and advertisers found it difficult to believe that people would invest time and energy in this kind of thing without there being some kind of financial reward attached – even though there are thousands of different Chinese fora where people are helping each other in this selfless manner all the time.

Never mind, let's press on. Next problem. Everyone who has a review site must not only try to attract honest, real and helpful reviewers, but must also give the brand the opportunity to respond in public. It is only when there is a right of reply that a conversation can begin.

This is the review that I wrote for the Gem Hotel in New York (back in chapter 1, if you recall). And I used the word 'recommend' deliberately in the title of my piece. It is worth noting that Tripadvisor also published my mistakes (hence the misspelling of 'discovered', which reads as 'dicovered').

"It is very likely I would recommend it."

◉◉◉◉◯ Reviewed February 9, 2012

Everything about this charming hotel was good. No real negative comments. Only if you need a big room no need to come here. There's also no breakfast, but plenty of opportunities in the neighbourhood. If you don't like the idea of being in the middle of the LGBT Chelsea-district in an hotel that really supports the community you don't have to book. The WIFI i my room was weak and the coffeepads in the room could also be stonger and tastier. I dicovered the hotel in the Flemish newspaper De Standaard beginning of Jan 2012. Good recommendation.

Room Tip: Ask for a room with a view. My view was a wall.
See more room tips

Stayed February 2012, traveled on business

◉◉◉◉◉ Value
◉◉◉◉◉ Location
◉◉◉◉◉ Sleep Quality

◉◉◉◉◯ Rooms
◉◉◉◉◉ Cleanliness
◉◉◉◉◯ Service

Less ▲

A CONCRETE
EXAMPLE FROM
A HOTEL IN
VIENNA WHERE
I RECENTLY
STAYED

Just a few hours after I checked out, I received a link on my mail that forwarded me to a fairly extensive survey. When I had filled everything in, there was a closing screen that asked me whether or not I would be prepared to recommend the hotel. Of course, I clicked 'yes', and then...

I was automatically offered a Tripadvisor screen, so that I could type in my review. From satisfied customer to recommender in one easy step!

And here is the answer from the hotel management.

GEMChelseaFOM, Front Office Manager at GEM Hotel - Chelsea, an Ascend Collection hotel, responded to this review

February 15, 2012

Thank you so much for sharing your review with us. We apprecciate your suggestions and cannot wait for you to visit us again in the future. Please feel free to contact me on your next visit to the big apple as I would love to personally welcome you back!

Best regards,

Julio Acosta
Front Office Manager

After this chat between myself and the hotel, Tripadvisor must have been pretty sure that I actually existed. The hotel had clearly read my review and could confirm, if necessary, that I stayed there during the period in question.

This is something that Tripadvisor introduced at the beginning of 2012: a system for verifying reviews. This interesting development allows hotels, restaurants, etc. to ask their customers to write a review for the site. In this way, the existence of the customer – and the reviewer – is immediately verified.

One of the leading European hotel booking sites (EasyToBook) has already replaced its own review collecting system with the Tripadvisor model. People who have stayed somewhere are sent a mail as soon as their stay is finished and are promptly asked to evaluate the accommodation. This is how it should always be: acquiring data at just the right time, immediately after the moment of consumption. The resulting evaluations appear then simultaneously on both the booking site and on Tripadvisor. The credibility of the latter is therefore bound to grow. In the past, there were often considerable doubts about whether all the reviews had been written by people who had actually stayed at hotel X or Y. There could be no certainty unless each review was followed up with the hotel itself: not only a time-consuming process but one that allowed the hotels to deny the existence of negative reviewers (or to confirm that enthusiastic reviewers had indeed slept there, whereas in reality it was the friend of a friend of a friend who had slept there). As the Good Book says: 'Let he who is without sin cast the first stone'.[50]

With Tripadvisor, we are obviously dealing with the very top of the review sites. But even the top sites have their opponents.

YELP: A RECOMMENDER? NOT FOR EVERYONE, APPARENTLY

Just as Tripadvisor seeks to help travellers find the hotel of their dreams, so Yelp aims to help consumers find their way through the maze of local shops and services. Everyone knows that this is a minefield sector, with hundreds of sub-standard suppliers and even gangsters. When they started back in 2004, the aim of Yelp was to separate the wheat from the chaff as far as local hairdressers, restaurants, plumbers, carpenters, dentists, etc. were concerned.

As far as it is possible to tell for an outsider, they have succeeded in this objective quite admirably. In the fourth quarter of 2011, the site had 66 million unique visitors each month. That's an awful lot.

Anyone searching the site for, say, a massage centre in San Francisco will find at the top of the screen a business with four stars (against a yellowish background), but it is mentioned clearly (both in the top right corner and on the map) that this is an advertisement. There is nothing wrong in that. The Diamond Centre has not yet had many reviews, but the average score is good and so the centre has decided to spend some money on advertising to crank up its rating still further.

◊ Diamond Massage & Wellness Center
Categories: Massage, Physical Therapy
Neighborhood: Marina/Cow Hollow

★★★★☆ 37 reviews
1841 Lombard St
San Francisco, CA 94123
(415) 921-1290

I am picky about **massages** and hate those fancy spa **massages** where they just slap oil on you and then it costs $200+. Don't go if you are looking for spa style **massage** with…

◊ 1. Earthbody
Categories: Massage, Day Spas, Skin Care
Neighborhood: Hayes Valley
◊ Special Offer

★★★★★ 227 reviews
534 Laguna St
San Francisco, CA 94102
(415) 552-7200

 Massage therapist Sharma is the real deal. She has a healing touch that is intuitive and strong. An hour and a half **massage** was just what I needed to reset, relax, and re-engage with the person underneath the mask

◊ 2. Oxygen **Massage** Therapy
o x y g e n Category: Massage
and massage therapy Neighborhood: Mission

★★★★★ 134 reviews
3389 22nd St
San Francisco, CA 94110
(415) 738-7708

I had a gift certificate for a 60 minute **massage** so I made an appointment with Mary Anne. Driving into the city all the way from Fremont, I hit traffic and could not find parking for 15 minutes. Since this place

Its competitors have already received more reviews, almost all of which have also given high scores. This is the difference between 'earned media' and 'paid media'. Those with four stars have to pay. Those with five stars no longer need to. They make it to the top of the list on their own merits. And every new massage centre will need to start at the very bottom and hope (or ensure) that its first customers give it rave reviews.

In total, Yelpers have written more than 25 million reviews. And the shops themselves (or plumbers, or dentists, etc.) can also open an account on the site that allows them to post messages for their customers and potential customers. The reviews and messages remain on the site in the order that they were posted (although some critics contest this point: they claim that shops can push bad reviews right to the bottom of the list, where almost nobody goes to look).

What's more, Yelp also does its own filtering – and this is where things get a bit murky. Reviews that at first sight seem honest are sometimes filtered out, because the site filter has decided – for reasons that are usually far from clear – that the source is no longer to be trusted. Critics says that this leads to a disproportionate number of negative comments on Yelp. And it does, indeed, seem very strange.

To make matters worse, the Yelper who wrote the review is not informed that his work has been removed. If you log in to the site, you will still see your review – but no one else will. However, if you just surf to read, without logging in, then you will also be able to see that it has gone. As I say: very strange.

It also seems that Yelp is not seeking to maximise its number of reviews. In a recent mail they asked shops not to go 'fishing' for new reviews. They assume that the spontaneous reviews from real, ordinary people will be largely negative. If something is absolutely awful, people are more quickly inclined to take up their pen. The more negative reviews someone gets, the more likely that the negatively assessed shop will be willing to pay and take 'necessary action' to restore the balance in the opposite direction: for example, by advertising, so that the negative reviews are pushed down to the bottom of the sort list. The Yelp reasoning? If companies encourage their customers to write reviews, they will probably ask only their satisfied customers to perform this service, so that all the spontaneous negative reviews get pushed even lower and lower. A shop or company that is already at the top of the list doesn't need to advertise and so brings in no revenue for Yelp. Does this then mean that good reviews are bad for Yelp's own business? Perhaps it does. It is certainly true that in general good companies need to spend less on advertising.

This makes me think of the (somewhat cynical) story about the doctoring profession. Doctors do not work in the health industry. Why? Because they have no interest in healthy people. Their income comes exclusively from unhealthy people. The sick are their customers. So the more sick people there are, the bigger their market becomes – a fact which only benefits the health... of their bank balance. And fortunately for them, new diseases and new cures are being discovered all the time. And as for the elderly, with their long slow decline into old age, with all its attendant problems and discomforts... well, they are a veritable goldmine!

Is this the course that Yelp is following? The more bad businesses there are, the better it is for Yelp's own business? If this is the case, then they are not my friend and, likewise, they are not the friend of the genuine recommenders. Time will tell.

In passing, it is worth noting that there are now a number of companies specialised in making bad reviews 'invisible': these reviews are so manipulated that they are no longer picked up and displayed by search robots.[51] What is the world coming to!

Yelp's revenue rose 74% to a total of 83.3 million dollars in 2011, with local ads accounting for 70% of income. The remaining 30% was largely made up from brand advertising.[52]

IF ONLY THERE WERE NO CHEATS IN THE WORLD!

The reviews of recommenders are the necessary 'compost' that helps to ensure fertile competition. Because let's be honest: it is still a war out there – notwithstanding all the hopeful claims about the increase in the number of conversation companies. When the *Cluetrain Manifesto*[53] was launched to such acclaim – now more than a decade ago – its first sentence was: 'Markets are Conversations': a slogan that has turned out to be as true (or rather, as false) as the claim that 'the socialist revolution will free the working class.' Markets are still battlefields, and the combatants who have the best organised guerrilla army of recommenders are the ones who will win. No doubt about it. That faith can move mountains has been proclaimed by Christians and Communists alike for the best part of the last 2,000 years. And both, have indeed, moved mountains. Unfortunately, new mountains have now risen to taken their place: mountains that are higher and more difficult to climb.

During the past decade consumers have had much more pre-purchasing information at their disposal than ever before, but the difficulty rests in deciding what is true and what is false. In days gone by, it seemed in the first instance that everything told to us by the brands and the advertisers was 'true': the 'false' only became evident after the purchase had been made. Nowadays, both true and false are evident before the purchase is made, but in fluctuating proportions. Some sources are false. And some true sources unintentionally pass on false information. It is all very complex.

Separating the wheat from the chaff requires a greater effort than blindly believing what an advertisement tells you. In much the same way that a democracy also requires a greater effort of its citizens than a dictatorship. Nevertheless, the risk of making a bad purchase is now significantly less than in the past – and that is very important. In fact, that is what people call 'progress'.

You need to be on the lookout for one or two elements that some people would like to make you believe are part of the recommender profile, but which are, in reality, nothing of the kind.

ı I do not recommend everything that I buy

Recommendation engines that tell you (if you are my friend) that I have bought something only tell you (logically enough) that I have bought something. Nothing more than that. And that means very little. If the same engines were to ask me a week after my purchase to give the product/service a score on the Reichheld scale and if I give that score in good faith, only then have I made a valuable recommendation for other searching consumers and also for the brand that asked me. This is a key element in the Tripadvisor scenario. They have nothing to lose and everything to gain by listening. A so-called 'recommendation' by someone from my circle of friends is actually a form of peer-pressure in disguise: the pressure to conform with someone else's taste. Because he has bought one, you feel that you have to buy one – if you want to stay 'in' with the in-crowd.

This is the kind of thing that you should do your best to avoid. Pressure is never good; not even the pressure of your friends. I realise, of course, that many hypes grow precisely because there are small clusters of people who almost unconsciously work to promote the new rage or fad – but that is not what we are talking about in this instance. However, if you browse through the reading list of your best friends because you know that they have a fine literary sense, that is something completely different: you are searching for something, you know a good source, you nose around, and you end up buying three books that suit you down to the ground.

2 Mentioning a brand does not mean that I recommend it

The fact that I mention a brand name in a tweet or in a status update on a social network site (SNS) is no basis on which to trust me and certainly no basis to label me as a recommender. Read the following hypothetical statements and judge their recommending power for yourself.

> 'I am drinking a glass of beer with some friends.'
>> This is just an announcement to your followers that you are (exceptionally/again) hanging out in the pub with your pals and that you are not as pathetically lonely as some of them might think!
> 'I am drinking a Guinness with some friends.'
>> This can mean that on this occasion you just felt like a Guinness (as opposed to something else).
>> It can mean that it is the first time you have ever drunk Guinness.
>> It can mean that you are drinking Guinness again – as usual.
>> It can also mean that you are recommending Guinness to someone who has just asked you to identify 'the best beer in the world'.
> 'I am finally drinking a Guinness with my friends.'
>> This can mean that you are dying of thirst and have finally found a pub that is still open.
>> It can also mean that your friends have at last persuaded you to try a Guinness, although they still don't know whether you like it or not.
> 'I am sitting with friends and am already on my third Guinness.'
>> This can mean that you are having a good time, but that you could just as easily be drinking Budweiser as Guinness.
>> It can mean that you are well on the way to getting blind drunk – again.
>> It can also be a kind of complaint; namely that Guinness is not the right kind of beer for a long evening in the pub, followed by a long drive home.
> 'After three pints of Guinness, my friends have also become Guinness fans.'
>> This is an indication pure and simple that you have once again acted as a Guinness recommender.

What would really be interesting is to send a mail to all those friends with a Guinness status update, asking them: 'Now that you have finally tried Guinness, what is the likelihood on a scale of 0 to 10 that you would be prepared to recommend it.' It is almost certain that some people will reply with a low score, because they found Guinness too strong, or too bitter or just too black (not everyone's favourite colour for beer!). But be on your guard against Twitter and Facebook analysts who claim that they can deduce sentiments from words. They are nearly always wrong, and will lead you well and truly up the garden path!

THE DIFFERENCE BETWEEN NEGATIVE SENTIMENT AND POSITIVE REALITY

Before moving on I would like to make one or two brief comments about a brave research project, the results of which recently circulated in the Netherlands under the title of the Greenpaper. For three months – between January and March 2012 – Greenberry examined in total all (!) 1.8 million messages about the country's top 100 brands. These messages appeared on Facebook, Twitter, Hyves, YouTube and various internet (web)logs. 'For the first time in the Netherlands a large-scale investigation has been carried out into sentiments relating to brands in social media.' Or so said the publicity blurb. This was obviously of interest to me and so I decided to take a closer look.

The first thing that struck me was that brands were only talked about on average 216 times per day. I have no idea how many individuals sent those 1.8 million messages into cyberspace, but 216 strikes me as being a very low figure. This confirmed my suspicion that people don't talk a lot about brands. And remember: we are dealing here with the top 100 Dutch brands. It is clear, therefore, that consumers use social media for other purposes. Spread over the top 25 brands, the total number of messages is 627. In other words, 80% of all brand messages are about just 25 brands. The most messages are about brands in the telecom sector, but the general sentiment about that sector (and the companies operating within it) was negative. The NS (Dutch Railways) was the absolute top in terms of number of messages per day. During the three months of the survey they were the subject of 274,000 of the 1.8 million messages.

In China almost half the Chinese between the ages of 13 and 45 years have something positive to say about a brand each day. About 12-15% of them do this online. If we convert these figures to the Dutch situation, this would mean that the 1.8 million messages should have been sent in about a day and a half – not three months. The conclusion is therefore once again confirmed: Dutch consumers don't talk a lot about brands. The most startling conclusions of all, however, relate to the sentiment analysis. Dreft was the most positive brand, followed by Lotto, Robijn and the National Lottery. The most negative brand was Telfort, followed by Carglass, T-Mobile and Tele2.

How did Greenberry draw up these lists? Teezir search technology was used to track down the brand messages and a language algorithm was applied to take account of sarcasm, irony, double meanings, etc. in order to assess whether the sentiment was positive, negative or neutral. These analyses were deemed to be 70% accurate.

But what does this sentiment analysis actually mean? And why should we regard it as reliable? Does the analysis express whether I am satisfied or dissatisfied? Does it allow people to deduce whether I intend to stay loyal to a brand or desert it? Will I recommend the brand or will I recommend against it? And how long do the sentiments remain valid. If my bank messes things up, I may be angry for a day. But once they have put things right, I may quickly return to being a satisfied customer. Or I may not, if mistakes continue to happen.

This is the key question: what exactly is the sentiment value of these 1.8 million messages?

Let's begin with the NS. Are the majority of the analysed messages generally neutral communications between passengers about trains that are likely to arrive late? Or messages from passengers to their families, announcing that they have almost arrived at their destination? Or about trains that are overfull? Or too cold in the winter? Or are the messages more positive in tone? Perhaps that travelling with the NS is better for the environment than travelling by car? Or that it is safer than a bus? Or cheaper than a plane? Naturally, some of the messages are also likely to be strongly negative. But how does the sentiment analysis deal with simple sentences such as 'I am sitting on a train' or 'The train is pulling into the station now'? If you want to know what the senders of those 274,000 messages really think about the NS, the only way is to ask them whether or not they would be prepared to recommend the NS to their friends, colleagues and neighbours. If they answer 'of course', then you know that the NS is doing a good job. If they answer 'never in a thousand years', you can be reasonably certain that the train service stinks.

In other words, the fact that the NS occupies position 91 in the sentiment analysis does not necessarily tell the whole story. On the other hand, the low position may indeed reflect the fact that there is something wrong. But there is only one sure way to find out just how good (or bad) things really are. You need to ask a specific question. And also ask the reason why.

So what about Carglass? My suspicion (which I expressed explicitly to Greenberry in a telephone conversation) was that the very negative score for Carglass could be attributed to a large degree to their advertising, whereas Carglass could actually be a very good partner if you have a crack in your windscreen, resulting in a very high percentage of satisfied customers. As it turned out, my suspicion was proved to be well grounded. Just ten minutes on Google told me an awful lot more. This is what Carglass itself had to say about its NPS score:

"The feedback from our customers plays a crucial role in our company. We do more than 500,000 repairs or replacements each year. 60% of our customers leave us their e-mail address. They each receive a mail from us after the work on their car has been carried out. 55% fill in the attached questionnaire. This results in a yearly total of some 150,000 completed surveys. Every customer reaction is linked to a specific branch garage and a specific mechanic. In this way, we gain a continuous insight into what our customers think about us, right down to the level of the individual members of staff.

At the present time our net promoter score varies between 59% and 61%. For this assessment we use the "official" NPS questions: "How likely is it that you will recommend Carglass to your family, friends and colleagues?" The people who give us a score of 9 or 10 are our promoters. We deduct scores of 6 or lower to arrive at our NPS coefficient. If people give us a 7 or 8, we contact them again to ask what we would need to do to turn this score into a 9 or 10. 90% of respondents say that they will call Carglass again in the event of further glass damage to their vehicles. Carglass is active in 34 countries and the NPS is measured in each of them. Although 61% represents a good score in comparison with other companies in the Dutch context, we are still nowhere near the top of the list in comparison with our Carglass colleagues elsewhere. This may, in part, be a question of cultural differences. An American is more likely to be effusively enthusiastic than a Dutchman. What's more, you can even see this kind of cultural difference within the Netherlands itself.

People in the Randstad are more critical and much less likely to give a score of 9 or 10."[54]

Jan-Willem van Beek of Greenberry.nl replied to my comments and confirmed that a large proportion of the Carglass messages were advertising-related and not service-related.

"Following my discussion with Jan Van den Berghe, I decided to dig deeper. As far as Carglass is concerned, we analysed 100 of their messages at random, to determine their subject matter. Of these 100 messages, 32 were about the service, 42 were about advertising and 26 were about other matters. It should also be noted, however, that Carglass is an exception in terms of negative sentiment. Of all the 2 million messages that we analysed, 16% were positive and 11% were negative. In other words, people are generally positive about brands on social networks. This in turn means that people on average are more frequently positive about brands than negative."[55]

Which, however, does not prove what really needs to be proved: is the negative sentiment relating to Carglass a consequence of advertising and/or a lack of awareness of their service, and are the customers who are 'forced' by circumstances into using Carglass satisfied in retrospect with their treatment? This also leads on to another question (my own particular favourite): what must a company do on social media if its sentiment analysis is a disaster and if its banner ads are no longer working? Simple. The brand must try to identify the senders of those millions of messages every day and attempt to get in touch with them. That must be (and remain) the essence of their activity. Do not jump to hasty conclusions on the basis of angry tweets. I know someone who is frequently very angry with Apple, but has been a loyal customer for more than 20 years. In fact, it's me! And it is precisely this paradox that many of the critics of the NPS method completely misunderstand and misinterpret. Customer satisfaction is different from an NPS score. I can be dissatisfied at times with Apple, the NS, my bank, etc. but still recommend them to my family, friends and colleagues. This is by no means contradictory. 'What does such a recommendation sound like?', I hear you ask. Well, something like this: 'Notwithstanding this, that and the other, I still think that Apple (the NS, my bank) is the best option for you.' This is the carefully considered opinion of a customer who can place his score of the moment in a wider context.

And in the case of Carglass, the recommendation might read as follows: 'They might make those irritating adverts in the Netherlands, but so what? Yesterday I got a crack in my windscreen and today it was repaired, as good as new. Quick, easy and cheap.'[56]

---

3   The almost zero value of a 'like'

The awarding of a 'like' or something similar on a social network has almost no real value. It means little or nothing. It is the social network equivalent of a handshake or a kiss on the cheek when you meet someone you know. And since Judas Iscariot, we all know that a quick kiss is not always as friendly as it seems.

You can give a 'like':

I   To keep in your friends' good books: if you fail to support them in their business, they will be unlikely to support you in yours. If you want to receive, you have to give.

II To demonstrate your knowledge: giving a 'like' to something new, expensive and luxurious shows just how up-to-date you really are and what excellent taste you have.

III To gain discount coupons in the future; for many people, this seems to be a sufficient reason to 'like' big brands.

IV To find out what is going on: you are curious and perhaps even a recommender, who likes to win friends by always being first with the latest news.

V   To earn points with Klout or other sites that give points for 'likes'. This is the web equivalent of women gossiping over a cup of coffee or men chatting about nothing in particular in the pub. I once saw a French friend who kept his followers informed about the progress of a rugby game between France and New Zealand for a full hour and a half. His Klout score rocketed, but my respect for him diminished in equal proportion.

VI Because you also have a page and will be asking for 'likes' in return in the near future. Have you ever heard of 'grooming'?[57] Well, this is classic grooming. Never use the number of 'likes' as a criterion for deciding anything. For example, the unquestionably excellent Holaba site had fewer than 100 'likes' on Facebook at the moment of writing. But this was and is probably because we are more John the Baptist than Jesus Christ!

VII Because many companies first require you to give a 'like' to their page before you can actually move on to the information you really want to see. This is the worst and cheapest kind of deception – but it at least allows desperate marketers to tell the CMO (chief marketing officer) just how well the latest social media campaign is going…

4 Do not assume that a retweet or a share means that I recommend something

As with 'likes', the fact that I have retweeted something or forwarded a status or shared something with friends means, in essence, very little. The same is true of my reply to your Guinness messages. I might reply dishonestly to promote my own Budweiser campaign. This is known as ambush marketing. For example, I can retweet your Guinness post to my followers just to confirm that you are still the same drunken bum that I have always claimed you are! This has little to do with recommending! Let's think back briefly to our Guinness sentences. The sharing or forwarding of these sentences can mean:

> I want to tell my friends what I am doing at the present moment with some of my other friends.
> I want to let my friends know that I enjoy a good night out – and would be happy to do the same with them.
> I want to make clear to my friends (if, for example, I am wine-seller) that beer is still nothing more than a cheap good-time drink for people with no class.

So don't kid yourself. The biggest activity on social network sites is neither the appreciation of brands nor the passing on of useful brand information, but is more focussed on mindless gossip intended to prove to other people that you are still alive. And to profile yourself. To recommend your personal brands to others, and vice versa. In other words, a search for a little bit of praise and attention. Keeping the lines open, with people both near and far. Its only real function is purely psychological: it is designed to make you feel good. Occasionally, a brand will be mentioned between all the other tittle-tattle, but let us not exaggerate the 'brand recommendation' phenomenon. SNS is about 'me': me>my friends>my brands.

EVEN ONLINE, NARCISSIST RECOMMENDERS
ARE NOT MUCH USE TO ANYONE

Narcissist recommenders are easy to identify offline. But it is more difficult online. Which is a pity: since they are even less reliable online than they are offline! They are simply displaying their ego for the sole purpose of self-glorification. And the others? Who are the others? In the best circumstances, they are the people who are supposed to stand there and applaud.

The narcissist's Twitter status is usually something like: 'Sitting in my favourite place right at the very top. First class. Front row. Wheels up.'

Their Facebook update is probably in a similar vein: 'With a pleasant glass of Ardbeg and a few crumbs of mature cheddar, lounging lazily in our new chaise longue – far too expensive, I know, but who cares? – with Bach's cello suites in the background, wrestling my way through a badly written presentation by one of my colleagues on the latest iPad model.'

Strange as it may seem, this type of self-kicker often attracts a huge number of followers. Usually desperate wannabes, who will never learn anything useful from their boastful idol, but who want to be just like him (or her, of course).

The University of Western Illinois calls this 'grandiose exhibitionism' and has even created a GE-meter to measure this explosive mix of self-satisfaction, vanity, superiority and the overwhelming desire to be the centre of attention. Having loads of friends on Facebook immediately makes you suspect. I currently have 1,800, so I imagine that my GE-rating must be rocketing through the roof by now.

Fortunately, however, I do not match the other aspects of the GE profile. Most GE's are young people with a high score in the Narcissistic Personality Test. As mentioned, they usually have a lot of friends on Facebook, tag themselves more often, update their status more frequently, change their profile photograph more regularly, react more tetchily to negative comments, and display manipulative behaviour.[58] They like to be helped by others (though are seldom prepared to return the favour) and accept everyone who wants to become their friend.

Researchers are not yet fully clear where this phenomenon comes from and whether or not it is caused and/or intensified by Facebook. Viewed from my more limited perspective, I have not yet been able to find out whether they talk much about brands online. And, if so, which brands.[59]

SO WHO ARE THE REAL RECOMMENDERS?
AND WHAT IS A RECOMMENDATION?

123

A recommender needs to drop his comments somewhere. He wants to place his opinions where he knows they will be found. But he never knows who exactly will find them. He cannot target people. Made-to-measure work is out of the question.

However, a recommender can also give a 'personal' recommendation. The good thing about a genuine recommendation is that not only is it based on an analysis of the offer ('In my opinion, the best thing to buy is…'), but above all is also based on 'knowledge of' and 'respect for' the person requesting the recommendation.

You will probably have noticed that I frequently argue my case on the assumption that someone somewhere will ask for a recommendation. If someone asks me a very concrete question and I know something meaningful to communicate on that particular subject, only then is it possible to speak of a real match. Just like the old shopkeepers of days gone by, who knew their customers personally and could tailor their sales pitch to the individual's specific requirements.

In a certain sense, this 19th century relationship between the shopkeeper and the customer has been reborn. Recommenders also engage in a virtual form of face-to-face trading, but without the need to actually be face to face.

We can talk of a real made-to-measure recommendation when it has its origins in the seldom spoken sentence: 'In my opinion, and knowing what I know about you, I think that at the present time X is the best buy for you.'

The recommender can even fine tune his recommendation in the question-and-answer session that sometimes follows:

1 'If you had more money, I would really recommend…'
2 'If you want to spend a bit more, I would aim higher and go for Y instead of X.'
3 'If you had no children, I would suggest…'
4 'If your children were older, I would certainly consider…'
5 'If I were you, I would postpone my purchase for a few months, until the latest new model comes on the market…'
6 'If you are travelling to X in the coming months, you can probably buy it cheaper there.'

7   'If you are not bothered about the country of origin, it is probably wisest to buy one from X...'
8   'If functionality is more important than design, I would definitely go for ...'
9   'If you want to take cost of use into account, you could do worse than consider...'
10 'If you aren't planning to use it a lot, X should be good enough for your needs...'
11 'If you are allergic, you should choose...'
12 'If you don't have to diet, then X is just the thing for you...'
13 'If you're not bothered about trying to impress your friends with something fashionable, X is just what you are looking for...'

THESE CONDITIONAL NUANCES ARE
A TIME-HONOURED FORM OF TARGETED ADVERTISING

As a recommender, you know the person who wants to listen to your advice so well that you can target your message with great precision. Targeted banner advertising aims to achieve much the same effect. This usually takes the form of small ads, and they can be very effective, depending on the context. The almost whispering tone of these small ads is not dissimilar to the manner in which the recommenders also try to exert their influence. They start from what they know about their friend, neighbour and colleague, and then take matters from there. And from people in your inner circle you can reasonably expect that they will also know something about you. This is much more comfortable for all concerned than the foot-in-the-door tactics of the travelling salesman. You can compare this salesman to the noisy intrusion of the pop-up banner. Of course, it has to be admitted that noisy intrusion sometimes works – but you shouldn't behave this way with your family and friends!

Why? Because it doesn't work with them. Research has clearly shown that with banners the combination of the two is ineffective. Even counterproductive. The consumers are frightened off twice over: how do they know so much about me and why are they making so much noise? If you use them apart, they are much more likely to be effective. Up to a certain point.[60]

5 What recommenders can and can't do. What they do and don't do

- Much has already been written about the recommender phenomenon from the perspective of the sender, the evangelist, the ambassador and the brand advocate, but very little from the point of view of the consumer who goes in search of good advice. That makes a big difference.
- If you look at the recommender phenomenon as a metaphor for an epidemic or a forest fire, you will miss the point completely. So don't do it! Choose the guerrilla fighter as your metaphor. That is a metaphor that lives, not destroys!
- There are tens of millions of tightly-knit circles of friends around the world, in which people influence each other, simply by a process of sharing, without any intention to exert influence.

Recommenders look things up, are informed, talk to others, like writing, and love answering questions. They are people. Not viruses. Not ants. Not bees.

They do not forward messages all day long on automatic pilot, without thinking. Precisely the opposite, in fact. And then the marketers are surprised that so few people know anything about their brands! Get real!

On average a brand advocate (40% of consumers according to the Zuberance technology) makes no more than 26 recommendations each year. Twenty-six! That's just one every two weeks. Not exactly what you could call 'viral'. A small minority of the brand advocates (who Zuberance[81] refers to as power advocates) make more recommendations, perhaps several times per week. These are the people that we refer to as recommenders.

And we are not talking about a lot of brands. An average of nine, in fact. I have about twenty that I occasionally recommend. How many do you have? More? Fewer? Only the power advocates come above the fifteen mark.

Moreover, the recommenders do not always have a deliberate intention to influence others. True, they have a certain authority within their immediate circle of family, friends and acquaintances, but they are not evangelists, fanatically preaching a particular religious, political or commercial gospel. I actually wonder whether any priest or politician can be considered a recommender. I suspect that they are all nothing more than influencers, convinced that they – and no one else – is right.

The place, role and power of the recommenders is all too frequently underestimated or overestimated. Both these perspectives are wrong. But they are both understandable errors to make, since we still know relatively little about how the influencing process actually works. There are so many different sources we can use to allow ourselves to be influenced, so that no single source is wholly responsible for our eventual decision to purchase. Sometimes our decisions are made by chance. And sometimes these decisions are a bull's-eye. Serendipity: a word – and a concept – that I like.

MANY PEOPLE HAVE ALREADY TRIED – AND FAILED – TO MAP THE EXACT DEVELOPMENT OF THE INFLUENCING PROCESS

Some experts have gone too far, claiming that such a thing as 'super-influentials' exist: a higher order of recommenders who can steer the influencing process, like some kind of viral marketing bacteria. Others say that this idea is ridiculous, but then go too far in the opposite direction by claiming that super-influentials might very well exist, but that they don't have any real influence! In other words, they exist in name, but not in nature!

None of the antagonists in this pseudo-scientific debate have looked at the matter from the point of view of the average recommender and the consumer who seeks to make use of his knowledge. It is this much broader population that needs to be investigated, not the 0.1% of super-influentials, who may or may not exist. The first nine of the following points of attention examine the situation from the perspective of the sender. In point 10 the situation is viewed from the perspective of the active searcher: the only proper way to view it.

1   We are talking about everyday things

Much more than I would like to see, the so-called scientific debate focuses on trends, fads and hypes. We should be talking more about everyday things and not about Black Swans, like the Kony 2012 video. In this book we will be trying to look further than the amazing coincidences and 'lucky shots' from which everyone wants to draw the 'right' lessons. The processes that Gladwell describes in *The Tipping Point* when writing about the Hush Puppies rage are not the processes that are relevant to the recommender phenomenon. Whoever is trying to build up a brand might certainly welcome a lightning start, but if you are not careful this can die away just as quickly as it came to life. It is important to build a brand sustainably, brick by brick. The twenty, fifty or even hundred super-influentials who carried the Hush Puppies brand to its dizzy heights are not the real key for a brand that is thinking in the long term. The super-influentials can be useful for a launch, supported by well-targeted PR, but it is vital to avoid the all too familiar phenomenon of 'from nothing to everything and back to nothing'.

2   We are not talking about 1% but about 15%

Gladwell did, however, hit the nail on the head when he said that 'in a given process or system, some people matter more than others.' But he was referring to just 1% or even less than 1% of the people involved. This is where I disagree with him. If we are dealing with recommenders, we are actually talking about 15% of consumers. In other words, we are talking about a sizeable group. And as a group, these 15% have an influence that should not be underestimated, even if many of them as individuals are not particularly assertive as recommenders. Some have no real network of their own and go no further than the straightforward writing of a review. But this review will appear on screen when others go in search of information on the relevant topic. Or it will count towards the global score that might be given by the relevant review site. There is much anonymity and behind-the-scenes influence in our recommender story. It is based above all on the democratic guerrilla principle: 'together we are strong'. This 15% do not all need to stand behind the same brand. On the contrary. There is often competition within this 15% to push forward their own favourite brand as 'the best'. And the winners of this internal battle will usually carry the other 85% with them, to achieve a position of market leadership.

Until, of course, they lose this leading position to the next challenger who comes along.

3   Real people are not trees. Nor are they bits and bytes

The wise and sensible Duncan Watts[62] (at Yahoo until May 2012 and now at Microsoft) has conducted and is still conducting many tests with the forwarding of e-mails and advertisements. In the e-mail patterns he found indications 'that highly connected people are not, in fact, crucial social hubs.' He has also devised computer models, but his programmed bits and bytes in test conditions on a personal computer or in a giant server network are not the same as actually dealing with real people. People still react differently to bits and bytes – thank goodness! And in our recommender scenario there is a huge difference between a digital laboratory and the real world. Similarly, a network of flesh-and-blood people – some of whom will always be searching for something – is not a tinder-dry forest, waiting to burst spontaneously into flames as soon as there is enough wind and a spark. Watts likes this forest fire analogy. In his reasoning, the super-influentials provide the spark and the ordinary consumers are the trees that catch fire. Once again, this is not the way things work in reality. Trees are immobile. They spend their whole life before the fire standing on precisely the same spot. And when the fire starts, they cannot go in search of water to put it out. Nor can they warn other trees of the danger. They can't even save themselves by simply running away. Self evidently, they cannot learn from experience how to prevent the next fire, or at least how to survive it. Trees have no self-will and are therefore subject to the vagaries of fate. And if some idiot drops a cigarette in the forest in the middle of a scorching dry summer, then fate will strike very quickly indeed! This, of course, is not the way things happen with people. In a human forest the 'trees' will rush off for a bucket of water at the first sign of fire, will warn others and perhaps even try to save them (sometimes at risk to themselves).[63] And if all else fails, they can just leg it to safety.

4   My excuses: but in the past I also referred to the phenomenon as viral marketing

The equally attractive analogy that ideas and trends spread like an epidemic is also sadly wide of the mark. Viral marketing is the wrong way to describe this process. There is nothing you can do about a virus. But you can do something about an idea that is trying to find its way to other people through you. You can refuse to accept the idea or you can refuse to pass it on

The proponents of these theories – fire and virus – always seem to overlook the fact that in a purchasing situation someone ultimately needs to pull out their wallet or purse – and lay their hard-earned money on the table. But a tree doesn't pay to be in fire and my body is infected with the flu without any need for cash payment.

The process that marketers are dealing with is a conscious purchasing process. And each purchasing process always contains a small amount of reason and much larger amounts of emotion and free will (unless someone is compulsively addicted to this or that brand – which can also happen).

5 Opinion leaders can also be recommenders
The recommenders we are talking about have little in common with the opinion leaders called into life in 1955 with the mechanical 'two-step' process.[64] Opinion leaders – or so they thought back in those days – pick up a message and pass it on, so that the rest will eventually follow. The situation is different in our analysis. There are indeed still opinion leaders who pick up a message and pass it on in a supportive manner. But there are other opinion leaders who pick up the same message and tear it to pieces, before passing it on. In other words, at any one time there are always different opinions fighting for supremacy. A never-ending fight between fire and water. Between virus and antibiotics. These opinion leaders are still the major target for classic PR, which has been reinvented to great effect in the new internet era and is therefore – in my opinion, at least – likely to gain in importance in comparison with classic advertising. Soft power.

6 The Six Degrees of Separation have little to do with our recommender story
The idea of the six degrees of separation was launched in the 1967 book of the same title by the sociologist Stanley Milgram. He claimed that the 160 people in his experiment on average needed six contact moments to get the message across to the people at whom it was aimed. Nowadays, thanks to the development of Facebook, the average

number of moments –at least for Facebook users – has been reduced from six to 3.74.[65]

The real question is whether or not Milgram's 160 test subjects were actually recommenders. Did they need to pass on a specific idea or convince others of the merits of a specific product? Did they need to persuade the recipients to tell others about this idea or product? No, not at all. They were given a task to complete and then searched in their network for people who they thought could bring them closer to their objective. What Milgram discovered – like Gladwell – is that some people are more important than others in the information transmission process.

7   So what about snooker or billiards: a valid comparison?
Watts carried out the 'Six Degrees' test in a more modern context. He built a website and recruited 61,000 people to pass on a specific message to 18 end recipients. He found that the same six steps were necessary, but also discovered – rather to his surprise – that the most strongly networked participants were no more important than everyone else. Only 5% of the test's e-mails were forwarded via these people. Watts argued that the 160 people from the original Milgram experiment formed too small a group. For this reason, shortly before their arrival at the final destination they came into contact with three people who already had direct contact with the end-recipient. But the more people you have, the more random and democratic this pattern becomes. Without super-influentials. This sounds a bit like a game of snooker or billiards. I have always admired the way that players can send the ball around two or three cushions before finally hitting the ball they want (something that I have never been able to manage!). Yet again, however, the comparison falls short. The object ball is not a moving target: it is just sitting there, waiting to be hit. It is only then that the ball is set in motion, before randomly colliding with other balls. In other words, the process lacks all intentionality. Balls are stupid: they roll in the direction they are pushed. But people in the pre-purchase phase are not stupid: they ask to be pushed in a specific direction.

8   Perhaps a little bit like The Influentials, but then again…
It is probably the work of Keller and Berry – who published their ground-breaking book *The Influentials* back in 2003 – that most closely

reflects the way I look at this subject. They argue that one in every ten people has a disproportionate influence on the other nine. For every-thing. Yet even this is taking things a bridge too far. I think that the group is 50% larger (15% instead of 10%) and that it has less influence. We are not talking about supermen and superwomen. They certainly recommend things, but they often need to fight to get their opinions accepted. Having said this, the following quotation from Keller and Berry comes fairly close to what I feel: 'They are the 10% of Americans most engaged in their local communities (..) and they wield a huge amount of influence within those communities.'[66]

9 Infection potency – and impotency

Another laboratory test with 10,000 programmed 'persons' also lacks the necessary degree of conviction. The test subjects were all issued with a few lines of code to start inter-personal relations with other people from their immediate circle. Watts argued that 10% of digital people have a higher level of infection potency: the ability to incite others to action. He chose one of his test subjects as 'the trendsetter' to initiate the 'passing on' (information transmission) phase. This trendsetter was supposed to be the spark that would set the whole forest on fire. Yet once again the results showed that this 10% did not have significantly more impact than the other 90%. Even when he later made them 40 times more influential, the results remained disappointingly consistent. It is fascinating to read Watts' own conclusions on this experiment.

10 At last! – the searching consumer

We have finally – if carefully – come to the place where we should have been all along: the searching consumer. After long considera-tion, Watts finally came to the conclusion that the adopting of ideas is less concerned with the power of someone who wants to project his ideas on others and more concerned with the number and willingness of people to be influenced. To which I would add: their willingness to be influenced and the eagerness with which they go in active search of solutions for their problems and dilemmas.

The world's greatest wine expert can give as many excellent tips as he likes in the period after Christmas and New Year, but he will have very few followers. The real wine drinkers will have made their purchases before Christmas and by now have probably drunk enough for the time being. Consequently, they will wait for the next spate of offers in March/April.

In contrast, someone seeking to recruit people for his revolutionary diet programme will probably have quite a lot of success in the immediate post-New Year period. Moreover, it is not only the permanently twittering sources of information that attract people. It is often the searching consumer who finds and actively approaches otherwise 'silent' sources of information.

Fifteen or twenty years ago I developed the concept of the 'invited persuader'. The concept was based on the following premise: 'When I am ready, I will invite brands to come and tempt me'. The headline (written by me) on the very first site for our advertising agency in Brussels (Quattro, now Saatchi Brussels) put it even more graphically: 'Invited persuaders don't get the finger; they get heard.' Let the brands come with their stories: they can amuse themselves with their arts of persuasion until I am ready to make a decision. It is often a matter of pure chance that I arrive at brand A, B or C – *while I am searching* – but the smartest companies make sure that I find them by the clever use of search robots.

It must again be underlined: this has nothing to do with trends. Some people may refer to it as content marketing and I have no problem with this description, as long as the content comes from a consumer who speaks about his own experiences. The content that a brand makes available will not tell the same story as the content made available by a recommender. I can immediately switch from a journalist's report about a hotel in New York to the Tripadvisor reviews of people who have actually stayed in the place, so that I can use and compare both sources of information before coming to my own decision. The first opinion was formed by someone who was probably on an all-expenses-paid PR visit. The second opinion was crowd-sourced from people who had to pay their own way with their own hard-earned cash. Whose opinion would you choose?

PROVING THAT RECOMMENDERS DON'T EXIST?

Let us now briefly return to Duncan Watts, who – curiously enough – continued to conduct experiments to prove that super-influentials with the power to influence everyone and everything simply do not exist – something that most of us have known for a long time.

In 2005 he launched an online music-downloading service. He made available 48 completely unknown songs by 48 completely unknown bands and invited 48,000 people to download the songs that they most liked.

Some of the participants were allowed to pick out their own favourites, without being subjected to outside influence by others. For this group, nearly all the songs received the same score: none of them was significantly more popular than all the others.

Another group of participants – which was further divided into eight sub-groups – received additional information before making their choice. For example, they could see what others had downloaded before them. In other words, they were given a kind of 'unofficial ranking so far'. In each of these eight sub-groups a limited number of songs became extremely popular. The rest were nowhere. Watts had created eight 'worlds' and in each of these worlds a different song was a hit. There was no relationship between the inherent quality of the songs and their chance of success.

In other words, the first song that managed – more or less by chance - to attract a number of fans later found it easier to attract even more fans, without the need to make any extra effort. Likewise, the recommenders were also not required to make any additional effort. They weren't asked to give a score. They weren't asked to write a review. All they did was make a choice. They downloaded a song or they didn't: as simple as that. But when a song was downloaded, the other people in the group could see what they had chosen. And so they became influenced, consciously or not.

Watts deduced the following conclusion from this experiment: 'Word of mouth and social contagion made big hits bigger. But they also made success more unpredictable. (And, it is worth noting, no one in the social worlds had more influence than anyone else.)'[67]

But is this the right conclusion? Does this mean that Watts has finally proved that there is no such thing as influencers? Certainly there were no influencers in his group of 14,000. And even if there were, they would have been unable to make their existence known and their musical knowledge/experience count, simply because they did not have the tools available to influence others. The only signal they could give was that they had downloaded 'something'. However, the non-recommenders – the tone deaf participants with absolutely no feeling for music – were able to send exactly the same signal. Consequently, Watts' conclusion was not correct; his experiment was organised in a manner that automatically provided the conclusion he was looking for. The experiment can certainly be regarded as a good example of social herding; the concept that says if enough people are waiting in a queue then it must be the right one to join, even if the queue alongside is much shorter. But Watts' test proved nothing more than that and is certainly no evidence for arguing that recommenders do not exist.

But what would have happened if four of the eight groups had been given the opportunity to explain briefly why they had chosen song X, Y or Z or why they thought song A, B or C was total crap? Perhaps they could even have been allowed to give an answer to the One Question.

And what would have happened if it became clear after a period of time that some of the reviewers had made more sensible, better grounded choices than others? Then it might have been possible to see whether or not these self-professed music 'experts' had more recommender influence on others, other than through their initial choice of song.

In the Watts' experiment share of market was influenced exclusively through a gradually developed share of voice and that share of voice was dependent to a large extent on the chance selections of the first – and therefore the quickest, but by no means the most expert – downloaders. How 'real' is that?

Watts understandably denies the charge, but the circumstances he created are far removed from the complexities of the real world. He thought that his test conditions were 'reasonably close to a "natural" environment'. But I do not agree. In a natural environment there is always a small group (15%) who give their opinions and a larger group (85%) that listens, assesses, judges – and only then makes a decision.

It is undeniable that the experiment – in part, at least – rightly took the searching consumer as its starting point, in the sense that it asked real, ordinary people to download the music they liked. However, searching for music, books, films that you like is a very different matter from searching for the best nappy for your baby's bottom. This perhaps explains why the test subjects in each of the eight subgroups allowed themselves to be influenced so easily as soon as the (random) trendsetters appeared. If you know nothing about music and suddenly see what others are doing – others who possibly (probably?) know more than you do – you will be more inclined to follow their lead. But this is nothing new. It is the oldest and very simplest form of 'influencing'.

Nevertheless, the eight sub-groups underline the fact that in reality there are millions of little groups in which information is circulating. And this is a crucial realisation for understanding and explaining the recommender phenomenon. When you are dealing with brands, there is no point going in search of the 0.1% or 1% of super-influentials. Even if they exist, their influence is not super, but relatively limited. Consumers take decisions at home in small groups. That is the real essence of the situation. And they have access to many more signals of 'excellence' than the chance acquisition of share of market.

There may even be as many as a billion of these small groups. Within each group there will always be at least one person who satisfies the recommender criteria. Sometimes because he is the first person in the group to recommend something. Sometimes because he has knowledge that the other group members do not possess. But if there are no recommenders, the flow of information will grind to a halt. The share ratio on Facebook is just 9 to 1. One person receives something and it is read by nine others. If the ratio falls to 8 to 1, the flow of information from person to person will gradually dry up. With Twitter, the average message travels no further downstream than the circle of the fifth recipient. With StumbleUpon this drops to the second person.

Krawczyck has rightly concluded: 'In looking to get content shared, marketers and publishers should focus on content that will resonate and get people talking to their colleagues, friends and families. Social media is about engaging people in conversations that mirror the offline world, as opposed to chasing mythical influentials.'[68]

TWO GRAPHICS THAT I LIKE TO USE

I would like to bring this chapter to a close by inviting you to examine the two graphics on the following pages.

These are my favourite two graphics for convincing people of the importance of recommenders. Because there are still many people who doubt the impact that these recommenders and their recommendations can really have.

The problem: advertising is no longer to be trusted (APAC figures)

I trust the recommendations from these sources when I am making a purchase decision.

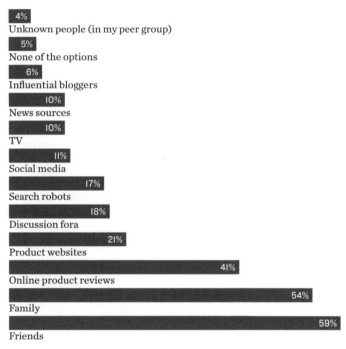

4%	Unknown people (in my peer group)
5%	None of the options
6%	Influential bloggers
10%	News sources
10%	TV
11%	Social media
17%	Search robots
18%	Discussion fora
21%	Product websites
41%	Online product reviews
54%	Family
59%	Friends

Source: http://www.slideshare.net/tbwa_hk/neilsen-apac-social-media-report-june2010

The first graphic comes from Nielsen (2010); the second from Gartner (2011). Elsewhere in the book you will find other examples and figures, but they all point in the same direction.

In the Nielsen graphic 'friends' come in first place, followed by 'family' and 'online reviews'. The Nielsen question is about credibility – 'Which sources do you trust when making a purchasing decision?' You can obtain information from many different sources, but the crunch question is always about which one(s) you believe. An average consumer in the Netherlands sees 377 advertising moments each day and he probably ignores all of them. But once each day something in his immediate environment catches his attention and he almost automatically accepts this as true. Why? Because the source is one he trusts; it is reliable.

Let's move on to Gartner. His question is about the importance of sources. Just 8% of consumers say that they are not influenced by the recommendations of family, friends and colleagues. 12% say that they are not influenced by consumer comments and reviews. This means that 92% and 88% are influenced; in other words, a sizeable majority.

Family, friends and online reviews are therefore not only extremely important but are also more trustworthy than other sources. These two aspects are complementary.

Consequently, the real trick – both for the brand and for the doubting consumer – is to combine the recommendations that you frequently receive from person to person with the information that you can read on the web. In other words, there is much more to the mix that leads to the taking of a purchase decision than the things that we can measure and (think we) know about social network sites.

This means that the brands will need to identify the 15% of online recommenders person by person for each of the markets in which they operate. And the web will play a hugely important part in this identification process.

An online 'recommendation from a friend' does not always have to appear in a Holaba-like survey.

The sharing/forwarding of 'something' to your immediate circle, coupled with a request for advice, is almost like begging for a recommendation.

So how do things work as the moment for making the purchase decision approaches? Take a look at the final graphic in this chapter and read the following text.

ı   In the distance, far in the background and as a background, you can see the moving theatre of advertising: always present, but without playing a prominent role. Precisely the opposite, in fact: advertising is constantly and consciously being pushed to the margins by the consumer, with the help of suicidal brands that fail to realise that enough is as good as a feast.

What influences a consumer?

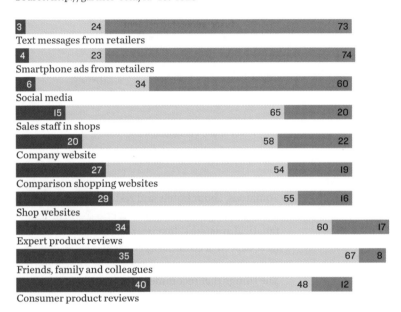

Text messages from retailers — 3 | 24 | 73

Smartphone ads from retailers — 4 | 23 | 74

Social media — 6 | 34 | 60

Sales staff in shops — 15 | 65 | 20

Company website — 20 | 58 | 22

Comparison shopping websites — 27 | 54 | 19

Shop websites — 29 | 55 | 16

Expert product reviews — 34 | 60 | 17

Friends, family and colleagues — 35 | 67 | 8

Consumer product reviews — 40 | 48 | 12

2 Sometimes – and this is bringing us closer to the searching consumer – I might try to find the results of a laboratory test that show me how things work, should work or don't work. Such tests are available from consumer organisations in every country.

3 What the experts then do with these tests – how they translate and evaluate the results – is even more accessible. Experts are people who give Oscars to films. Or Michelin stars to chefs. Oscars and Michelin stars are always likely to increase confidence – and promote sales.

4 Even closer to me are the sources that I stumble across accidentally or search for deliberately. They influence not only my opinions, but also the opinions of the recommenders around me. This 15% of consumers add an extremely important element to all the other relevant sources: they make their experiences and/or the experiences of people from their immediate circle available to the wider public.

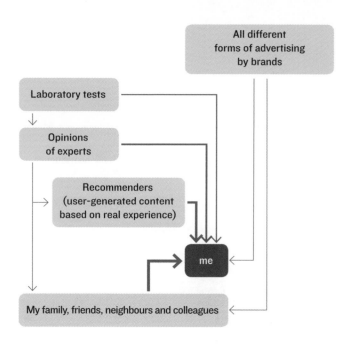

These are the people who write reviews about films on Rotten Tomatoes, about hotels and restaurants on Tripadvisor, about wine on Kurkdroog. They are not experts. Sometimes they are not even fanatical amateurs. Just people who can't help sharing what they have experienced and what they know.

The things that recommenders recommend find their way in a perfectly natural manner to the top of my message list. Good things always rise to the top. Just like water-lilies float gently upwards to the surface, so that they can add beauty to a lake. If these true-life stories correspond closely with the messages that I am also hearing from my immediate circle, then my decision will almost make itself.

An example? We are going to Vienna with friends. Their son (a musician) has recently slept in one of the city's hotels. He was very enthusiastic about it. We look it up on Tripadvisor. It is rated in position 3 on the list. Without looking at any other alternatives, we immediately book two double rooms, simply on the basis of a mix of individual and collective positive experiences.

And if the hotel is as good as we hope, then I will confirm that with enthusiasm on Tripadvisor once I have returned home. If it turns out to be a disappointment, I will notify that as well, so that the hotel's average score on the site will fall. Too bad. That's the way it works. If you are interested in finding out what we experienced, why not read the Tripadvisor page for the hotel in question?[69]

6 Don't turn social media into advertising media. The money-lenders are being thrown out of the temple!

- 'The Rockies may crumble, Gibraltar may tumble, they're only made of clay. But our love is here to stay.' Surely you don't still believe this anymore?!
- Social media are there for the consumer. Like playgrounds, churches and cultural centres. So why not leave them alone and give them a bit of peace? They are on these sites to communicate with each other. Not to be bombarded with commercial promotions.
- A market stall that picks a spot outside the market square is almost certain to do exactly that: stall. Consumers on social media are first and foremost people, not potential customers. So let them act like people and don't keep bothering them all the time. But if they do talk about your brand, listen closely and answer immediately.

20 to 40% of consumers change brands each year.
Just 20% of your customers are truly loyal.
The remaining 40 to 60% change brands every two years, or perhaps every three.
In commerce there is no such thing as 'forever'.
Most of your customers are permanently ready to drop you.
They can go almost anywhere. There is choice enough.
And how do you respond to this situation? You faithfully measure the RFM (Recency, Frequency, Monetary Value) of your customers and

conclude (in part understandably) that those who have recently bought a lot are the key to your future success – and so you concentrate on them, in the hope that they will stay. You tempt them with loyalty bonuses, offer them an extra discount (occasionally), shower them with free samples, give them a regular pat on the back...

Unfortunately, you soon discover that focusing on loyalty in this manner only works with difficulty, if it works at all. As the Beatles knew as long ago as 1964: 'Can't Buy Me Love.' Love needs to be earned, not bought. For a long time I have been a loyal '5 times per year' customer of the Dutch airline KLM (I fly regularly to Shanghai) and occasionally I am given a well-deserved upgrade to business class, something for which I am very grateful. I also belong to their Golden Card club and KLM saves my points for me. But this is as far as it goes. You may remember that I have already criticised them once or twice in the preceding pages. And if tomorrow I can find another airline that can get me to Shanghai and back with the same degree of ease and comfort, but at a cheaper price, then I would be silly not to take a look, wouldn't I? So far, I haven't found any such company (although I have searched), and so I will stay with KLM – for now. You might call this 'forced loyalty' – loyalty based on a lack of any better alternative. And let's be honest: the service – and in particular the ever-smiling, ever-polite in-flight stewardesses – is very good. They could certainly teach their counterparts on internal flights in China a thing or two – and anyone who has even flown from Shanghai to Beijing will know exactly what I mean!

ARE YOU SATISFIED AND ARE YOU COMING BACK FOR MORE?

In response to the typical loyalty research question that you regularly ask your customers –'are you satisfied?' – the easiest, politest and most obvious answer is 'yes'. This allows the customer to 'escape' before the more difficult questions start coming. Consequently, the 'yes' answer is often given automatically, almost without thinking. It therefore has the same inherent lack of meaning as the answer to the question 'do you still love me?' when posed between a couple that have known each other for 40 days or 40 years. 'Yes, of course I still love you...'

Much the same applies to your second loyalty question: 'will you be buying with us again'. Once more, the answer 'yes' trips easily – and meaninglessly – from your tongue. Back to our loving couple. 'When will you be home tonight, sweetheart?' 'Late, probably. Not sure when, exactly...' You say something, simply because it is potentially trickier if you say nothing. But what you say is vague and imprecise – particularly if you were planning to have drink with the lads after work. And so it is with customers. They say something, anything, just to get the researcher of their backs and avoid further embarrassment. And nothing is better calculated to send a loyalty researcher away happy than a few well-placed 'yes' answers.

Perhaps your customer buys with you because he has always bought with you. There is nothing wrong with that, but will he actually tell you so? Probably not.

Perhaps he buys from you because your shop is just that little bit closer to where he lives than your competitor's shop. Closer, but not necessarily better. Will he willingly admit this? What do you think?

Maybe he buys from you because you are the cheapest shop in the area. But will he publicly confess that he is interested in saving every eurocent he can? Very unlikely. (I recently bumped into one of my neighbours in the Aldi and she immediately began explaining why she was shopping in such a low-budget supermarket, in case I might think she was just penny-pinching. She assured me that she usually shops at Tesco or Sainsbury's! But what's wrong with shopping in the Aldi, for goodness sake! I do it all the time!)

Or does he buy from you simply because he is too lazy to try any-where else? Very possibly. But if he is not going to confess to being a penny-pinching miser, he is unlikely to admit – to you, at least – that he is just an idle bum.

Or did his choice of your shop all begin by accident? Just popped in for a packet of cigarettes because he happened to be passing. So why does he stay? Maybe because he fears that it might be worse elsewhere (hardly a glowing recommendation).

How many of the 20% of so-called loyal customers simply carry on doing the same old things in the same unthinking manner, simply because they don't really care or perhaps because they have better things to think about? I have no idea. But I would call none of the people in the above examples 'loyal customers'.

One day you might decide that you want to find out more about your current customers. More particularly, why they shop with you and why they stay. But let's be clear on this point: this involves more than just being 'social' with your customers – even if it involves the use of a social medium. It is not just a social chat on Twitter or Facebook, playing up to what your customers want to hear, while hardly listening to what they have to say. If you try and conduct this kind of exercise on automatic pilot, you will crash and burn. Consumers are not idiots. They are people, like you and me.

And even if you do listen and learn from these entertaining chat sessions, the information you glean is likely to be superficial. What you hear is seldom what they are actually thinking. For this reason, your key task is to try and establish the real meaning behind their words. Will the person you are chatting to really recommend your brand to his family and friends? This kind of question will cause your conversation partner to pause for thought. If he gives a 6, 7 or even an 8, you know enough. He had the option to give you a 9 or a 10, but he declined to choose that option. Why? This is the next thing that you need to try and find out, because it can give you important insights into where you might be going wrong. Deeper insights. The matters that irritate the consumer, whether moderately or seriously. The matters that prevent him from taking the step from 'yes, maybe' to 'yes, of course!' And you can be certain that he will become a recommender if you listen to him carefully and do what he asks. Because this will give him a feeling of respect. And that is a thousand times more powerful than all the sales jargon in the world. Because let's be honest: your loyalty programmes are little more than a fairly unsubtle attempt to con the consumer. Advertising in disguise.

Yet many companies still fail to see this. Consider the following. 'While customer retention is a top concern for most organisations, the percentage of overall marketing budgets our respondents devote to customer retention doesn't mirror these priorities. A full 84.4% devote less than half their marketing budget to customer retention, while 39.9% devote less than 10% of their marketing dollars to customer retention.'[70]

As if more marketing dollars can help to solve the loyalty problem! Besides, for whom does a lack of loyalty constitute a problem? Certainly not for the consumer. If he wants to be loyal, he can stay. If he doesn't want to be loyal, he can go. He is a free agent and can do what he likes.

It is time to stop following the wrong path. We must start giving the best of ourselves to the customers we have, making them so happy that they will be willing to sing our praises to the whole wide world. When I was still in the advertising business, we often used to have such customers. But even they never stayed for long, let alone for ever. Sooner or later, they all went away, no matter how good our performance was. And that is true of 80% of all consumers in all sectors. Variety is the spice of life, as they say. You can't change this, so don't worry about it. Just do your best. In many cases you are not the problem; the customer simply wants 'a change'. Whatever that might mean. Alibis are easily fabricated!

I AM A BIG FAN AND WAS A VERY EARLY USER OF SOCIAL MEDIA – BUT NOT BECAUSE OF THEIR MARKETING POTENCY

I seriously doubt whether your loyalty problem can be solved by the use of social media, no matter how popular they are. They can certainly be used to build up 'engagement' – as it is called. In this context, conversations can indeed have an added value. But I am getting sick and tired of the whole engagement business. Hypes that we create and then whip up into a religious frenzy that we even start to believe ourselves. For many, the Facebook-IPO was the moment when the scales fell from their eyes.

I am a big fan and was a very early user of social media – but not because of their marketing potency. I like them simply because they make it easier for people – and I do mean people, not consumers – to remain in contact with each other than the 'old-fashioned' methods of conversations, letters or telephone calls. As early as 1994, I was already wandering around the eWorld of Apple[71] – a world that they closed down much too quickly.

And yes, social media do have a wider social (and political?) role. Just as in centuries gone by pamphlets, books and even operettas (for those of you who know Belgian history) played a role in the overthrow of foreign and/or authoritarian regimes, so modern-day social media will likewise play a role in the game of 'changing to remain the same'. These much lauded media do not cause these pseudo-overthrows themselves, but are cleverly used by clever people with liberating or subjugating intentions. In February and March 2012, the Chinese authorities detained more than a thousand people who had written – on social media – that a coup d'état was on the way.

It is certainly true that some people – and regimes – are afraid of social media, but for the time being the powers-that-be can rest easy. There have already been a number of pseudo-overthrows – one thinks in particular of the Arab Spring – but very little seems to have changed for the better. The world is becoming more cynical. And in spite of recent history, the banks are still stealing our hard-earned savings, just like they did before the 2008-2009 financial and economic crisis. Or have I missed something in the news?

Notwithstanding their strong belief that social networks offer them a new route to the promised land (a belief that they are prepared to support with ever-greater investments), I do not see much future for brands in the social media. Their activities in these networks will yield them little positive benefit in the long run. I am not sorry to say this: nothing is more pathetic than watching a brand trying to behave 'socially'.

Whether the brands refer to their interventions as conversations or engagement triggers, this new-speak does little to conceal the fact that the messages being projected by the brands via social media have little effect, because they are inherently ineffective. These 'messages' are little more than an irrelevant, irritating and interruptive attempt to earn money from 'private intimacies between friends'. Of course, I agree with one of my proof-readers who told me angrily that there are brands that also do good things (it would be strange if there were not!). And I agree with the argument that brands can still achieve better segmentation and targeting. But this is missing the point. Segmentation and targeting were possible before the arrival of the virtual social networks. *The crux of the matter is that brands simply do not belong on social media.* The Christian Bible tells how Jesus once threw the money-lenders and the traders out of the temple in Jerusalem. The temple was God's place. And the only people who should be active in a church are the members of the Church itself.

The time has now come to apply the same principle to social media. These media are the people's places. And it is not because people choose to come together in these places that the brands should try desperately to infiltrate their activities. Brands belong primarily in shops, malls, e-commerce sites, review sites, etc. This is their natural biotope. These are the places where they can rightly say: 'here, we are the boss!' Brands only work their way into the thoughts of the average consumer during the immediate pre-purchase phase. And once the purchase is made, most people are no longer interested.

Brands expect too much love from consumers in general, too much engagement from their most loyal customers, and too many conversations with their prospects. And they don't get any of these things. We need to move away from this utopian/idealistic model. The love between consumers and brands is even more fragile and short-lived than the schoolyard love between teenagers, because in the relationships between consumers and brands promiscuity is not a sin but a virtue: you can always go and check whether the grass is greener somewhere else, without any risk of retribution. Unless your iPad contract has lumbered you with the same telecom-operator for a whole two years. Then change can really be hell!

WHEN THE CONSUMER IS READY TO START SEARCHING, YOU NEED TO BE READY TO REPLY – WITH ALL GUNS BLAZING!

The conversations between brands and people and the conversations between people about brands are relatively few. In China, less than half the consumers speak about a brand once every two days. This means just 150 brand conversations per person each year. On Holaba alone there are some 5,000 brands. This means that it will be almost thirty years before two average Chinese people get around to mentioning all these brands in their conversations. Madness!

The reality is that people only think about brands when they need to replace something in their home, whether it is food, a broken light bulb or a four-poster bed. And they continue to think about brands while they are deciding what to buy. This period can sometimes last for quite a long time. Perhaps months if you are dealing with a car or a new house. After all, these are not things you buy every year. But you will probably decide more quickly for a washing machine or a television. And for your tea and biscuits you will almost certainly decide on the spot, once you get to the supermarket.

Yet again, we are talking about the searching consumer. Searching for a solution to a problem, whether great or small. Or searching for a new source of pleasure and enjoyment. During this search, he will want to track down arguments (whether true or false) that will help him to make a selection from the almost limitless range of choice available to him. A choice that he hopes will be the right one. At this moment – and only at this moment – his willingness to listen to what brands have to say is high. For a short period (the duration of the pre-purchase phase), he is happy to receive all the arguments pro and contra that the relevant brands are able to send him.

And at this moment of uncertainty, before he knows what he really wants to buy, a single question is first and foremost in his mind: who can I trust? By now we already know the answer to this question: his family, friends, neighbours and colleagues, together with all the stories that they have experienced and all the product reviews they have read. It's as simple as that. All the rest is just entertainment. Passing on YouTube films for fun.

Of course, some of these consumer stories are indeed to be found on Facebook and Twitter. But the place where you find your information is essentially unimportant. You can find good stories and bad stories just about everywhere. Five minutes on Google will give you more stories than you will ever be able to read. In the final analysis, the crucial stories – the ones that really convince - are shared and evaluated in face-to-face encounters. This is the decisive moment when the conclusive argument gives the coup de grace to all the other would-be arguments.

Occasionally, these conclusive arguments may be rational ('It is cheaper to travel to Paris by train than in your car.') More often, however, the final choices are based on emotional factors. ('I'd rather sit in a traffic jam in my car, so that I can at least listen to music or phone my friends.'). Unless you think that this latter argument is also rational, based on a false illusion of freedom. Or control. Or they way others look at you.

What have social media got to do with all these things? No more and no less than any other comparable media, such as television, radio, cinema, the newspapers, etc. I am, of course, exaggerating. The huge search possibilities offered by internet are crucial in the search phase. Google (and Baidu in China) have become such a monster success precisely because of their ability to help searching consumers. Above all, by convincing brands to place small text advertisements on the pages that the consumer gets to see in answer to his search question. This allows Google (quite rightly) to earn money, but not Facebook – or not yet. Viewed from a purely utilitarian marketing standpoint, Facebook has little to offer. I state this as an opinion, not as a value judgement. After all, we all do lots of things that have no useful value.

It is also at this moment of intense searching that the battle between the different recommenders is won and lost. The battle to decide who gets the consumer's final 'yes' of approval. Until this final point is reached, the recommenders still have everything to play for.

The consumer allows everyone to say their own piece, perhaps picks up one or two useful pointers elsewhere and then makes his decision. Only then will it become apparent who was the biggest influencer. And by allowing himself to be influenced in this manner, the consumer enhances still further the influencing status of his chosen recommender.

It is important in this context to note the use of the phrase 'allow himself to be influenced'. If the battle is finally won by the marketing guerrilla army that Apple and its host of volunteer fans have put into the field, this will result in an Apple being bought – and not a Nokia, or an HTC, or a Samsung. And if more searching consumers worldwide allow themselves to be influenced in this manner Apple will win market share at the expense of Nokia, HTC and Samsung. Market share is the result of thousands of individual decisions each second. In a single quarter, there are probably hundreds of millions of decisions about which mobile phone to buy. But nobody can 'force' the consumer to be influenced. It remains at all times a voluntary process. And it is a process that is not decided by social media. They simply play a contributory role – just like street posters and cinema commercials.

UNCERTAIN CONSUMERS ARE LOOKING FOR SOMEONE THEY CAN TRUST; IF YOU CAN WIN THEIR TRUST, YOU WILL WIN THE BATTLE

But if the role of social media in this process is contributory, the role played by the recommenders – and by the recommenders alone – is central. If we can believe McKinsey, recommenders have a decisive impact on 20 to 50% of all purchasing decisions. For this reason, the point is worth repeating. Uncertain consumers are looking for some-

one they can trust; if you can win their trust, you will win the battle.
This doesn't mean you need to look at the recommender as though he
is some type of salesman. He is nothing of the kind. He is just someone who puts forward his arguments with conviction and allows his
friend, colleague or neighbour to decide. He does not cajole; he does
not insist. Why should he? After all, who allows themselves to be persuaded by a salesman? Losers and dummies!

Philip Sheldrake.[72] 'Overall, it seems that each of us is more influenced
by the 150-odd people nearest to us than by the other six or so billion
combined. Influence is truly complex. And this is a considerable chal-
lenge – and opportunity – to marketing and public relations firms. So
far, many have claimed to be able to identify influentials, get to know
them, and influence them. They are effectively claiming to be the influencers of the influencers, a sort of influencer-in-chief, if you like.'

The current discussion about whether or not the recommenders are
important and, if so, just how important, is a sterile and unnecessary
one. This argument has already been settled: they are very, very important. Amongst others, for the 100 million people who need to decide
each quarter what new mobile phone they want to buy. And what
happens to the recommenders after the purchase has been made?
They retreat with their knowledge back into the anonymity of cyberspace, until next quarter another one of their friends asks if anyone
knows anything about the latest mobile phones... Recommenders do
not get up each morning and ask themselves which of their friends
they are going to influence today to buy Apple or Guinness or KLM.
But as soon as Apple, Guinness or KLM are mentioned in conversation (online or offline), they will be there in an instant to defend their
favourite brand.

What's more, it must be remembered that we are not talking about
Famous People (with capital letters!) or super-influencers with hundreds
of thousands or even millions of followers on Twitter or Facebook.

These are not 'our' recommenders. It is not because Justin Bieber suddenly starts recommending Guinness that all his followers will start drinking the stuff. Although…

No, back to reality. We are talking about the 15% of ordinary consumers. Normal people. 200 million Chinese, 45 million Americans, 2.5 million Dutchmen, 1.6 million Belgians, and so on. It is a relatively small group, but it is still 15 or 150 times bigger than the select band of celebrities from the world of stage, screen and sport, who will never form more than 1% or 0.1% of the population.

MASS-TURBATION. NO MATTER HOW SOCIAL SOCIAL MEDIA ARE, THEY ARE STILL MASS MEDIA

This brings us back to the religion of mass media. Time after time, advertising agencies and other consultants seek to reinvent the wheel by claiming to have found the secret of mass media success. Most brands have scarcely recovered from decades of television addiction before these new messiahs are knocking on the door, ready to convert them to a belief in the newest mass medium: the social network sites. Because that is precisely what social network sites are. No matter how social they might seem, they are a mass medium in their own right.

The only difference between these two mass media is that with television there were a few thousand broadcasters with billions of viewers worldwide, whereas with social network sites there are billions of broadcasters, but hardly anyone who bothers to read their output.

On Twitter there are now between 250 and 300 million tweets per day. PER DAY! That is 25 billion words, if each tweet contains an average of ten words. Or 40,000 books of this size. Per day. What chance does your brand tweet have amongst this tsunami of information? Who is waiting to hear from you? Nobody! Is anybody actually waiting to hear any of these messages? Do I really need to know that my friend has just landed at JFK or is standing in a bar in Time Square? No. Am I even interested? No again. But I am interested to read the links that my friends send me about films they have seen or books they have read. But for me, that's about as far as it goes. I am not a gossiper. My friends and I live our own separate lives and that's the way I like it. Facebook and Twitter have helped me to learn more about them: we have discovered more points of common interest that can help to make our friendship tighter. But the opposite can also be true: if I find their tweets ridiculous and their Facebook shares banal, our friendship might become less close…

Facebook has become the digital equivalent of a friend sitting you down and forcing you to page through every single photo they've ever taken, whether during their last holiday or even during their last meal! The good thing about Facebook is that you don't actually have to look at them, if you don't want to.[73]

SO WHAT SHOULD A BRAND DO ON FACEBOOK AND TWITTER? SIMPLE: LOOK FOR THE RECOMMENDERS

So how do you start? Well, first you should finish reading this book. And other books of a similar kind. Next, you should follow who is saying what on the web. Who is defending what position? What are the new trends? What is the latest news? Ask your staff and your customers what they think you should be doing. Talk to a few external partners who claim to know a lot about it. There may be one or two digital agencies worth contacting. And maybe some consultants with a wider remit: after all, we are talking here about business, not just doing 'fun' things on social media.

What you ultimately do will depend on your sector and the SWOT analysis of your brand. I also do one or two things with Holaba on Facebook and Twitter. What are the results? I don't really know! A little bit of name awareness, I hope. But what's the point of a bit more awareness if half the world already knows your name?

So you do indeed need to be active (no doubt about it), just like you need to be active in all the other media. Doing nothing is worse than doing something, even if at first this means learning from your mistakes.

But there is one thing I know for sure: you have to go in search of the recommenders! The people who have something to say about the products in your market sector. But remember: these are not necessarily the same people who give you a 'like'.

If you look again at the Nielsen figures, there is little doubt that you need to embrace the social media in (South-East) Asia. According to Nielsen, the Americans and the Europeans have a generally more passive attitude toward social network sites.

In America, 76% of users just follow and don't actually do anything. Ditto, 69% in Europe.

The rest – roughly a quarter – are the good ladies and gentlemen who create content. For ease of reference, we will assume that our recommenders belong to this group of content creators.

The figures for Japan reflect the US/EU situation, but the picture is very different in China and India.

In China the number of creators stands at 76%. In India, it rises to an astonishing 80%. In these countries it would seem that almost everyone wants to be heard. You might be asking yourself who reads this mass of information. A censorial government? Surely not!

Of course, marketers in every country love to collect the opinions of consumers on social media, but a large majority of South-East Asian consumers – 73% in fact – claim to be influenced to a greater or lesser degree by advertising on the web. They give 'likes' to brands much more readily, while at world level this only happens in 52% of cases. Is this perhaps in some way related to the 'newness' of consumerism in this part of Asia?

On the other hand, you can interpret the results of the study as follows: 85% of consumers worldwide say that they are not influenced or only marginally influenced by advertising on the web. The comparable figure for South-East Asia is 81%.

Including a little bit of social media in your media plan can do no harm, but its influence will not be great. You shouldn't think that winters outside will suddenly become warmer, simply because you open the windows! The only difference you will notice is in your gas and electricity bill – not on your garden thermometer.

So what to do? Focus your efforts on identifying potential recommenders and build up brand recognition (unless it already exists) with… the famous 15%. Because the rest are just spectators or seldom say anything about brands.

Some of the people you think you are reaching on social media either don't exist or don't even know that they are following you. Because the internet also has its own form of plague: some people

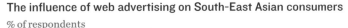

% of respondents

■ Strongly influenced / ▨ Slightly influenced / ▨ Not influenced

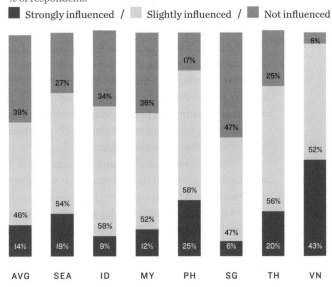

Source: http://blog.nielsen.com/nielsenwire/consumer/southeast-asians-like-ads-on-social-media-sites/

Online ads that are delivered to consumers, based on previous purchases or other websites visited, also resonated with South-East Asian consumers, with 74% saying they found this technique 'made their lives easier', compared to just 58% globally. Consumers in the Philippines and Vietnam were most receptive to such ads (83% and 82% respectively).

---

only exist virtually. And some others are duplicates or divisions of people who do exist.

It was with this phenomenon in mind that Kevin Kelly recently asked himself where the more than 500,000 followers of Google+ actually come from. He quickly concluded that the majority were ciphers.[74] People (or perhaps clones of people) who have registered for something in the past – in this case Google+ – but have never published anything. No text, no photo, no profile.

In other words, they stumbled into things more or less accidentally and their names were forwarded by Google+ to others – including Kevin Kelly – as followers. It is not impossible that they may become active at some point – a number of them do indeed exist – but the level of activity of 70 to 80% of social media users is low anyway. Because Kevin Kelly's name is on the list of people that you 'must' follow, new Google+ recruits clicked enthusiastically on his name. In the sample that he checked only 30% of them had ever written anything on Google+ and I suspect that this figure is unlikely to increase in future.

This same cipher effect has also been identified on Twitter. Twitter newbies also receive a list of 'names to follow' – and so they click 'ok' and follow as asked. But what do they follow? A pair of journalists decided to check a sample of a thousand followers. Just 24.6% were real people. 14% were real companies or other organisations. The identity of the rest was unclear, fake or spam-related. It would be useful to know if such figures for China also exist.[75] They could be interesting. Very interesting indeed.

'The initial results show that on average 31% of online display ads aren't seen by users. Why? Sometimes the ads appear "below the fold" and users don't scroll down the webpage far enough to see them. Other times ads that are placed "above the fold" are scrolled past before they have a chance to load. As for the geo-targeting of display ads, this appears effective with, on average, just 4% of impressions wasted on folk that aren't located in the right geographic location or where a product wasn't even available. This figure rose to 15% in some analysed campaigns. Bad ad placement is also tracked. Inappropriate display ad placements were evident in almost three-quarters (72%) of campaigns. Apart from a wasted ad, these could also do damage to the brand.'[76]

31% OF WEB ADVERTISEMENTS ARE NOT SEEN: THAT SOUNDS TO ME LIKE A VERY OPTIMISITC ESTIMATE

So what about the people who do exist and who have a real interest in the people they follow? Do they also have an interest in what is being

advertised on social network sites? Do they always see these ads? This
is open to serious question.

Comscore calculated that 31% of advertisements are never seen. Based on my own experience – for example, of Facebook – this sounds like a very optimistic estimate.

I experimented for a few months with a small ad for Holaba on Facebook. My target – as indicated in the self-service screen – was 1,146,360 users: just a fraction of the 1 billion Facebookers. I attempted to reach this target with a budget of $15 dollars per day. The users had to live in either the United States, the Netherlands, the United Kingdom, Belgium or China and they had to have an interest in # Digital marketing, # Internet marketing, # Management, # Market research, # Marketing, # Mobile marketing, or # Search engine optimisation. Of course, I also stipulated that only university graduates should see my ad. Who else in God's name could possibly understand what we do!

The graphic shows the results for the final month of what was quite a lengthy trial. In total just 172,121 people were able to see the advertisement. 172,121 in comparison with a target of 1,146,360. A mere 281 people clicked on the ad, which gave a CTR (click through rate) of a very modest 0.008%. And this for a cost of $350 dollars during this last month. Is that expensive? Yes and no. At the beginning of February 2012 I spent 14 days in San Francisco for an NPS conference and a number of related interviews. This cost me ten times as much and I am yet to see a single cent (Euro or American currency) in return. However, a section of this present volume was also written there. So if you have paid full price for the book, thank you very much! That at least is some form of return!

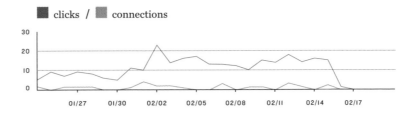

The average CTR should be around 0.1%. The CTR for Facebook is 0.051. For Google it is an impressive 0.4%. It is perfectly normal that Google should win. Google is the place where everyone goes if they want to buy something. Hence the reason why one in every 250 Google advertisements is clicked. There are a hundred and one reasons for being on Facebook, but buying something is not one of them. Hence the reason why only one in every 2,000 (1/2000) Facebook advertisements is clicked.[77]

'Not being seen' seems to be the fate of many online ads and many feeds from your friends. In terms of my own situation, I must confess that with nearly 1,000 followers on Twitter and almost 2,000 on Facebook, I do not always read what the people I am following write. I might have a nose around once or twice per day, just to see if I can pick up anything interesting, but nothing more than that. Not for anyone. The official 'read' figure is somewhere between 10 and 35%. This sounds about right. I think I read around 10% of the feeds sent to me by the people who I consciously follow. But on the reverse side of the coin, I hope that I am also being read by others. A question of vanity, I suppose: a failing of which we are all guilty. But this, too, is an illusion. Fortunately, I don't write very much. But I do read a lot about what is happening, both in the real world and in the marketing world, and I try to share the links to pieces I find interesting.

I sometimes ask myself about the people who in addition to all this 'routine maintenance' still find time to engage in real conversations with each other or with brands. I suspect that this is just another illusion (the umpteenth in this book already). People who are not closely involved with the internet as part of their daily work usually spend time on the web during their lunch breaks, in the evening or at weekends. And these are precisely the moments when we – the web-warriors who serve the brands – are no longer working and are actually doing our own thing. After a cautious reply that arrives in the company mailbox a day or two later, the conversation usually just fizzles out. I do not know how many iterations occur on average between the so-called conversation partners. If they occur at all.

Even if some people have seen your ad on a social media site, even if they have clicked on the ad and even if they have given your brand a 'like', there is still no guarantee that they are genuinely engaged. Perhaps first of all someone needs to explain to me what engagement really is and to what these people actually become engaged. Do they want to enter into a relationship with your brand? I don't think so! With very few exceptions (a limited number of recommenders, perhaps), they are all more interested in discounts, promotions, competitions and lotteries. This seems to me to be perfectly normal. But enter into a relationship? You must be joking!

In this respect, I would echo a suggestion made by another one of my wide-awake proof-readers. 'The question is also whether you want to enter into a relationship with all those fans. Is this absolutely necessary per se or is it just the heritage of the old style media reach thinking? Might it not be better, for example, to have as your ambition the desire to hold a single conversation each day with someone who has obtained, say, 20 likes per post? One such conversation per day is equivalent to 365 potentially genuine recommenders, who are probably worth more for your market share than the 365 fans that you attract each day for your page. Time for a little experiment, perhaps?' Time indeed!

'Liking' a brand has become routine, rather in the same manner that we say goodbye to people. 'Sure, it was fun. We must do it again sometime. See you later…' Fortunately, these formulae are often meant when expressed between friends, family and colleagues. But not between total strangers. 'Thank you, Mr. Van den Bergh. That was a very interesting presentation. We will get back to you as soon as possible.' If I have heard this once from possible investors in China, I have heard it a hundred times – almost always without further contact. People are very polite – but politeness doesn't help you to pay the rent.

If you temper your expectations and do not cause too much irritating interruption to the 40 to 50% of users who would prefer not to see your stall on the Facebook market, it is certainly worth while trying to come into contact with the 0.45% of users who are prepared to talk. Because that is the percentage (according to the Ehrenberg-Bass Institute) that is willing to engage. Whatever that might mean.

Facebook has a metric (*People talking about this*) which charts 'likes', posts, comments, tags, shares and all other forms of interaction with a brand. This metric has shown that 1.3% of Facebook users are in active communication with brands. But if you deduct the people who clicked on 'like' just once during the survey period, than you arrive at the same 0.45% figure. If these people all turn out to be recommenders, your fishing expedition for engagement has resulted in a good catch. But I somehow doubt it.

This is what Karen Nelson-Field – senior research associate at the Ehrenberg-Bass Institute and an ardent Facebook advocate – had to say on the matter. 'People need to understand what it can do for a brand and what it can't do. Facebook doesn't really differ from mass media. It's great to get decent reach, but to change the way people interact with the brand overnight is just unrealistic.'

So there we have it: Facebook is just another mass medium to go along with all the mass media we already have. Okay, so let's use it like a mass medium – and accept that any engagement we pick up along the way is just a gift from the gods.

During my years in the advertising business I often misused Ehrenberg in discussions about the importance of creativity. What I can still remember of his theory is that the act of creation, putting together the content of the advertising message, plays a much smaller role than the precisely planned (and usually excessive) frequency of its exposure. Ehrenberg did not really believe in the power of creative advertising to convince people.

And I am now discovering that he had an equally low regard for all forms of loyalty marketing. The continuous bombardment of loyal customers (for example, via Facebook) gets you nowhere. You cannot readily persuade people who are already drinking two or three pints of Guinness a day to drink two or three more. Unless you (and they) have absolutely no respect for their livers. 'Drink, but in moderation' is the message of today's modern brewers.

Ehrenberg's disciples argue in favour of 'broad reach through mass media'. A brand that wishes to grow should not target a few loyal customers, but should seek out its light and medium buyers. Using mass media.

Fans on Facebook are already heavy users. 'So what's the point of trying there?' they say. Just because someone is a fan, this does not necessarily mean that they will buy more. 'If there is an overall cau-

tion, it is against, in the words of Ms. Nelson-Field, putting a disproportionate amount of effort into engagement and strategies to get
people to talk about a brand, when you should be spending more
time getting more light buyers.'[78]

If this is true, the key question therefore becomes: how do you reach
these important light users? According to the followers of Andrew
Ehrenberg this can only be achieved through the use of mass media.
Not on Facebook. In answer to my comment that many Facebook users
might also be recommenders, who, if dealt with correctly, could also
help to track down and approach light users, the institute replied with
the same old story: 'But my dear Jan, the reach of your recommenders
is much too small! We are talking here about mass markets and mass
products, which need the use of mass media to build up the required
levels of reach.' How can you respond to that? It is difficult to convince
people who believe – who know – that they are right (although I suppose I am no better, really!). Perhaps in the near future there will be
successful cases of FMCG's (Fast Moving Consumer Goods) that have
relied primarily on recommenders to sprint from 0% to a reasonable
level of market penetration in no time at all. Let's hope so.

MONEY WASTED ON SOCIAL MEDIA

In addition to heavy, medium and light buyers of products, there
are also heavy, medium and light users of social media:
> heavy users spend 26% of their online time on social media;
> medium users spend 4.1% of their time on social media;
> light users spend just 0.41% of their time on social media.

We might as well start with the comments of the researcher who carried out this survey. Speaking of heavy users, he said: 'These consumers may not be worth all the attention and marketing dollars spent
on them.'

Online purchases by users of social media

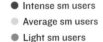

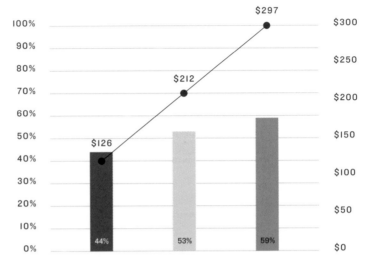

Source: http://www.forbes.com/sites/ciocentral/2011/08/14/how-valuable-are-heavy-social-media-users-anyway/2/

He continued: 'Not only are heavy social media users less likely to purchase online, they spend a lot less money when they do. Again the consistent theme: heavy social use doesn't translate into desired behaviours. Does this mean that heavy social users aren't valuable to brand advertisers? It depends on the brand and the budget. But our results do suggest that the rush to social should be tempered with more than a little caution.'[79]

In other words, just because someone is active on social media does not mean that they will also buy a lot when they are there. So what do they want to do? The following table makes this very clear: they want to keep in touch with their family and friends. This is right at the very top of the list, whereas 'interacting with brands' is somewhere near the bottom. It is to be hoped that the majority of the 23% who indicate this as one of their social media activities are also recommenders! 'Accessing reviews' is only a little higher in the list, as is 'airing (and sharing) my opinions'.

Sample size: 1,066

0,4%	
Other	
20%	
Looking for work	
22%	
Access to training	
22%	
Writing a blog	
22%	
Networking for my job	
23%	
Interacting with brands	
26%	
Finding deals	
28%	
Work-related research	
36%	
Sharing media	
38%	
Meeting people	
39%	
Accessing reviews	
42%	
Sharing opinions	
46%	
Relaxation	
49%	
News	
70%	
Contact with family and friends	

Source: IBM Institute for Business Value analysis. CHM Study 2011

The differences in the rankings become even more painful when you ask the internauts why they want to interact with brands and when you ask the brands why they think consumers follow them on the web – as the following table illustrates.

Consumers are not dummies. What do they want? They want to be able to buy (after all, they are in a purchase phase), they want a discount and they want to read reviews and product rankings. No messing about and no bullshit.

Differences in what consumers think and what brands think

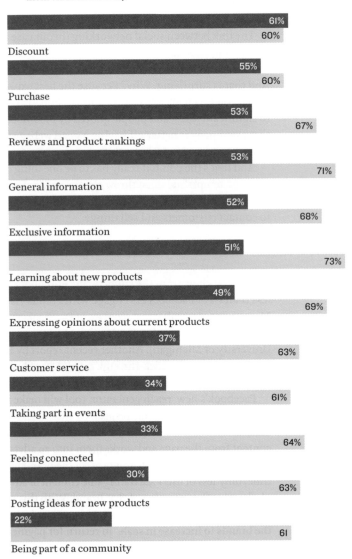

■ Consumer ranking (the reasons why consumers interact with brands via social media)
□ Brand ranking (the reasons why brands believe consumers follow them via social media)

61%
60%
Discount

55%
60%
Purchase

53%
67%
Reviews and product rankings

53%
71%
General information

52%
68%
Exclusive information

51%
73%
Learning about new products

49%
69%
Expressing opinions about current products

37%
63%
Customer service

34%
61%
Taking part in events

33%
64%
Feeling connected

30%
63%
Posting ideas for new products

22%
61
Being part of a community

The idealistic brands with a naïve image of the relationship with their consumers at least appreciate their desire for reviews, but they seem to think that their followers just can't wait to hear about the latest products and are also hungry for more general information. I'm afraid that this latter assumption is only true (again) of recommenders. The rest couldn't care less. And so they don't come to your website.

The link between social networking (in our case a review site) and purchasing seems to be very strong. Consumers want to 'buy' on these social sites. Whereas the brands think they don't want to buy at all. And that is surprising. Why? Because the first experiences of store owners on Facebook all spoke of a major flop. 'The stores didn't lead to significant sales, and people quoted by Bloomberg seem to suggest that a company is better off having a good website for e-commerce than a store inside of Facebook'.[80]

And that's the point. It really has to be one thing or the other. Either you are a temple and must throw out the money-lenders and traders, or else you are a market, so that you must embrace those who are there to contact customers and sell things.

THE STRENGTH OF A BRAND IS IN THE WAY IT WORKS – AND NOT IN THE FIREWORKS IT PRODUCES

We already know from the study by the Ehrenberg-Bass Institute that less than 1% of Facebookers engage with brands via the Facebook site. Moreover, it seems that just 0.0019% of Facebookers click on a link sent to them other Facebookers (according to a January 2012 study by the University of Michigan). Another recent report by EdgeRank Checker established that the click-through rate (CTR) of links that were posted by brands with 100,000 fans was a very unimpressive 0.14%.

Facebook's new 'reach generator' tool will make the marketing world much happier in this respect. Or that, at least, is the intention. 'This tool will allow marketers to buy reach. The tool takes elements of content from the page and works them into an advertisement. The cost is dependent on the number of fans on the brand page. At the present time, only 16% of users see the organic content of advertisers; for example, because they are a fan of that brand. With this new tool a brand can achieve 75% greater visibility. This will make it much easier for the brands to increase in scale. In return for payment, of course.'[81]

Must brands have a higher CTR?[82] If they can, why not? It would certainly be useful. But the reality is different. You can probably drive up the rate by putting your best creative minds to work in combination with the reach generator. But once the initial fireworks are over and the smoke and ash fall gently back to earth, the effect of all your creative power is also lost.

The strength of a brand is – and always has been – in the way it works. And not in the fireworks it produces.

IF SHOPPING IS THE OBJECTIVE, GO TO A PLACE WHERE PEOPLE TALK ABOUT SHOPPING

Even so, let's imagine that a brand can increase its click-through rate to 1%, 2% or even 3%. What then?

We are still not where we need to be; namely, in the market! That is the place where things are bought and sold, that is the place where we should be, but we prefer to hang around in the temple, where people go to meet other people, and not to shop. And even this 'social' aspect is coming under pressure . An article recently appeared which claimed that '41% of Brits are getting bored with social networks'. The headline read: 'YouGov predicts a rise in social networks with a purpose'.

Sounds like a nice idea, doesn't it? We are all going to ditch those useless, pointless social media sites where we have been wasting all our time, and switch instead to more useful, worthwhile sites. One of the sites in the UK that already has more users than Twitter is Money-savingexpert.com. 'The site not only offers financial information, but also lets users create profiles, leave comments and interact in similar ways to other social media sites. (…) "This points towards a new phase – the rise of social sites with slightly more purpose than just connecting to people for the sake of it", YouGov said.'[83]

LinkedIn seems to be making progress in the same direction.[84] There are many people who have no money and no work. *Moneysavingexpert. com* can help you to solve the first problem, but you have more chance of finding a job if you have a proper professional network. And this is where LinkedIn can help. 53% of British netizens say that they now use LinkedIn more than 12 months ago.

YouGov is clear: there will be less and less for brands to earn on social media.

44% of British internet-users indicated that they would have a more positive feeling about a brand if they saw that it was followed or 'liked' by a friend. 44%. Is that a lot? Or relatively few? I am inclined to think that it is actually quite a lot. And I can live with the 43% who 'admit' that they 'probably' don't talk about brands on social media. This means that 57% of users on Facebook do talk about their positive experiences with brands. And that is a good percentage. 53% of the respondents even claim to like the ads that are targeted at them – which also strikes me as being reasonably positive. Even so, the real question is this: just how negative are the negatives?

SEARCH FOR THE RECOMMENDERS AND MEASURE THEIR PERCENTAGE IN EACH SOCIAL MEDIUM YOU USE

Look at the following graphic carefully. What is missing? Exactly! No mention is made of the identity of the real recommenders, unless it is supposed to be included in the measuring of 'favourability'.

http://mashable. com/2012/05/23/social-marketing-infographic/

This graphic brings us to the thing we really want to measure on social media. Namely, how large is the percentage of recommenders in every social medium you use? In relative terms, where do you have the most recommenders? On Facebook? On Twitter? On Pinterest? Or on one of the many niche social network sites?

You will not be able to find this information from TV or in the press. You can only start your crucial identification process on the web and, in particular, via social media.

The rest of the graphic is a bit vague. What is the value of a 'like'? And what does it mean if, as a brand, we have 'a good conversation with the customer on the web'? How good is good? And how do you measure this level of 'goodness'? Likewise, how can you measure which tool is ideal for building up a relationship? I love Illy coffee, and have done for years. But I can't remember that I ever received a relationship-development tool to cement my love. What really clinched it, in fact, was a chance visit to their coffee-roasting house in Trieste!

So what exactly is measurable? If you had 7% of recommenders amongst your Facebook 'likes' last year and if you have 9% this year, that is something measurable, something capable of being followed, monitored, evaluated and – ultimately – improved. So counting names is the first step that needs to be taken, before moving on to establish precisely who and what is behind those names. And to do this, you can use the One Question – to start with.[85]

'Activities like conducting qualitative surveys to understand why customers are behaving as they are and what sentiments are driving interactions, should be at the top of marketers' minds. Until this is done, conversations with consumers will only serve to harbour good sentiment, but without clear value.'[86]

If I have something to tell a brand, I will...

6%
Go to one of their events

12%
Tweet them

12%
Send them an sms

23%
Join a discussion forum

25%
Go to a shop

29%
Post it on my Facebook page

33%
Post it on the Facebook page of the brand

44%
Call their customer service team

50%
Fill in a form on their website

65%
Send them an e-mail

Source: http://www.slideshare.net/ricardodepaula/social-brand-experience

35.5% of 900 recently surveyed UK marketers admitted that their social media activities to date had so far not been effective. 13.7% said precisely the opposite. But what had they measured to reach these conclusions? I would be surprised if they even know. Nevertheless, 74.5% said that they intend to invest more money in social media during the coming 12 months. So what are they planning to do with it? How will they change next year's approach if they don't know what was wrong with last year's approach? 16% claimed that their results on Facebook were 'good'. But good in terms of what? The development of a loyal group of fans? Direct sales? No one seems to know.[87]

Besides, if I am a consumer why would I want to communicate with a brand every day? Even a brand that I am a fan of? It is for me to decide when I 'need' my brand. When the time is right, I will go in search of them. Usually when there is a problem. And that is precisely the moment when they are no longer quite so interested in contacting me! Suddenly, the warm, cuddly world of social media (*'Tout le monde il est beau, tout le monde il est gentil'*) collapses around your ears and you are sent packing without help and without explanation. That is the reality of the situation.

So what tools should you use to get your point across? In the past, people used to go to shops for information and then went back to the same shops to make their complaints. Sometimes, they might have telephoned instead. For the last 15 years, most brands have had an e-mail address and so nowadays you send a mail. If your Google search fails to reveal an address, you might fill in the info-form that you find on every brand website. If you are the restless type, who wants an answer here and now, you may pick up the phone and call the brand's head office. Who knows: after 15 minutes of muzak and menu choices, you might actually get through to a real, live person! If you are feeling very angry, you might even post something on Twitter or Facebook – but only when the other tools have first let you down or if you really want to 'name and shame' your brand in public. But this won't happen very often. Social media are not really the place to hang out your dirty washing. In this respect, they are a tool of last resort.

This again underlines the importance of good customer service. Being there for your customer when he needs you is much more important than having a nice chat with him when he doesn't need you. Brands that excel in this department get a much higher recommender

THREE ODDITIES
TO FINISH OFF
THE CHAPTER

1 68% of women in the UK no longer use traditional TV guides when they want to know what they should be watching. They prefer to rely on the Facebook recommendations of family and friends.[90]

2 That real or would-be recommenders can earn money from the promotion of a brand is apparent from the following message: 'Dear User. There is a new opportunity for you at Zuvvu. Spread the word about this new Bing search engine, which uses data from the whole of the social media to improve its results, and earn up to $0.10 per click your friends make on your shared tweets or Facebook posts about this cool new search engine. Check out the advertiser's link: http://socialmedia-pagerank.com. Grab your easy $ 10-50 bucks now, login now: http://zuvvu.com. Thank you. Zuvvu Admin'

3 And what about the women who recommend to other women on Facebook what they should be watching on television? Do they get paid as well? I don't think so. Having said this, Martin Lindstrom – and who am I to contradict him? – thinks that ordinary people will soon be paid to promote brands offline.

---

score from their customers than their less interested or less efficient counterparts. '58% of shoppers would "definitely recommend" brands achieving excellence in this area, compared with 38% for their less successful rivals. A 52% majority displayed similar certainty when it came to re-purchasing goods and services if the providers had delivered a superior experience, declining to 37% when discussing more average competitors.'[88]

What more proof do you need? 1,000 adults were recently polled in the UK. 810 of the respondents had already publicly expressed an opinion about a product or service. 688 of them had never been contacted by the brand in question. Of those who had been contacted, 32% were 'very happy' with the response and 47% were 'satisfied'. 600 of the respondents had actually made positive comments about the product or service; the remaining 210 had made a complaint. A large majority of the complainants had at least expected some form of apology (74%), or financial compensation in the form of a voucher (39%) , and/or cash compensation (29%).[89] Most of them got nothing at all. Not even an answer. Enough said.

7 The regrettable – and hopefully temporary – impossibility of giving an exact score to individual recommenders

- I know a lot about China, but do I also know which disposable nappies are best for my grandchildren? No, I don't.
- Social Medial Monitoring, Measurement & Management Systems (SMMMMS) attempt for better or worse to measure people's digital influence. And those who earn money from digital media are doing very good business indeed. But it is very difficult to check if they are actually measuring real influence. In reality, they measure the likelihood that a message from someone will be seen and read. But is that the same thing?
- We badly need reliable SMMMMS. So let's not kill them with kindness or allow them to burst like a bubble.
- You get a slightly more accurate score if you add up the results of 15 to 20 measuring systems and then divide the sum total by 15 or 20.
- What should brands do with this measuring apparatus? They must go in search of people with reasonable scores and then try to find out how strong their recommender profile really is.

I always knew that this was going to be a difficult chapter to write – and so it turned out. How can you attach a meaningful score to the digital influence exerted by different people? I have discussed this thorny question with Klout, Kred, Peerindex, Peerreach, Viralheat, Engagor, SocialBakers and Metavana. To name but a few.

At one point I feared that I was going to lose my way, drown in the murky depths of this complex theme, which has only recently started to attract the attention it deserves. Fortunately, an illuminative piece was published on 21 March 2012 by Brian Solis – and suddenly everything became much clearer. In his short, 33-page book he explained things far better than I ever could. For this reason, I would strongly urge you to download and read *The Rise of Digital Influence*.[91] Certainly if you want to understand the moves and finesses of the different players. And if, as in my case, you discover this gem while flying high above the Gobi Desert (not the best place for an internet connection), you will probably experience the same frustration at not being able to download it immediately. Remember, however, that patience is a virtue.

Yet even if the theme is a very complex one, we will start at the beginning with something simple, and see where we end up. At the end of the chapter I will also return to Solis and his conclusions.

As you already know, this book is about recommenders, some of whom have a great deal of influence on their friends and their purchasing behaviour, and others who have next to no influence at all. It is my firm belief that you must identify the individual recommenders for every company in every sector. This is a necessary and continuing activity, in much the same way as you seek to continually assess the media (social or otherwise), journalists, experts, competitors, trendsetters, etc.

Consequently, I want these recommenders – who also air their opinions on social network sites – to appear in large numbers on the dashboard of at least one of the many providers offering SMMMMS's. That is all I ask. No more, but also no less.

I do not immediately need to know whether they are light, medium or heavy buyers of my brand. For all I care, they can even be buying another brand. The essential thing is to know that they are people who like to write about brands in general.

I am not interested in their no doubt valuable opinions about the situation in Iraq, the Olympic Games and the affair their next-door neighbour is having with the woman across the street. This digital tittle-tattle is an inevitable (and often fascinating) part of social media, but for the time being I just don't want to know. Not here. Not now. All I want to know about is brands. And what they have to say about brands. And to whom. And how often.

This is a long list of SMMMMS players. We are not going to look at them all. Brian Solis examined a number of them for his book The Rise of Digital Influence. They all give demonstrations, and even free trials. If you need to choose between them, it is worthwhile consulting a specialist analyst. They have a better idea of the companies that are good players in your sector and also know which of the newcomers are worth watching:

1. Alterian / 2. Arvato online services / 3. Appinions / 4. Attentio / 5. Attensity Respond / 6. bc.lab / 7. Beevolve / 8. Brandchats / 9. Brandmonitor / 10. Brandseye / 11. Brandtolgy / 12. Brandwatch / 13. Buddymedia / 14. Buzzient Enterprise / 15. Buzzom / 16. CIC / 17. Cision / 18. Custom Scoop / 19. Dialogix / 20. eCairns / 21. Engagor / 22. Ethority / 23. Infegy / 24. Jive / 25. Klout / 26. Kred / 27. Lithium / 28. Meltwater Buzz / 29. mPact / 30. Mutual Mind / 31. Netbreeze / 32. Netvibes / 33. Peerindex / 34. Position 2 / 35. PROscore / 36. Radian6 / 37. Shoutlet / 38. SocialBakers / 39. Spiral 16 / 40. Sprout Social / 41. Synthesio / 42. Sysomos Heartbeat / 43. Traackr / 44. trackur / 45. Tweetlevel / 46. Tweetreach / 47. Twitalyzer / 48. Twittergrade / 49. UberVU / 50. Viralheat / 51. Visible / 52. Vocus / 53. Wildfire

---

There are experts and influential people in almost every field of human endeavour on the internet. But if the man who knows everything about Iraq never says what he thinks about the breakfast cereal he eats each morning, then his opinions are of no use to me – if I am the marketer of a breakfast cereal.

Perhaps he is someone who buys price-consciously. Or maybe he is a routine buyer, who always buys the same cereal. Or an impulse buyer who simply pulls the first packet off the shelf. Or does he just eat whatever his partner buys for him?

For the time being, it seems that the SMMMMS providers are best placed to help you solve your identification problems. They monitor 24/7. But how effective are their systems really? They are certainly moving in the right direction, little by little, but there is still a long way to go (in my opinion, at least).

During the writing of this book, I was tipped off by Engagor about one of the specialist analysts I referred to above. The analyst in question was Goldbachinternational.[92] Their website offered a highly interesting comparison of the SMMMMS that were on the market at that time. Even so, when I tried to establish which of the screened companies could best help me to identify the recommenders (and, if possible, establish their respective powers of influence), I found myself up against a brick wall. It seems to be an aspect of the social media landscape that even the specialist analysts know little about. Of course, they can all identify people who are digitally active on Twitter, Facebook, Google+, LinkedIn and Pinterest. And that's fine. But it is also relatively easy. Sometimes they might publish a popularity poll or relevant summaries (for example, who shares messages with whom and how frequently, or how often the original message is responded to). In other words, a whole mass of data that you can extract from your application programming interface for social media.[93] In this respect, both Facebook and Twitter can provide endless streams (if not rivers) of data, to which everyone has access. Put simply, the threshold is too low.

Consequently, my provisional conclusion is that we are only at the very beginning of the gold-rush and that the struggle to find the perfect system will continue for some time yet. Hopefully, there might be a breakthrough towards the end of 2013 or the beginning of 2014.

DON'T JUST FOCUS ON MEASURING SUPERFICIAL CRITERIA – DEVELOP MICRO-MONITORING ACTIVITIES. AN EXAMPLE

The importance of the continuous (and preferably automated) identification of recommenders can be well illustrated by the following example.

I investigated a long list of influential bloggers using Brandwatch (one of the more highly rated SMMMMS). I was surprised to find Alex Bogusky[94] – who is highly regarded in marketing and advertising circles – occupying a lowly 189th position in the ranking.

188	If this is a blog then what's Christmas?	1932		
189	Alex Bogusky	1909		
190	Lies, damned lies and statistics	1891		
191	Renegade agency confessional	1884		

I clicked on the 'T' of Twitter after his name and was automatically forwarded to his Twitter page. At the same time (it was 15 February 2012) and purely by chance, I noticed a fragment of dialogue between Bogusky and a certain Benny Blanco. Bogusky was trying to find some 'made in America' sneakers, but without success. Benny had done a little research and discovered that a 'made in America' brand did exist: Lasco.

I don't know if Bogusky clicked on the Lasco link or what he thought of their shoes, but I did click the link and immediately placed a link to them on my Facebook page.

I thought that the story, the positioning, the film and the shoes were all very impressive. And the four words next to the flag exude the necessary pride and confidence that the United States currently needs: 'designed, machined, supplied, manufactured... by American citizens in the U.S.'

What I did with Lasco is one of the millions of micro-monitoring activities that every brand should do: search, search and search again. Search every day. Search every night. Like an astronomer searches for stars. Search for relevant topics in everything that people post. Search for the things that people say – and whatever they say – in the course of the day about a specific brand or product ('shoes'). Or about 'made in America'.

Someone who tweets something about shoes can be potentially very interesting for a shoe manufacturer. Perhaps this tweeting shoe-searcher is a recommender. Perhaps he is already influential in shoe circles, or even very influential. And now he is looking for… an American shoe! As was the case with Bogusky.

But when I discovered this dialogue, not one single shoe company had responded 'publicly', even though the ball was sitting up, just begging to be hammered into the goal. A top advertising guru says that he is looking for 'made in America' sneakers. A buddy tells him about a brand called Lasco. And what happens next? Nothing!

Any searching consumer – and certainly a consumer like Bogusky – must be capable of being found by brands searching for customers. That must be the raison d'être of the 'human search engine'. What's more, it is by no means a search for a needle in a haystack. Anybody could have read that Bogusky was looking for a specific type of shoes. But nobody bothered.

THERE IS A HUGE DIFFERENCE BETWEEN GIVING ADVICE, RECOMMENDING AND HAVING INFLUENCE. AND BETWEEN SOMEONE WHO RECOMMENDS AND SOMEONE WHO INFLUENCES

Influence operates both before and after a recommendation.

I might be a very influential person in the field of digital photography and might be recognised and respected as such. But as soon as the question turns to the recommendation of a specific type of camera, if I only mention Nikon I am in danger of influencing no one, since I know that my circle of friends all have Leicas and Canons, with an occasional Sony here and there.

Exerting influence – persuading someone to do something that he doesn't naturally want to do – is a difficult and complex business. As an ex-advertising man, it was a problem that I was faced with for decades, so I know what I am talking about! People simply do what they want to do – and not what people tell them they should do. They are stubborn. Stubborn as mules.

Phase 1. I choose who I will allow to influence me

Influence is involved right from the very beginning of the purchase process; namely, the orientation phase of the searching consumer in which he seeks some general knowledge about the sector that interests him. I want to buy a new car and so I familiarise myself with the automobile market. Are there specific points to which I need to pay attention, such as safety, engine capacity, price, fuel consumption, environmental friendliness, technical advances since my last purchase, etc.?

If I am environmentalist, there is a strong likelihood that I will allow my choice of car to be influenced by environmental considerations more than others. Consequently, I will go in search of websites that give me the feeling that I am looking at cars through 'green' eyes.

But if, in spite of my age, I decide that I want to tear around bends at 160 kph, in true James Bond style, then I will most likely go in search of articles and reviews about speedy seniors.

Alternatively, I might be at an age when the (road) safety of my children is my most important concern, so that my reading list will once again be very different, focusing on the results of crash tests and reviews written by people of influence.

In other words, I chose my own sources, the people who I will allow to influence me for the duration of this purchase. It is almost as if I invite them to come and sit next to me on my sofa or at my desk, so that I can share their information and knowledge. Back in 1994, when the web was only just starting, I had already christened them the 'invited persuaders', because their predecessors – the 'hidden persuaders' – had already been exposed as frauds.

In function of my preferences of the moment, which can change at any time, I might decide to peruse other sources, read different reviews, google for other input, tap into different conversations. If I am also a fervent social media user, a part of the knowledge I acquire will be fed back out into my social network. Even so, unless I am fanatically occupied with the subject in question, there will be very little trace of my searching so far online. It is only when I have found the answer to my problem that I will share the solution with others – and with pleasure. But making your search process explicit to others serves little real purpose.

The above-mentioned SMMMMS tools (which should help the brands to find me!) will not at this stage be able to make very much use of my Twitter and Facebook updates. Nevertheless, they should at least be able to discover that I am looking to buy a car.

However strange it might sound, brands are never talked about as much as every marketer would like. Even if I have a bright red Lamborghini standing in front of my palatial villa, I am still unlikely to tweet about it all day and every day. Unless there are problems. In which case my posts will be picked up by the analysis tools as a complaint. After all, that's what Twitter is for, isn't it? Complaining?

Phase 2. I choose again who I will allow to influence me

When I am ready to move to the next phase of 'buying a new fast car', my search becomes less general and more specific. I am now gradually becoming more open for concrete recommendations. I start to assess which models are currently 'hot' with people I know and with my 'friends' on the web. Which ones are praised by the reviews in car magazines? What is the J.D. Power satisfaction score? What is the NPS score? This is the mix of input, on the basis of which I will make my final choice.

Some people may advise me against buying a Porsche, because there are already too many of the damned things in our village. Whereas others might regard that as an argument in favour of Porsche. Vox populi…

At this moment in time, you still don't know which of your several sources you will ultimately allow to influence you. They all give their own opinions and all recommend what they think is best for you, but in the final analysis the choice is always yours. You pick your own influencer. It's a bit like: 'First choose your lover, then love your choice.'

If in a particular region at a particular time the people who recommend Porsche (for whatever reason) acquire the greatest influence over potential customers who are planning to buy a sports car, the market share of Porsche in that region will increase. For the time being, the positive word of mouth spread by the Porsche-lovers is stronger than the advice given by the Ferrari, Lamborghini and Jaguar-lovers.

You will not hear me say that this final choice is a rational one. It almost certainly isn't. We may kid ourselves that it is, but purchase choices are never made on the basis of reason alone. You might even have an XLS list inside your head, which (you are convinced) explains why you chose model X instead of model Y. In reality, this is little more than a crib-list, which will allow you to seem smart when discussing your new car with your neighbours, friends, etc. after you have already made the purchase. In fact, your choice of model will unquestionably be emotional rather than rational, something stupid rather than something sensible. Stupid? 'I only want shoes (or cars) made in America!' 'There are already too many Porsches in our village.' 'What will my customers think if I turn up to meetings in a Ferrari?' None of these arguments have anything to do with the essential qualities of model X or model Y. You will never find them in any of the reviews. They are purely emotional considerations – but they are always decisive.

These 'secret' considerations are seldom or never discussed with others. Revealing your inner thoughts in this manner only happens, if it happens at all, in face-to-face situations; conversations with people from your immediate circle, who in return will offer you their own personal opinions. Once in China I was sitting at dinner with two of my business contacts, when I noticed that both of them were wearing a Rolex. Because I cheekily commented 'Surely you're not going to tell me that both of you are wearing a real Rolex', they both admitted that they were cheap copies. But this is not the kind of 'confessional' moment that you come across frequently. And certainly not in China.

So where does this all leave us? The phase of the searching consumer, who also asks questions on social media, offers brands the possibility to respond to this search, thereby helping the consumer (and hopefully finishing off with a purchase). Other consumers who help people to find brands and who interact on the same media are perhaps the real recommenders – and it is to be hoped that they also have influence. The fact that they are prepared to open their mouths proves at least that they have an opinion and are prepared to express it. So go and talk to them. But first find out where they are.

Phase 3. Finally, I choose my influencer

And what about after the purchase? When it is clear that the purchase has been made ('Wow, I finally have the Ferrari I always dreamed about!'), the brand once again first needs to 'find' the buyer. If the buyer bought the car from your garage, this is obviously a piece of cake. If you have a database, he will be in it somewhere, so you can easily contact him and start talking. But even if he didn't buy the car of his dreams from you, it is still worthwhile trying to track him down and engaging him in conversation. Every consumer's loyalty hangs by a silken thread nowadays and if this customer discovers that the service at his normal garage is useless, he may think of switching to you next time. People who tweet that they have bought a new car – whether it is a Ferrari or a Lada – are extravert people. And it is better to have them as a friend. So go and find them.

WHY MAKE THE EFFORT?

Why should you go to all the effort of tracking down consumers to the individual level? Because you need to fight for every customer you can get. And you can only win him over to your side if you know who he is and what is his relationship with your brand. In the final analysis, you can only measure the totality of someone's relationship with your brand if you quite literally ask them our now familiar question about their willingness to recommend it. I might find lots of positive twitter about Porsches, but if all these tweets come from young wannabes who have never driven a Porsche in their life, then I would be well advised to ignore their influence – unless, of course, I only want to buy a Porsche to impress all the people in my neighbourhood. Which is perfectly possible. If I think that others think that buying a Porsche is the ultimate symbol of success, good taste, virility, superiority, etc., then I might well be tempted to take the plunge. Does this 'discrete' reason for my purchase mean that I am a recommender for Porsche? Well, yes it does. But it is not something that I will make a great song and dance about on social media. But if I am asked by Porsche directly whether or not I would recommend them, the answer will be 'yes'. No doubt about it.

FINDING WHERE THEY ARE AND FINDING OUT WHO THEY ARE

We not only need to identify the people who have influence. It is also important to try and find out something about their brand ranking, which in part can be deduced from the war of words on Twitter, Facebook, LinkedIn and other social media.

The ranking of brands is not straightforward (fortunately, that is why we have the One Question) but the hierarchical ranking of people on the basis of their recommendations and the influence they have on prospective purchasers is even more difficult. In fact, at the present time it is impossible.

Nevertheless, this is the direction we need to work towards. A brand wants to know where it stands in relation to its competitors and also wants to know who the recommenders are, who they recommend, what they recommend and how much influence they have.

The first problem is that most of the current measurement systems determine someone's influence on the basis of a mix of tweets, status updates, shares, forwards and commentaries. These can all be counted on Facebook and Twitter.

This means that your digital influence will decline if you are less active or inactive for a period on these social network sites. And that is perfectly correct. There are people who claim that they measure my 'online influence', my Twitter influence. If I stay away from the digital podia for a month or so, it is only normal that my digital strength will temporarily diminish. If do nothing and say nothing, I will not attract new followers and my current followers will have nothing to read – so that my ability to influence them is also reduced. This is something that happened to me during the period January/February 2012, when I was very busy with the writing of this book and also had to spend a number of weeks in San Francisco and New York. My Twitter and Facebook presence dropped almost to nil and I could see my Klout score falling each day. No problem. Totally understandable.

The following screens make clear that Klout really 'sympathised' with me as my score kept on falling (at my peak, I had a score of 60).

Klout is nothing but a marketing database organisation that used the Twitter 'influencers' to build up their database, so Klout can in return 'sell' the user profiles to brands such as Subway, Audi, AXE, etc. for marketing campaign and promotional purposes. This is the money-maker for Klout and, unfortunately, they will continue with this business model if they want to maintain a positive stream of VC funding.

It is also understandable that people who are obsessed with having a high score become nervous, sick even, when their score begins to plummet. For someone who is a 'medium' (these are all fanatical Twitterers and Facebookers), their daily look, read and listen figures are just as important as viewing figures for a television station and circulation figures for a newspaper.

Klout-aholics spend the whole day hunched over their computer screen and are very conscious of the fact that they must continue to 'perform'. If they fail to do so, the influence rug will be pulled out from under their feet and their value as a consultant, analyst or blogger will decline. So too will their income, since most bloggers make good money from having Google ads on their blogs.

And in these circumstances, perhaps not surprisingly, Klout suddenly gets more critical blogs and reviews from certain quarters than it would otherwise care for![95]

MAKE NO MISTAKE: KLOUT PROVIDES ITS OWN CLOUT!

That the boys and girls at Klout are masters of (self-promoting) PR is evident from the fact that the company has won for itself a place in the list of the world's 50 most innovative businesses. And they are not categorised with the web and internet companies, nor with the social media companies. No, they are classified as… an advertising company. Surprising. So read on:

'Klout. For evolving the art of "the influencer" into a science. For decades companies have spent big money to try to identify and nurture word-of-mouth influencers. Klout is finding the people who are experts at creating, aggregating and sharing content that moves online, and measuring influ-

ence for marketers, based on that. Some of the biggest and brightest marketers and brands, such as Disney, Audi, Starbucks and Nike, have incorporated Klout influencers into their traditional marketing efforts. And it is working. According to Klout, each influencer in one of their perk programmes generates an average of 30 pieces of content and millions of possible impressions. The cost per thousand impressions is incredibly low compared to other forms of advertising and it is organic, since it is being generated by people who already love the brands.[96]

That Klout – an excellent marketer in its own right – fully understands the value of the One Question is evident from the fact that the question occasionally pops up in their inquiry activities. They have not yet revealed how high their own score is…

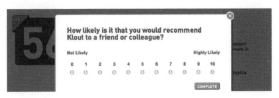

IF RECOMMENDERS ARE IMPORTANT, THEIR TWEETS AND STATUS UPDATES MUST ALSO BE IMPORTANT. AND THE MORE IMPORTANT THEY ARE, THE MORE IMPORTANT THEIR COMMUNICATION BECOMES

One of the reasons why we, the brands and our immediate environment, all want to know 'who counts for most and how much' is related to the average life expectancy of a tweet. A tweet doesn't last for ever. Far from it. In fact, they are more like a flash in the pan. Here today and gone tomorrow. You might pick out one or two or ten each day, but the rest pass by unnoticed, never to return. Having said this, tweets that are sent by people with a high Klout score live longer. Much longer. 67 times longer than a tweet sent by an ordinary mortal. For a brand, this means that you need to get consumers with a high Klout score talking about your products.

'If you have a Klout score between 40 and 70, you can expect your tweet's half-life to last for just five minutes. If you have a Klout score between 70 and 75, that duration quintuples to 25 minutes.'[97]

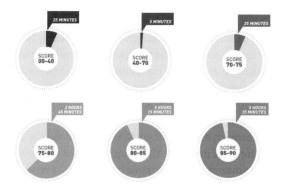

*http://mashable.
com/2011/11/04/klout-
twitter-half-life-study/*

(And yes, you have read it correctly: the half-life of tweets is identical for low scores between 0 and 40 and high scores between 70 and 75. I have not yet been able to discover the reason.)

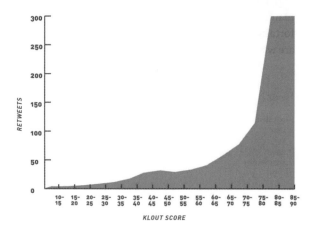

KLOUT MAKES PLENTY OF MISTAKES – BUT SO WHAT?

Let us go back to one of our provable starting points: more than 90% of all recommendations are made offline. And these are the people I want to find. They are also active online, but hard to identify. For example, I have written very little online about brands such as Canon, Illy, Guinness and Saab, even though all these brands are close to my heart. And if I posted anything about Apple or Nike, it was usually in a business (marketing or management) context, by way of highlighting a good example of something. So how would an SMMMMS find me?

I do use social media to send links about China, management, marketing and online marketing to the people who follow me on those media. And since I read a lot about these subjects, I also publicise a lot of links. This is something that an SMMMMS could find out about me.

However, one day recently, when I opened my list of Klout topics (the fields of expertise that I am supposed to know something about) I was amazed to see the name 'McDonalds'. I have no idea where that came from. I am not a fast-food lover – and that's putting it mildly (I watch my weight and my cholesterol level). So how did the world's leading fast-food chain suddenly appear in my Klout topic list? Other popular brands, like Apple and Nike, are also in my list, but this is true of many people.

This McDonalds bug (or did Klout or one of my friends add me manually as an influencer to the McDonalds list?) gives me the uncomfortable feeling that Klout has not yet fully got its act together. They are working at it and are prepared to stick their neck out.

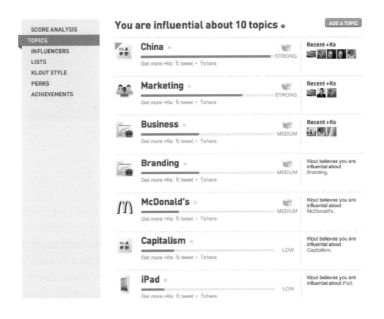

And that's fine – even though it means they will still get blasted by the critics from time to time. But they at least seem to realise the importance of ranking influencers and I assume that they will be one of the eventual winners in the race to discover the real truth about this key subject. The evolution of search robots in recent years is probably a good indication of what is likely to happen in this field in the future. In 1999 Yahoo still had 55% of the market, and there were other major players as well, such as Excite, Altavista, Lycos, etc. And Google? At that time they had just a 1% share of the market. It just shows you how quickly things can change.

WHY DO PEOPLE FOLLOW OTHER PEOPLE? AND IS THAT IMPORTANT IN THE CALCULATION?

The number of followers should be directly proportional to the quality of tweets and updates. The greater the number of tweets and updates with links, the greater the number of followers. The cold transmission of content (hopefully relevant content) is therefore deemed to be more important than whether or not people choose to reply to this content, expressed in your number of retweets and your number of followers. Sending them 'good stuff' is enough. They will mix all the input they get – including yours – in their own cooking pot and you will only get to see what they have done with it later on. Don't interfere too much. Just let them get on with it. I have said it before, and I will say it again: don't make the mistake of thinking that these are real conversations. This is simple, old-fashioned 'broadcasting' by consumers. But it is not broadcasting to convince the others, which is what the brands used to do, steamrolling their listeners into submission, until they were ready to part with their hard-earned cash. No, this is broadcasting by millions of people; people who broadcast because they have an opinion and want it to be heard. That is the reason why they share their opinions. They don't necessarily need to have a conversation with you. They simply say: 'This is what I know, what I have read, what I have experienced. You can do what you like with this information. It's up to you.'

This was confirmed in a small web-poll conducted by Jeff Bullas[98] – one of the mega-bloggers who always seems to be online. In answer to the question 'what makes a brand or a person an influencer?', his followers came up with the following list:

1 the quality of the links that are posted (22%);
2 the possibility that the tweet offers readers to take action (18%);
3 the number of followers who retweet a tweet or share an update (17%);
4 source: the site or blog of the sender (16%);
5 the quality of the followers (14%).

This poll again suggested that your number of followers or the number of tweets you send both play a much smaller roll.

So the number of followers is not important?

I doubt that very much indeed. The above question is not about whether a tweet influences you or not; it is about the person who sends the tweets. I suspect that this is once again a case of wishful thinking; finding the answer you are looking for. If you make the comparison with political elections, then the number of a politician's followers is a very exact expression of his influence in respect of a particular area or topic. 'Area' and 'topic' can be interpreted both globally and locally.

And the number of tweets you send or receive is also not important?

Don't make me laugh! The age-old advertising model is still based on repetition, repetition, repetition. In the past, that was repetition on TV (enough to drive you barmy). Nowadays, it is repeated exposure in all kinds of different places. And the tweets and status updates that mention brands are all part of this non-stop bombardment. No doubt about it. Even so, it is something that we (the advertisers and marketers) are reluctant to admit. Because we want to engage the consumers in a meaningful, worthwhile manner. But this is not a game that Klout is prepared to play. It openly gives its customer perks to the highest scorers.

A HIGH KLOUT SCORE IS WORTH A EURO OR TWO!

For many people a high Klout score is a noble objective. But in addition to respect and reputation (crucially important for a recommender), it also bring you loads of extra perks.

Brands do not know exactly who you are, but you still get presents from them. The Airbnb voucher shown below is one of the many extra bonuses on the Klout site.

Just perfect for me, to be honest. And I would have liked to have tested Airbnb, since my Klout score is well over 40. But, unfortunately, I live in China, not in the UK, and so I am not eligible. Damn!

Whoever has tweeted together enough social capital gets rewarded. A sound theory - and on Groupon or Living Social everyone can buy these perks. But at Peerindex only the people who have 'earned' it are allowed to enjoy the perks. For a brand, its twittering evangelists are more important than the rest.

We have you in Shanghai, China. Please confirm so we can find the best perks for you.   That's correct! or Update

Airbnb UK

Back to Perks Index

YOU DESERVE A HOLIDAY   £50 TRAVEL VOUCHER

airbnb

Sorry, this perk is open to other influencers.
Like 26
Klout scores above 40
LOCATIONS: GB

Go and take a look at the site for yourself; you will see the perks currently on offer. Brands that decide to work with Klout (in this instance Airbnb) are not given any information about the person who finally receives the free voucher. It will obviously be someone with a high Klout score, but as far as the person's feelings towards Airbnb are concerned… these will remain unknown. The company has to satisfy itself with the knowledge that the person in question is a +40K influencer and lives somewhere in the UK. Not much to be going on, if you were hoping to contact him, but Klout is adamant on this point: 'No matter what, brands do not get access to your private data'. Besides, you are free to decide whether you accept the Airbnb offer or not. If you do nothing, you get nothing. But if you do accept, the people who welcome you at your final destination will certainly know who you are once you arrive. Moreover, getting a free gift of £50 is not something that happens every day. On the contrary, it is the kind of thing that you are likely to talk about. Not that there is any obligation. As Klout says: 'You are welcome to tell the world you love the perk, you dislike the perk or say nothing at all.' That's all well and good, but once you start chatting with your network (which is obviously what Klout is hoping), you will almost certainly blow the secret – and with it your privacy. And from then on you are lost; or rather, Klout and Airbnb have won. You can rubbish the room you booked (through Airbnb) as much as you like – but it is hard to hit back directly at Airbnb itself. Or Klout. They have both got what they wanted.

IN WHAT FIELDS CAN YOU EARN A HIGH KLOUT SCORE?

It goes without saying that it would be much easier for brands if they could see directly who is recommending what. Without the need for free gifts. A kind of brand passport; that is what they need. And that is what we are working on in China with Holaba.

I realise that in terms of scalability (and for potential investors who are fixated on this point) this is not the easiest option, which explains why every company with SMMMMS gold fever is currently jumping on the same API bandwagon, in the hope of doing things better or differently or more efficiently that its present and future competitors.

And so you start looking with your SMMMMS at the things that people are talking about. If someone is primarily talking about China, then that is topic no.1 for them. That is the case with me. My topic no.2 is management. Topic no.3 is marketing. And so on. This is not very useful information for a brand. Yet it is precisely the brands that must provide the income for all these SMMMMS's.

If other consumers who have also discovered Klout then give me a +K for those topics (a +K means 'this person has influenced my opinion of this topic'), then the whole thing can quickly snowball. Some Klouters end up with a huge number of +K's, which they have picked up from here, there and everywhere.

This is what happened to Brian Sollis. When I last looked, he had an astronomical 280 K's. Of course, he is a very influential person in the marketing world, which helps. And he is an American writing in English, which helps. And some people will have given him a K in the hope of staying in his good books, which helps. A Lithuanian marketer, still living in Lithuania and writing in Lithuanian, will never get as far, no matter how good he is. The land of origin not only plays an important role with brands, but also with the accumulation of influencing power. I am not suggesting for one moment that Klout is backed by a pack of hawkish American imperialists and exceptionalists, but the net effect of their activities is certainly to strengthen the position of the United States. Just wait until the Chinese discover how the law of big numbers really works! In China it is relatively easy to quickly acquire a few million followers, and in view of the fervour with which they communicate with each other, it should be equally easy for the top Chinese influencers to obtain Klout scores that are off the scale. In fact, the scale will need to be increased from 100 to 1,000! Will Klout ever come to China? And, if so, can they win? I doubt it.

The second issue relates to the strength of a person's influence in a particular domain. According to the Klout method of assessment, I am more influential about China than about marketing, management and branding. It is certainly likely that I post more links about China and also that people share and forward these links more frequently than my links on other topics.

But if this results in me being labelled as an influential in matters Chinese, that strikes me as being a bit of an exaggeration. How can people who follow me but know nothing about China give me a +K that has any meaning? On what is their opinion of me and my knowledge based? Not very much.

What's more, I seldom express personal opinions in my China posts, but simply spread the opinions of others I have read about, some of which I might agree with and some of which I might not. Sometimes, I simply use these opinions to try and provoke a reaction. In other words, I do not regard myself as a specialist 'about' China. In fact, I think I know more about marketing (my no.2 topic), branding, the web and the whole recommender story.

To make a valid assessment of this kind, you first really need to decide how big your pond is, how many fish (waiting to be influenced) are swimming in it and how much they already know. But try quantifying that! It is almost impossible.

The Chinese pond is very big and very complex, with very many fish, most of whom know very little but want to know much more, and are therefore very enthusiastic about reading, sharing, forwarding and reacting to stories of many different kinds. It is a situation that allows even someone like me to build up a large Klout score. But it is much more difficult to do the same thing in a more limited field of expertise. For example, the single malt and very peaty whisky from the small Scottish island of Islay.

The leading influencers in whisky all have a lower Klout score than I do (proving that there really is no justice in the world), whereas in reality they are all at the absolute top in their own country and in their own specialist field.

So how can this situation be corrected? Let us imagine that I am a single malt drinker, that I also produce my own good whisky and that I want to get to know the top influencers in my field. Shouldn't Klout and their SMMMMS competitors first chart exactly how many updates over this topic have appeared in a given period? And should they not then establish who are the sources and who are the followers, so that they can determine who has the largest share of voice within a specified corpus of comments, posts, reviews and messages? Isn't that the way it's supposed to work?

If there are 1,000 quotes per day from and about the Islay distilleries, and if 300 of these come from Ardbeg, and if Ardbeg also has the

highest percentage of followers amongst people who are lovers of single malt whisky, then there is a more than reasonable chance that Ardbeg is the top influencer and possibly also has the largest market share. Who knows, they might even be selling the best and most widely praised whisky in the world.

The SMMMMS must be capable of bringing all these elements to the surface, because this is the information that people in the sector need. This is elementary media-planning logic. Because we are dealing here with human media planning. And the results that I receive must be immediately actionable. And relevant.

CAN THE DUTCH PEERREACH PROVIDE US WITH PART OF THE ANSWER?

From a long discussion I had with Peerreach, it became evident that this is the direction in which they are also moving. This is clear if you look at their dashboard of top influencers. Part of it is based on worldwide results, part of it on country results (at least for the Netherlands). These are the kind of actionable lists that we need, a bit like the restau-

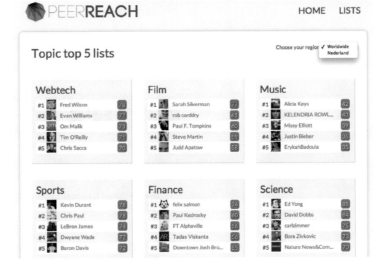

rant guides (Michelin, GaultMillau, Frommers) that also, in effect, give scores to people (chef, waiters, hostess, etc.). At the top it starts with a list of experts within a particular public group, who are regarded by the other experts in that same group as being the most influential. This is an important distinction: we are dealing here with experts talking about experts, and not consumers who have become 'experts' through their experience with disposable nappies or some other FMCG (Fast Moving Consumer Goods).

Scientists and academics who are regularly followed by 'many others with influence' and who are frequently re-posted or with whom there is a great deal of interaction will also, no doubt, be pleased with their high score. They live from their 'fame', whether it is justified or not. And it is a simple fact of life that people who are often quoted enjoy greater respect than people who remain in the shadows.

At this high level – and we are talking about an upper layer of some 15% – success in other media is also necessary to obtain a good Klout score. People who have achieved a certain fame through television and/or radio and people with an outstanding professional reputation in their area of expertise are more likely to have followers who will quickly forward and respond to their posts. The online battlefield is an additional arena where the fight against your competitors must be fought – and won.

Of course, these measurements often record matters that are part and parcel of daily life in such expert circles, so that the results come as no great surprise to those involved. Young scientists and politicians who are fighting for a place against the 'established names' of the old guard generally to know their place and status in the pecking order.

Things only start to get really interesting when you look at the layers just under this top crust of 15%. Which more 'ordinary' people are interested in reading about single malt? And how often do they pass on this information to their followers, who also know a thing or two about good whisky? We are now at the level of the recommenders, who form the subject of this book.

As already mentioned, Peerreach ranks experts on the basis of the follower-behaviour of other experts – for the time being within a single continent/country/city. This seems to me to be a sensible delineation. A house doctor in Ohio will have very few GP's from Rotterdam in his peer group. Even if he does, their level of influence is likely to be very low. Consequently, it is reasonable that the Peerreach scores are calculated on the basis of the number of experts in a limited area of expertise who follow their expert-colleague.

Consider the following example. Imagine that there are 1,000 twittering doctors in a country and that one of these doctors is followed by the other 999. Not surprisingly, the single doctor will end up at the top of the ranking. This is only logical. Unless there are two doctors who are both followed by the other 999 – in which case they will both share the top spot. Which is also logical. The last place will be occupied by the doctor who is followed by none of his colleagues. It all makes perfect sense.

The highest ranking expert is the influential in his peer group and also (probably) in the field of expertise in which he works. The lowest ranking 'expert' finds no one who is prepared to listen to anything he has to say. However, this does not mean that he cannot be an expert in some other field. Our lowest ranking doctor might be a great wine buff, who is regularly followed on Twitter by other wine-lovers. And in all probability none of them (or very few) will be a doctor. As a result, this man will have a high Peerreach ranking in the wine group, but not in the group of doctors. In other words, he is an expert in a field other than the field in which he studied. But there is nothing wrong with that. He might even be followed by hundreds of his patients, who know him as 'the doctor who knows everything about wine'!

What can you do with this kind of list that is only made public in part? Peerreach does not expect that companies will make use of their lists to approach people for commercial purposes. The lists give no e-mail addresses, but do mention a Twitter name. And twitterers hate to be approached directly in this manner on their favourite SMS, so that any attempt at contact would almost certainly be counterproductive. Similarly, contact details are not sold to outsiders: everything is internalised within the platform for further analysis and development.

In theory, Peerreach can investigate and classify an endless number of peer networks:
1. All doctors.
2. All doctors in Europe.
3. All doctors in the Netherlands.
4. All doctors in Rotterdam.
5. All doctors in Rotterdam-South
6. Etc.

Peerreach can also create further segments within each of these groups: anaesthetists, cardiologists, dermatologists, neurosurgeons, orthopaedists, oculists, etc. And even provide additional tags for other 'specialities' not connected with medicine, such as wine, sailing, skiing, luxury cars, thereby allowing an even more precise delineation of the individuals involved.

In theory, it is therefore possible to produce an influence ranking for a small group of twittering oculists in Europe. I assume that this is interesting information for the marketers of medical products within that field of specialisation. Also for media who regularly need to approach specialists (in any subject) for guidance and/or explanation. At the moment, we regularly see and hear the same faces on television and radio: once an expert, always an expert.

Of course, there will always be experts who are not active on Twitter, and have probably never even heard of it. Consequently, they will never appear in the Peerreach rankings. Does this mean that they are not influencers? Of course they are! You must remember that 90% of 'influencing recommendations' are made in the real world, and not online. That, at least, is the rule of thumb in consumer marketing. In general, talking about products occurs more in the local pub and at the breakfast table than in cyberspace. Perhaps it is different in the exalted world of ophthalmic surgery and other medical specialisations, but to date we have no research data on this subject. Unless they are married to a fellow oculist, their breakfast chit-chat will probably deal with more routine matters than the latest technical developments in the world of corneas, retinas and irises. Professional people of this kind are more likely to discuss and influence each other in scientific journals, at congresses, by mail and on Twitter.

Notwithstanding the 90% rule, I believe that in time the increasing penetration of the internet in general and Twitter in particular will serve to increase the influencing power of oculists with a high Peerreach score. In this sense, the online score will increasingly come to reflect the real score of the specialist. Professionals who only speak at congresses or in e-mails will gradually be overtaken by their colleagues who seek to extend their reach and visibility by operating through the social media. Being well-known in a broad online circle offers more potential to someone who wants to become an influencer than simply being known by a small group of colleagues in Rotterdam-South.

Becoming an influencer in Peerreach is a bit like an athlete who has achieved the Olympic minimum and now looks forward to competing for gold, silver and bronze: the top spots. It is not something that everyone is cut out for. Not everyone is prepared to twitter like mad all day long, just so that they can be recognised as top-dog in their discipline. Even so, it is this stubborn and persistent few that will eventually make it to the medal rostrum.

Peerreach is transparent. They are prepared to explain to the world how they calculate their scores. Consequently, everyone who is interested in achieving a high score knows exactly what he or she has to do in order to make their dream come true. In the final analysis, a good score is closely related to the content that you offer to your peer group on Twitter (and later on other social media). This means keeping your eye firmly on the ball, monitoring the latest trends, offering interesting links, writing sensible introductions to those links, publicly answering your colleagues' questions – and doing all these things regularly and seriously. To climb up the Peerreach ratings – or at least to prevent your score from dropping – you need to do much more than just twitter any old nonsense. That is the surest way to lose your credibility, your followers and your peer reach.

It is also important to remember that the term 'influencer' can have several different meanings, or at least several different origins. Here are just some of them:

1. I have a high score because I read a huge amount and my colleagues use me as a filter to make their own reading that much easier.
2. I thank my high score to the fact that I am an interesting content producer, who my colleagues like to read (research, cases, comments on the posts of others, etc.).
3. My high score is the result of the fact that I have already built up a reputation as a specialist in other media; a reputation that immediately opens doors on Twitter.
4. My rating is high because I am a controversial expert, who is followed because of the controversies my opinions create, even though I might not actually influence the people in my peer group in this manner.
5. Perhaps people follow me simply because it is beneficial for them to do so. The peer group pressure to follow me is great.
6. The reverse can also be true. Perhaps people follow me because I say the opposite of what they claim to be thinking themselves.
7. The ultimate caveat: following someone on Twitter is not the same as recommending someone.

It would be interesting to ask the peers of a top expert if they are actually influenced by him and, if so, to what degree. How does this express itself and in which areas of expertise? Have they learnt something new? Have they abandoned an old point of view? Do they now think differently? Do they behave differently? In what way? Are they guided by the meaning of just a single expert or by a number of experts who are all simultaneously moving in the same direction?

An expert is someone who excels, is admired and followed in his own field of professional specialisation. It is tempting to believe that this kind of 'expertness' can be transferred to other fields of endeavour, almost as if it is built into his DNA… Is an expert someone who always carefully weighs everything he says and does, before launching his opinions on a wider audience? Is an expert someone who is cautious in every aspect of his life, even the non-professional ones? If an expert wants to buy a cell phone (or a camera, or a car, or a bottle of dandruff shampoo), does their investigative pre-purchase phase last longer than average and do they share their conclusions with others in their peer group? The expert seems to be the antithesis of the impulse buyer, who often makes quick purchases based on gut feeling and just a fraction of the available information.

WHAT DOES PEERINDEX ADD TO ALL THIS?

Peerindex also measures your social authority on a topic by topic basis. They actually follow some 8,000 references, but only 2,000 of them are made public. The confidence that other people have in you they call 'authority'. This is different for each of your eight listed topics, but they also give you an overall authority score.

In addition, they also give ratings for concepts such as 'audience', 'activity' and 'resonance'.

The 'audience' score does not measure the number of people who follow you, but rather the impact you have on them. Accounts that follow you simply to send spam are not included.

The 'activity' score, as the name implies, expresses how active you are within your particular group. Being too active is bad, since you simply overwhelm your listeners. But being quiet for too long is also not good, since you lose influence and impact. The statistics show that it is best to be just above the average of your group.

The scores are all normalised. If you are in the top 20% of a particular category, this obviously means that you have more authority than the other 80%. But the normalised score that you are awarded is not 80, but somewhere in the region between 55 and 65. In fact, a score of 65 means that you actually score higher than 95% in your topic. What's more (and in contrast to Klout), the scores remain fairly stable. It takes months to fine-tune a score to the right level, but once it is at that level it is not easy to gain or lose ground over a short period of time (which is certainly possible with Klout).

Peerindex does more than simply chart your performance on Twitter (which is also true of Klout). They measure your activity on the entirety of the social web. For this reason, you can still check your Peerindex, even if you don't have a Twitter account. When I last visited their site, they claimed to have measured more than 50 million people. Not companies or organisations. Just people.

Viralheat has launched the Viralheat Social Sentiment Plugin, which is free and can be integrated on Chrome (the Google browser). 'It gives users the power to analyse the sentiments of tweets, Twitter streams and Facebook new feeds, timelines, fan pages, posts and comments too – from within your browser.'[100]

Their analysis lists look like this:

> TV show reviews (ex: The Office) – sentiment for The Office (a popular American TV sit-com) page is 56% positive, 12% negative and 32% neutral (59 messages on Facebook).
> Company pages (ex: Facebook) – sentiment for the Facebook page is 30% pos, 32% neg and 38% neu (126 msgs on Facebook).
> Product reviews (ex: Canon Powershot) – sentiment for the Canon Powershot page is 56% pos, 13% neg and 30% neu (82 msgs on Facebook).
> Current events (ex: Occupy Wall Street) – sentiment for 'occupywallstreet' is 56% pos, 16% neg and 28% neu (231 tweets).
> Product announcements (ex: iPhone 4S announcement) – sentiment for iPhone 4S is 44% pos, 17% neg and 38% neu (59 msgs on Facebook). (Consumer Revolution: The Power is Now in Our Hands)[101]

METAVANA

The most surprising experiment is currently being conducted by Metavana.[102]

You know already that the NPS system attempts on the basis of the One Question to determine a net promoter score for each brand. The accuracy of the score depends on the explicit questioning of the respondents. This is the same principle that Holaba applies in China. After years of research Metavana now claims that it has managed to calculate an approximate net promoter score on the basis of spontaneously generated tweets, updates and other communications in the public online space. It argues that for each sector there are a number of precise, concrete trigger words that allow their system to determine whether an online communication is either positive (leaning towards a recommendation) or negative (leaning towards a non-recommendation). It is also possible to define a third group of neutral communications. If the software 'decides' that the communications with regard to the One Question for a particular brand are 37% generally positive, 30% neutral and 33% generally negative, the estimated

NPS is +4. If the respective values are 47%, 25% and 28%, the NPS is +19 (47-28, ignoring the 25). At the time of writing, this search engine has not yet been launched (and very little has been written about it), but that is more or less how the system works – although I personally doubt whether they have a neutral pot. Or to put it in Metavana's own words, their classification engine first 'brings order to the chaos of unstructured human language', following which a sentiment engine does the analytical work.[103]

WE ARE TALKING ABOUT MEASURING PEOPLE, BOTH IN THE BROAD CONTEXT OF MARKETING AND FROM THE PERSPECTIVE OF THE PURCHASING CONSUMER

1   We know for certain that the purchasing consumer is searching for information and guidance and that his ultimate decision will be influenced by the people who are closest to him. They are not interested whether or not these people have a high influence score or a low one. The experience they share with a friend, neighbour, colleague or member of the family is more relevant to them than any influencing statistics – for the time being. In other words, when the final decision-making moment arrives high or low digital influence scores are largely irrelevant. 'After all, there were no figures to help us decide before Klout, Peerreach and all the others came along,' the modern Luddites will tell you with glee.

2   We also know that product reviews likewise have a decisive impact in the wider circle around the searching consumer. Instead of placing more importance on a single score from one person in his immediate environment, this consumer attaches greater weight to the crowd-sourced global score, on the basis of the democratic principle of 'one man, one vote'. You can compare it with the mass of stock analysts, who ply their trade on Wall Street and elsewhere. You may have one or two analysts who you regularly follow, but the overall trend of your investments – buy, sell or hold – will be set by the general sentiments of the market. It is safer to assume that the wisdom of the group is greater than the wisdom of the individual. The measuring of digital influence pushes the individual 'hero'/performer too much to the forefront, conferring on them the status of 'expert'. But this idea of 'a nobody becoming a somebody' is not what we want or need. The hundreds of thousands of mums who daily influence the nappy-buying

behaviour of millions of other mums are already 'somebodies'. They
don't become more of a somebody simply because they do it online.

3   These first two circles of trust are only minimally influenced by external campaigns. In my opinion, Solis places too much emphasis on campaigns. His analysis is too heavily focused on the brand that broadcasts (partly through the use of people with a high digital influence score) and too little on the searching consumer, who has developed a high level of resistance of all forms of push marketing. Nothing is more likely to put off a potential customer than to discover that his 'friend' is actually on the digital influence payroll of a brand!

4   There is much less activity about brands and products on Twitter and Facebook than the SMMMMS companies would like to have us believe. Most of the traffic is about much broader topics than brands and their products. Digital influence is therefore to be found at this broader level, where general information about a subject is more important ('shoes made in America'), rather than at the brand/product level of specific recommendations.

5   Recommenders are much less of a 'flexible tool' in the hands of the brands than Solis seems to think, and the more they do actually 'bend' in the direction of the brand, the less reliable they become in the eyes of the consumer. Recommenders not only have a 'propaganda' role in respect of their favourite brands, but also by virtue of their honesty act as a kind of 'purifying agent', making the brand information more trustworthy.

6   The 'measuring people' approach is interesting as a tool for evaluating the most powerful influencers. Some super-influencers just keep on going, rising to the very top of the influencing ladder (and even occasionally going beyond). However, these constitute just 1% of the consumer population. Recommenders in a marketing context (our 15%) will follow the clash of the influencing titans at the top of the ladder with interest, but will then distance themselves from it. It is not always the people who are best able to manipulate public opinion who have the best opinions themselves. Just as in a democracy the free vote of the people does not always lead to the best president.

7   The danger inherent in this battle at the top is the same danger that is inherent in any contest, whether it be sporting, economic or political: intrigue. Contests of this kind are all too often won (or lost) by hackers who plug, lobby, bribe or invest huge amounts of money in an attempt

to 'massage' the algorithms. For many it simply becomes a game to find new ways to trick the measuring systems. What's more, it's a game that everyone can play. For example, your friends can help you to earn 'extra' +K points on Klout: it is not unusual to see someone's score rise from 60 to 65 on their birthday, if all their friends send virtual 'best wishes' via Twitter and Facebook!

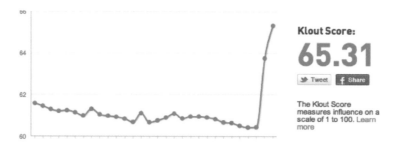

8 Paying consumers for an online lead (tweet, update) is a very welcome bonus for some people, but at the same time it affects the digital influence score of the sender. 'Dell's Share and Earn scheme, launched this week, enables customers who promote Dell products to earn £5 if one of their "shares" leads to the sale of a Dell product worth more than £70.'[104]

9 We already have the ultimate measuring tool for influence, but sadly it only becomes evident after the sales event. The tool in question is share of market. What we need to understand is what happens in the seconds, hours, days, weeks and sometimes months that precedes every individual decision that can have an effect on market share. The NPS can help in this respect. So too can people who state explicitly that they recommend or do not recommend a particular brand. It is this dynamic that we need to identify, quantify and turn into meaningful figures.

10 It is still a mystery to me which units most companies (except Peerreach) use as the most decisive element in calculating a person's influencing score. The number of followers? Plus the number of tweets? Plus the number of retweets? Plus the number of interactions between people? And this all against a background of a topic domain in which other actors are also playing? And if a top 10 or 20 per topic is gradually formed in this manner, how is their digital influence expressed? And how far does this influence reach? And (the $64,000 dollar question) to what extent do consumers take account of these scores and

allow themselves to be influenced by them? Is there a measurable conversion between digital influence and effective influence?

A Klout Score / B Peerresearch ranking for 'marketers in the Netherlands' / C Number of tweets since they started twittering / D Number of people they follow / E Number of people who follow them.

	A	B	C	D	E
Menno Lanting	56	1	12.447	19.070	19.059
Ronald van den Hoff	49	2	12.206	6.901	6.864
Jan Willem Alphenaar	69	3	36.635	6.864	8.922
Roos van Vugt	67	4	82.834	3.496	7.639
Thomas Marzano	67	120	86.365	28.052	41.816
Berrie Pelser	63	1022	36.633	49.935	135.761
Jan Van den Bergh	57	*	4.587	1.619	839

*Belgian in China = no ranking

A RE-EVALUATED LOOK AT SOME 'HUMAN MEDIA' SCORES IN THE NETHERLANDS

During my conversations with Peerreach about their ranking system, we came (or rather, I came) to some strange conclusions about their scores for Dutch marketers. The first four positions are occupied by 'marketers' who, more than anyone else, are linked with each other. The reasoning of the system being that if someone is followed by all the other influential marketers, he/she must also be important.

In this manner, Menno Lanting finds himself at the top of the Peerreach list, even though he does not regard himself as a marketer! A few weeks before I telephoned him to discuss this seeming anomaly, he had been invited to attend the première of a Hollywood film, without having the faintest idea why. When he asked the organisers, it became apparent that this unexpected VIP treatment was the result of his high Klout score. Then the penny dropped. At another event he once attended he had also seen – and been surprised – that parking space had been specially reserved for participants with a high Klout score. Taking account of Klout scores is not yet such a rage in the Netherlands as it is in the U.S., but even in Europe this kind of special treatment is becoming more and more common – whether we like it or not, and notwithstanding the fact that the ranking is hardly based on reliable scientific foundations. This was much the same message that Roland van den Hoff gave in reply to my e-mail. 'I have had a quick look, but cannot really do very much with this kind of thing... this type of site currently gives little added value, possibly in the future, but at the moment they are not really relevant for us.'

Menno Lanting mentioned in our conversation that he also found the lack of transparency (how do you calculate a score?) disappointing and said that it would be better to develop a standard in open source, to which everyone could contribute. He understood that this would not be simple, because if the Google boys had done that in the second half of the 1990s we would now have a result hierarchy that is supported by everybody... but we would not have Google! He rightly commented that the scores only relate to digital influence and that the real influence exercised by someone in his domain of professional expertise is based on many other and more important things than digital influence – which itself is capable of being 'influenced' or manipulated. And if something can be manipulated, it is usually the people who have least to say who shoot to the top like a rocket. Hacking search results on Google has now become a profession in its own right!

It was the same story with Thomas Marzano. He, too, has had experience with score manipulation. It is certainly something that is possible in the short-term. And until systems like Klout become more 'waterproof', people should not attach too much importance to them. Having said that, these systems are a fun addition to what you know about the other people who are active in your professional environment. These people judge the influencing power of someone on the basis of the content that they receive from that someone. Separately from the real content of the things you actually do. (Kred is trying to also take account on this offline influencing.) Moreover, what exactly is meant by professional environment? Peerreach ranks him as a marketer in 120th position. But he, like Menno Lanting, does not regard himself as a marketer. He writes far more about design, user experience and photography than about marketing. Another feature of the lists is the way that consultants seem to be drifting towards the top. Thomas thinks that this is normal, but not necessarily healthy. Consultants do a lot, talk a lot, write a lot and blog a lot. But in essence they are one-man companies. Do they really have influence?

Or do they just have a large reach, because everybody knows them?
They twitter because that is a good way to generate leads for their
business.

Thomas Marzano is a Philips man – a regular corporate guy. His influence
is measurable every day on the work floor. And it is probably much greater
than the influence of any consultant. Of course, the mega-twitterers
are important for any brand. They are rather like human flyers, and
brands are grateful to make use of them to extend their own reach.
By why do they desire to have such reach? If these twitterers all had
real influence, because they understand a whole sector and how it works,
companies could then do much more with them. Integrate them more
fully into the company's operations. And I am in full agreement with
Thomas when he argues that it is more important to identify the 'real'
and 'ordinary' consumer, rather than the professionals. The real consumer, who has no specific area of professional expertise but has nevertheless somehow acquired an 'expert' knowledge of a particular disposable nappy, type of yoghurt, make of smartphone, etc. A young
mother who has changed five nappies a day for the past five years
knows more about good and bad brands – and is a more credible recommender – than a man in a three-piece suit who has never changed
a nappy in his life, but claims to know everything about it. Thomas fears
that the focus of, for example, Peerreach on professionals is over-exag-
gerated and misleading. There are other angles of approach, which
are as relevant (if not more relevant) than professional expertise.
He says that consumers should also be given greater opportunities
to give credibility scores for other people. I think he is probably right.
At the moment, there is too big a difference between on the one hand
following someone or giving a 'like' to their posts and on the other hand
stating publicly that someone has influenced your choice because of
his credibility and authority. His own estimate is that as few as half of
his 40,000-50,000 followers are 'real', in the sense of being genuinely
interested, and that just 4,000-5,000 of these people regard him as
credible in the three or four professional domains about which he
writes the most. This also explains how it is possible for someone like
myself, with my paltry just-less-than-a-thousand followers, to achieve
a relatively high score. The large majority of my near-I,000 will be real
followers, with very few passers-by. This means that whatever I post
has a greater chance of being retweeted or shared, to the benefit of

my overall score. Put simply, I probably influence fewer people more, whereas the influencers with a high percentage of fake followers influence more people less.

Odd-man-out in the list is Berrie Pelser. He is founder and CEO of a hosting company in the Netherlands that operates primarily in the field of search engine optimisation (SEO). He, Jan Willem, Roos and Thomas Marzano were amongst the very early Twitter adopters a few years ago. They were already highly active on Twitter before most of us had even started. To join their club you need to have 10,000 followers – and that is a huge number if you are only twittering in Dutch. They had agreed between themselves to artificially boost their scores by systematically retweeting each other. And their plan worked perfectly. Until Klout adjusted its algorithm in the third quarter of 2011 to outlaw this practice, at which point their scores fell dramatically. As with search engine optimisation, you need to stay alert and seek to discover how you can get a high position in the list and, just as importantly, how you can stay there or get even higher. Berrie Pelser is highly quoted in just about every list that has anything to do with social media and the measurement of the influencing power of people. He is not wholly wrong when he states that a score at this present time cannot be anything more than the re-weighted amalgamation of the scores on the ten or fifteen systems that are publicly available. By this he means Klout, Kred, Peerindex, Peereach, Social Chiefs, Empire Avenue, etc. His score in all these lists is astronomically high. He is proud of this fact, but has worked hard for two years to make it possible. And for the customers who take their SEO problems to Berrie, it is a big advantage to be working with such a network cluster-bomb. In fact, he probably has an unassailable position within his sector. His lowly position – 1,022nd place – in the list of Dutch marketers leaves him cold. He does not really belong in that category. But on the general list of Dutchmen and women with a high Klout score, he stands in a very impressive 54th spot (in May 2012, but in the meantime he has probably climbed even higher – check it out at http://www.influentials.nl/klout/).

8 What do Kurkdroog, Mobile Vikings and Apple all have in common?

In this chapter three different types of recommender will play the leading roles. For one reason or another, they can all be categorised as 'extreme' types.

1 Kurkdroog. A review site for wines (the name literally means 'Cork Dry') that are available for sale in most large supermarkets in different price categories.

2 Mobile Vikings. A local mobile phone operator that offers a low-price talk-and-data subscription without shops, without sales teams and without advertising. Their only method of promotion is through their fanatical customers, who get extra subscription benefits if they bring in new customers.

3 Apple. We all know that the gigantic success of Apple is in large part due to its fanatical promoters. I am also one of them. What you probably didn't know is that some of these same promoters are also giving Apple a wake-up call in respect of a number of important social themes.

YOU CAN BUY BETTER AT BETTER PRICES
IF YOU FOLLOW THE TASTE OF THE RECOMMENDERS

– The Holy Trinity is no longer what it used to be. Until the end of the 20th century it was the Father, Son and Holy Ghost (in Christian theology, at least). In the 21st century it is now the smartphone, the shop and user-generated evaluations (UGE). Much easier to understand and very down to earth!

– This mobile application cannot change water into wine, but it can – and has – offered rankings for hundreds of different vintages.

The Christians amongst you will obviously be familiar with the original concept of the Holy Trinity, and naturally it is not my intention in any way to belittle the key tenets of your faith. However, in recent years I have used this powerful metaphor to underline to unbelievers the importance of a new marketing trinity:

1 a smartphone, tablet or any other portable device that allows you to make use of mobile internet;
2 a shop (online or offline);
3 the user-generated evaluations of products and services, coming from various social networks.

If all these three elements are present, alert consumers and equally alert brands can both be winners. As sure as night follows day. This is the situation we want to move towards in future: that wherever you are, that whatever you are looking for, you will always be able to find it thanks to the miracle of technology that you have in your jacket pocket or handbag.

These possibilities are the subject of this story about wine. But the story is also about something else. The striatum.[105] This is the spot in your brain that lights up when you get your pay-cheque at the end of each month, but which also becomes active when you feel respected and appreciated.

You might imagine that most recommenders write their reviews in the open, so that everyone can see what they are doing and value their contribution accordingly. How can you hope to experience that delightful striatum feeling if no one gives you praise, because no one knows you exist?[106]

Not so! The Kurkdroog[107] story proves that you can experience the pleasurable emotions of the striatum in silence and secrecy. The hundreds of wine recommenders on Kurkdroog have been tasting wine for years. But they all remain anonymous, content to help others without stepping into the limelight. Being part of a collective and much respected reservoir of wine wisdom and altruistically sharing this wisdom with your fellow wine-lovers: it sounds almost Buddhist!

But how exactly does Kurkdroog work for the consumer?

I have been a true follower for more than 10 years and I will explain shortly how this UGE (user-generated evaluations) wine site actually operates. But first follow me on little voyage of discovery, which will

'We live in a world where the little things really do matter. Each encounter, no matter how brief is, a micro interaction which makes a deposit or withdrawal from our rational and emotional subconscious. The sum of these interactions and encounters adds up to how we feel about a particular product, brand or service. Little things. Feelings. They influence our everyday behaviours more than we realise' (David Armano).[108]

---

give you some impression of the charm of this 'divine' website and its 'heavenly' contents.

One cold winter evening I was clicking through their site, doing some research for this book (because I knew right from the very beginning that I would want to write about them). I stumbled across a wine that wasn't cheap, but also had a historic high score and was available for sale in Delhaize – a supermarket that operates in every town in Belgium, and one with excellent wine taste. 'Interesting,' I thought. 'Perhaps I should give it a try'. I don't often pay €15 euros for a bottle of wine, but on this occasion the opportunity seemed too good to miss.

As you can see on the following screenshot, the wine in question was a Château Haut-Millon from 2009. Or, if you prefer, Château Haut-Milon (without the typing error).

A few days later I received a mail in my mailbox from Delhaize (I buy wine from them from time to time), advising me that if I clicked on the link I could enjoy six bottles from a selection of their finest wines for the price of five. I clicked as instructed and was delighted to see that the highly-praised (and highly-priced) Haut-Milon 2009 was included in the selection.

And so I immediately ordered twelve bottles, on the assumption that I would only be paying for ten of them.

Next day I trotted down to my local Delhaize to collect my twelve bottles. However, a charming lady from Delhaize Direct immediately placed not twelve but nineteen bottles in my shopping trolley. She told me that I had not ordered twelve bottles, but fourteen! By now I was totally confused. It seems that the deal was actually 6+1 and not 5+1. And twice 6+1 = 14. I still wasn't certain how she arrived at nineteen bottles, but I wasn't inclined to argue. It seemed like this was going to be my lucky day!

If I had wandered into Delhaize on a normal shopping day and bought nineteen bottles of Haut-Milon off the shelf at €14.90 euros per bottle, I would have made the supermarket chain some €283 euros richer.

I now had the same nineteen bottles but was pleasantly surprised that I only had to pay for fourteen of them. A quick bit of mental arithmetic told me that with my discount this meant a total bill of just €182 euros. Or €9.50 euros per bottle instead of € 14.90 euros per bottle. Not the kind of offer you can allow to pass by!

PAUILLAC CHATEAU HAUT MILON 2009 (5 plus 1 gratis)	14St.	€ 208,60 - € 29,81
Subtotaal:		**€ 178,79**
Waarvan statiegeld:		€ 0,00
Bereidingskost:		€ 3,50
Totaal kortingen:		- € 29,81
Geschat totaal:		**€ 182,29**

Even better, this story was an e-commerce story.

Apart from the drive to Delhaize to pick up my ill-gotten gains, the whole transaction had been conducted at my kitchen table. These were the early days of e-commerce and m-commerce, and both are still in their infancy.

In China the turnover from e-commerce increased by 66% in 2011 (in comparison with 2010), reaching a total of $124 billion dollars. This sounds like a lot, but it isn't, really. It actually represents just 3% of total retail sales. It is estimated that this will rise to 7% by 2015. And remember that web penetration in China is still only 37.7% – even though this means a massive 505 million netizens in 2011.

Among British mobile users 64% said mobile ads were offensive and banner ads particularly so. Over three-quarters find banner ads irritating. Only 11% of UK mobile users said they had ever clicked on a banner ad on the mobile web and even less, 1%, click on banner ads frequently.[109]

In the United States, where there are almost 200 million netizens (less than half the Chinese total), the e-commerce turnover in that same year – 2011 – was $202 billion dollars.

According to the latest prognoses, this should increase to $327 billion dollars by 2016, which would represent approximately 9% of total retail sales. This is quite possible, since research has shown that buying with a tablet is easier than with a laptop or a smartphone.

But the essence of this story is not the irresistible growth of e-commerce and m-commerce, but the role of user-generated evaluations within the holy trinity that drives the e-commerce and m-commerce system. And to understand this, we first need to understand how ordinary wine-lovers become recommenders on Kurkdroog.

Once upon a time, I was the co-founder and co-director of an advertising agency that was later taken over by Saatchi & Saatchi. At that time, one of our copywriters was someone who loved both wine and the web: Dirk Rodriguez.

In 2000 he began to publish some of his wine-tasting comments online. He limited his choice to the wines that were available in the large retail outlets in Belgium and he assessed bottles in different price categories.

Little by little, a group of anonymous wine fanatics grew up around Dirk, who focused their reviews on the reasonably priced wines (less than €15 euros) on sale in local supermarkets. Each wine was given a score by each reviewer. Since then, Dirk has collected, collated and published the resulting wine hit-list on the web. They claim to be objective – and I believe them – because they publish the average of all the scores submitted and do not sell any wine themselves (they just drink the stuff). Viewed from a commercial perspective, this is pretty dumb. If they had placed links under their chosen wines, then they could earn money from every online order (such as my own personal contribution of € 182 euros for the Haut-Milon). And even in those circumstances I would still be inclined to regard them as an objective source.

These amateur wine writers are not experts. Nor do they want to be. Experts – according to Kurkdroog – often only publish their own taste preferences, which is not always what ordinary people like to drink. The film that wins an Oscar or the book that wins the Booker Prize or the wine that wins the Golden Snail are not always the film, book or wine that are popular with the man (or woman) in the street. Kurkdroog is therefore a perfect example of wine democracy at work: created by the people for the people. What's more, when you ask for something, they always give you more. What could be more democratic than that?

That amateur experts are gaining ground on professionals is also evident in the book sector. 'Amazon reviews have as much weight as professional reviews, says a new study.[110] Perhaps more surprisingly, professional critics and Amazon reviewers tend to have similar opinions about a book's quality on average, with the report stating that "experts and consumers tend to agree in aggregate about the quality of a book." That isn't always the case, however; the report also points out that "relative to consumer reviews, professional critics are less favourable to first-time authors" than Amazon.com reviewers in general.'

Their price categories are also democratic. They choose wine in four price ranges: less than €4 euros, €4-6 euros, €6-9 euros and €9-15 euros. Within each of these categories there are 'winners' per supermarket and per type. If Aldi is the supermarket where you buy your wine, you can soon find out which Aldi red in the €4-6 euro category has the most amateur recommenders.

And since recently, you can do more with Kurkdroog than simply order everything from the comfort of your kitchen (e-commerce) or check online before you go shopping which wine you want to buy (offline commerce). Now you can also use a (paying) app that allows you to do exactly the same on your mobile while you are actually shopping in the supermarket (m-commerce).

It doesn't get any easier than this: the power of the recommenders packed into your own mobile phone! A do-it-yourself (and deliciously tasty) version of the holy trinity.

The big advantage of the Kurkdroog lists is that you can find the 'winning' wines in almost every town in Belgium, and not just at specialist wine importers, who are often located nowhere near where you live and who only do their business offline. This is a point that is worth repeating. We are not talking here about expensive and exclusive wines that are difficult to find; the wines that the experts like to taste, simply because they are the 'top of the range' vintages with which they are presented in specialist wine houses. No, we are talking about everyday wines for ordinary people.

THE KURKDROOG FORMULA

WR = (v: v+m)) x R + (m: (v+m)) x C. This is the so-called Bayesian average, where the letters stand for:

WR: weighted ranking

v: the number of opinions submitted

m: the minimum required number of opinions

C: the average opinion over the entire sample

R: the normal average (the sum total of all opinions divided by the number of opinions)

This results in the collective opinions of the contributors being expressed as a percentage: 100% is absolute top, 0% is absolute flop.

The web also has the added advantage that the list remains constantly up-to-date. Wines that are 'out of stock' simply disappear from the list and new ones are added almost daily. Sometimes the 'newbies' nestle themselves amongst the lesser gods in the lower regions of the lists, until they can climb higher, but occasionally they shoot straight to the top in no time at all. As always, the people decide.

Dirk also writes a weekly column in the *De Morgen* newspaper, in which he selects and evaluates three or four supermarket wines. These are either wines that he has discovered himself or tips that he has received from one or more of the Kurkdroog volunteers.

KURKDROOG:
THE FIGURES

> The site continues to grow, with 54% of new visitors last year.
> The 'pages per visit' total (4.16) is not high, but the site is a quick-working 'search-and-find' tool. If I always shop at the X supermarket and only drink red wine, then that is the only score I need to check.
> This also explains the low average time on site: just 3.06 minutes. Kurkdroog is quick in and quick out. It is not an informative site. It is a find site – a sort of Google for wine.
> For the Apple lovers, it is worth noting that the number of Mac visitors to the site has increased from 4% when the site was first opened to a more healthy 12% today.
> 72% of the visitors come from (1) Ghent, (2) Brussels, (3) Antwerp and (4) Leuven, but there are as many visitors from the Netherlands as there are from the Belgian province of Limburg.
> Kurkdroog site visitors spend on average 6.36 euros on a bottle of wine (the Belgian national average is 4 euros). They are not necessarily looking for the cheapest wines, but for good value for money. Some of them are happy to pay the maximum price of 14.99 euros per bottle.
> Since 2007 Kurkdroog has been the best-scoring Belgian wine website. If you type in 'wine' on the Belgian page of Google, Kurkdroog appears at the very top of the answer list.
> Kurkdroog was awarded tenth prize in the 'food and drink' category during the 15th edition of the Belgian 'internet site of the year' awards. The first nine prizes were all given to 'food' sites, making Kurkdroog the first – and best – 'drink' site.

Category Food & Drink

1) Dagelijkse kost / 2) njam! / 3) Lekker van bij ons / 4) Resto.be /
5) zesta.be / 6) Libelle Lekker / 7) Solo Open Kitchen / 8) Koken.be
9) Kok op Kot / 10) Kurkdroog

The clever use of a mass medium (Kurkdroog is editorial and not advertorial) ensures that the site is always able to encourage its regular volunteers to taste, review and evaluate a wide range of wines – time after time. This is necessary, since Kurkdroog's own house rules stipulate that a wine must be the subject of at least 15 reviews before it appears on the web.

> Available in Dutch, English, French, Spanish and Italian
> 95,000 wines and 65,000 addresses
> 95,000 assessments from wine-lovers
> 350,000 photographs
> 400,000 unique visitors each month

The site also makes abundantly clear that anyone – and they do mean anyone – is free to submit their own reviews and scores. There is no money to be earned; simply the satisfaction that comes from doing something for nothing for the benefit of others. Kurkdroog also organises regular tastings that are open to everyone. Ordinary members of the public pay an admittance fee of €25 euros, but people who have contributed five scores in the three months prior to the tasting get in for just €5 euros. This is the only form of reward for the site's anonymous 'workers'.

Vinogusto began as an amateur site, but has now gone professional. Very professional indeed. Whereas Kurkdroog after twelve years is still a hobby activity for Dirk and his few hundred impassioned volunteers, Vinogusto is a very different matter.

They began in 2005 with the simple collection of data. The site went online with the intention of being a 'find-and-buy' indicator for all types of wines in every European country. When Marc Roisin (founder and CEO) was still a banker, he was irritated by the fact that he could never find the wine he wanted and that there were no comments or recommendations for the wines he did find. But instead of concentrating (like Kurkdroog) on large supermarkets, Vinogusto had higher, Google-like ambitions. It wanted to list all wine houses and all wine shops, as well as all wines from every recent year, with comments, tasting reports and recommendations. The site only has five members of staff, working from an office in Brussels, so to achieve this huge objective they need to rely on the input of hundreds of volunteers.

In the meantime, a section on wine tourism has also been added, where you can easily find places for a short or long stay (wine farms, guest houses and hotels in wine-growing regions, etc.). In Sardinia alone, for example, the site offers 302 accommodation alternatives, all directly connected with wine, a number of which have been evaluated by people who have stayed there. In essence, this is the beginning of a Tripadvisor for wine-lovers on holiday. The real Tripadvisor has reviews for 835 Sardinian hotels of all types. With its 302 specifically wine-related locations, Vinogusto is not all that far behind! It certainly has a very complete list within its category.

Wijn Toerisme : Sardegna

The same is true of restaurants. These are also included in the database and people are free to write reviews and give assessments not only of the food, but also the wine. During my preparatory work for this book I invited Marc Roisin for lunch. It was agreed that I would pay, but that he would choose the restaurant and the wine. He chose Chou, a restaurant for which there were already five reviews on the Vinogusto site. Of course, Belgium is already covered by the famous restaurant guides, such as Michelin and GaultMillau, but they frequently focus on the more expensive end of the market. Chou also has a high score in GaultMillau (15) and my meal with Marc wasn't cheap. And the restaurant is also mentioned in Michelin, but has no star. But how can a wine-lover/restaurant spotter decide what's what when the two major guides contradict each other? He consults the opinion of the people.

But where should he seek this opinion? From Kurkdroog or from Vinogusto? Which is best? If I look at things from my personal perspective, I find Kurkdroog more useful. All I need is the collective bundling of opinions, so that I can decide what wine to buy when I pop down to the local supermarket. With Kurkdroog I can find this quickly and easily. If, for whatever reason, I am not shopping this week at my normal supermarket, but at a supermarket on the other side of town, where I have no idea about their selection of wines, Kurkdroog will provide me with a list of six recommendations, all of which have been assessed by at least fifteen reviewers.

€ 119 voor een exclusief wijnabonnement van een jaar, samengesteld door de beste sommelier van België 2010: 4 maal per jaar 6 flessen wijn (waarde € 400)

Wijn heeft ons al in vele benarde situaties gebracht. Een gezellig avondje met vrienden op restaurant. Om de één of andere reden krijg net jij de wijnkaart op schoot, vol met wijnen uit elke uithoek van de wereld, met smaakprofielen en oogstjaren allerhande. Begin er m...

Nu vooruit bestellen   - 70%

The broad approach of Vinogusto, which seeks to cover everything about wine, also has its charm, but you need to invest a lot of time and money to turn this 'all-in-one' concept into reality.

Both Kurkdroog and Vinogusto can benefit from local wine-tasting sessions, which encourage people to write reviews about wines that are available in or near that locality. The forwarding of individual tasting packs at low cost is also an option for the more dedicated wine recommenders.

The above offer from Cuistot (via Groupon) is a good example of a packet that will please wine amateurs, wine recommenders and wine buyers. You pay just 199 euros for 4 x 6 bottles each year. If you like the stuff, you can recommended it and order more at the same discounted rate. Which is what I did. And I recommended Groupon to other people. So the mechanism works. And a mechanism that helps to identify recommenders is crucial for any brand. For your brand as well.

And just so beer-lovers won't feel left out I want to close this section with a brief mention of BeerAdvocate.com. This site does for beer what Kurkdroog and Vinogusto do for wine. It is a grassroots community of beer enthusiasts who drink and evaluate their favourite brews – and in this manner give recommendations. Jason and Todd Alström began the site in Boston in 1996. They are still owners of the complete set-up. Collectively, they want to do exactly what we want to do with our recommenders:

1) Wake up the masses to better beer options.

2) Give beer consumers a voice.

3) Empower them to learn, share and advocate.

There are now 75,000 beers in their database. Guinness is there, but so too are no fewer than 433 beers from Belgium, including my own favourite, Duvel. This excellent strong ale scored high with the brothers Alström, and also with 2,303 amateur tasters. 'Guinness is good for you,' a classic advert once told us. But Duvel is better. Trust me. I'm a recommender!

Duvel

BA SCORE	THE BROS	rAvg: 4.3
96	**100**	pDev: 10%
		High: 5
world-class	world-class	Low: 1.58
2,333 Reviews	read more »	Ratings [7]

Brewed by:
Brouwerij Duvel Moortgat NV 🏭
Belgium

Style | ABV
Belgian Strong Pale Ale | 8.50% ABV

Tweet 31

Notes:
Year-round. Serving types had: bottle (2315), on-tap (14), growler (4).

No other notes at this time.

ARE ALL RECOMMENDERS MOBILE VIKINGS?
YES, BUT WITHOUT THE LONG BOATS!

- Mobile Vikings have more recommenders working for them than there are staff on the payroll.
- A company that calls its customer 'members' and plans to make them 'shareholders' is the very epitome of the recommender philosophy.
- What will happen to a small, very 'human' company when it is forced to take on the big boys of the corporate world? Will it be forced to become big itself, in order to survive? Or can that be avoided? How far can you get with recommenders alone? And are they then still 'ordinary' recommenders?

In December 2008 CityLive announced with a great deal of hoo-ha the launch of a new mobile operator by the name of Famous. Some time later, Famous was changed to Mobile Vikings. God knows why! It seems that the change was inspired by the reading of the classic *Good to Great* by Jim Collins (clearly I should be reading more management literature!). Besides, Mobile Vikings sounds less corporate b.s. than Famous.

The Famous slide illustrated below (and dating from 2008) makes clear that the fan/idol aspect played an important role in the company right from the very beginning. It was in their DNA. And that is why they have a special place in this book. Because this book is essentially about their customers. Who they call members.

Shortly after this slide was made, Mobile Vikings sent its first sim-card to its first customer (sorry, member) in Belgium. It was January 2009, a historic moment. One day they should erect a statue to commemorate that moment!

I only met the chief Viking, Frank Bekkers (founder and CEO of Mobile Vikings) for the first time at the start of 2011. In Beijing. In a smoke-filled conference room. Together with three other business relations, he was the guest of one of the large Chinese state holdings. As was I. For business, of course. Two Belgians who don't know each other meet in Beijing. It sounds like an episode from a spy thriller, doesn't it? Frank asked me a lot of questions, which made it clear to me that he was as sold as I was on the evangelist theory. I was certain that I wanted to do business with him if he ever came to China. But he didn't. Not then.

Once before, a long time previously, I had heard the name Mobile Vikings. Former minister Rik Daems mentioned it to me in a private conversation about 'investment in China'. But it is not always wise to believe what ministers say, and so I thought no more about it. Not then.

After the Beijing meeting Frank and I had a number of follow-up conversations, since there were common points of interest in our Chinese story and their Belgian one. We both had a database with 'users'. The customers/users/members of Mobile Vikings paid for the privilege; ours didn't. When I began writing this book, it was only natural that our contact should become more intense.

At the end of February 2012 I finally had the chance to talk with Hans Similon. His business card declares that his profession is 'evangelist'. That's all. No other fancy corporate titles. It made me think that I might need to alter my own cards. But what does the word 'evangelist' mean to people in an atheist country like China? Like his CEO, Hans is the living embodiment of the evangelist creed. Dangerously fanatical. He is the incarnation of the whole Vikings shrine, giving it shape and form, spreading its gospel to a world of unbelievers.

Without having done much comparative field work on the subject, I think it is safe to say that Mobile Vikings is on the way to becoming the first company anywhere that is built from A to Z around its recommenders. World-class in the making. Soon to be operating outside Belgium as well. At the time of writing, they had just launched the company in Poland and they have other countries in their sights. Between the eighth and tenth centuries the original Vikings voyaged as far as southern Spain and Turkey in their long boats, thousands of kilometres from their cold Scandinavian home. The ocean is vast and limitless, just like the ambition of the Mobile Vikings.

But let's return to the beginning. They started their MVPN[III] in Belgium in 2009 with precisely zero customers. By the middle of 2012 they had 100,000 paying members. In a small country like Belgium, with a population of just 10 million, that's a big slice of the market for a small company. When they passed the magical 100,000 mark on 14 May 2012 all their members were allowed to phone each other free for an hour (or two hours, if you knew the right trick).

As already mentioned, they don't refer to their customers as 'customers', but as 'members'. That speaks volumes. It is the members –

and the members alone – who have made this spectacular growth possible, since it is they – and they alone – that recruit new members to the Mobile Vikings shrine. For every new member they bring, the old member gets 15 euros of free call credit. Unless, like me, you are constantly on the phone between Belgium and China each day, this is enough to pay for your telephone conversations and data transfer each month. Some members have already recruited as many as 100 converts. They probably won't have to pay a telephone bill for the rest of their life – certainly if they carry on that way!

What's more, attracting these converts seems to be fairly simple. As soon as someone becomes a new member and has paid his first month, he receives a 'ready to tweet/ready to facebook' text that contains a personal ID code. Everyone is able (if they so choose) to post that banner, so that people in their network can see that they have become a Mobile Vikings member. And for every friend that clicks on the banner and eventually becomes a member, you get your free €15 euros of call credit. As easy as pie.

69% of new members are recruited in this manner. The remaining 31% find their way to the company via the various different routes that Mobile Vikings employs. This figure of 69% is huge. It means that the members are not only satisfied and loyal, but also that they are very active in spreading the word to their network. Without even being on the payroll.

Of course, this 'member-gets-member' system does allow the existing Vikings to win 150 Vikings points or one free call recharge as soon as the new member registers. This can be done by the new member sms-ing the old member's mobile number to the company and then mentioning that number again when he registers. For many Vikings this is an extra stimulus to promote Mobile Vikings both online and offline within their circle of family, friends and acquaintances. And it works. You can frequently track down twitter messages from members claiming precisely what we suggested above: namely, that they almost never need to pay to have their call credit recharged.

There are even Vikings who put together their own adwords campaigns to place Mobile Vikings in the spotlight. If people click on this link, the Viking in question again earns 150 points or a free credit recharge: a win-win situation for both the member and the company.

But the existing members do much more than simply advertise the brand and provide sales leads (and sales). They even take care of the after-sales service! Vikings, Vikings-to-be and even non-Vikings who ask questions about Mobile Vikings on Twitter and Facebook are often helped further by the members. We are speaking here, of course, about the hard-core Vikings, who have an excellent knowledge of both the company and mobile internet, and who are prepared to share this knowledge for the benefit of the community. What do they get in return? The gratitude and respect of that community. Whilst at the same time pushing the level of Mobile Vikings service higher and higher.

Frederik Geeroms ▶ **Mobile Vikings**
10 minutes ago near Londerzeel, Brabant

Hey! Ik heb een iphone 4S aangekocht en kan alles behalve sms'en versturen. Het ontvangen van sms'en, bellen en data netwerk werkt perfect. Kan iemand mij helpen?

Like · Comment

Jens Veraa Dit al eens gedaan?
iPhone users can set the SMS central by entering *5005*7672*+32486000005# and pressing the send button.

Probeer het dan nog eens.
4 minutes ago · Like

To date, Mobile Vikings haven't spent a penny (or a eurocent) on advertising. And they have no plans to do so. They do, however, make extensive use of the two largest social media sites available to a company operating in Belgium: Twitter and Facebook.

In their initial Facebook group they had some 9,000 followers. This group has since been removed from cyberspace and has been replaced by a page on which 'likes' for the brand can be posted. They currently have just over 21,000 'likes'. A message that they publish on the Twitter and Facebook sites gets between 25,000 and 35,000 impressions.

Vikings who 'like' the Facebook page are highly engaged. They frequently share the messages they receive from the company. The popularity or virality of a message depends on its nature and content. The announcement of a new action or project gets the largest response. And it is not only the hard-core who seek to help others. 'Probationary' Vikings also assist in answering questions on Twitter and Facebook, often before their 'probationary period' has even begun.

Twitter is used in much the same manner as Facebook. There they also have 14,000 followers.

While I was writing this book, Mobile Vikings and myself had exactly the same Klout score. And in my opinion that score is pretty high. It means that Mobile Vikings use social media wisely and with discretion.

It is curious, however, that Telenet – a major classic triple-player telecom operator in Flanders – should have a slightly higher Klout score than Mobile Vikings, when it has significantly fewer Twitter followers. Perhaps the Telenet Facebookers and Twitterers follow 'their' Telenet more frequently via their televisions and fixed internet connections, and less through their mobile applications.

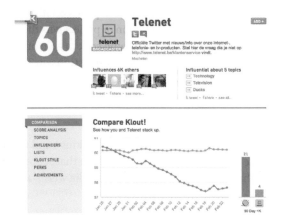

Be that as it may, one thing is clear: Mobile Vikings use social media correctly, in a manner befitting a genuine 'conversation company'. They know that they talk enough and they recognise the importance of listening and responding. But it is not a lonely conversation manager who is facebooking and twittering. The entire help team at the company's main office has an obligation to deal as quickly as possible and to the best of their ability with any request that comes in via social media or the telephone help desk.

During the first half of 2010 the company drew up a list of the five largest pain points from the 300 or so they received (in just a matter of hours) in response to an online inquiry held on Twitter. This was meant constructively. Vikings want to help their brand to move forward. They are expected to open their mouths to praise the company and attract new members. So it is only right and proper that they should also open their mouths when discussing ways in which the company can be improved still further. This is the list – and it is worth noting that all five were corrected within two months.

1 In the past bills were drawn up on the basis of minutes started; now this is done on the basis of seconds used.
2 In the past data-roaming in neighbouring countries was too expensive; the rates have now been reduced.
3 In the past, the number of SMS-messages included in the subscription was too low; this has now been increased to 1,000 external sms's and 1,000 to other Mobile Vikings members.

4 Right from the very beginning, there were complaints about the quality of the 3G connection; KPN (the service provider) quickly put this matter right.

5 In the early days, the network was not always reliable; KPN has improved this aspect as well.

This type of 'good listening' also meant that Mobile Vikings were the first company on the Belgian market to introduce a 100% 'data only' subscription for iPad users – two weeks before the iPad was even launched in Belgium.

Likewise, Mobile Vikings was also the first to offer a new type of sim-card that is micro-sim compatible, so that it can be used in different pieces of mobile equipment.

What Mobile Vikings does not have is a trendy flagship store. Nor do they have any sales staff. Not even at their headquarters building. The boys and girls of the help-desk team are there to guide and assist members and enquirers, not to sell them things.

They might not have a store, but they do have... a caravan! Their own unique and slightly eccentric version of a Viking long boat: the knarr.[112] This rides from town to town, making the ignorant aware that the company exists and allowing the enlightened to ask questions about the service. Yet once again, the idea is not to sell, but to inform.

Sales only take place through the company's website, where prospective customers can find everything they need. The site is updated weekly, not only in the two most frequently spoken languages in Belgium (Dutch and French) but also in English. There are about 8,000 visitors each day. For those who want to know all the fine detail, there is a supplementary blog with plenty of background information.

But perhaps the most startling thing about Mobile Vikings – it was certainly the thing that most startled me – is that the application that allows you to follow what is happening on your account was not developed by the company or by an external supplier, but by Mobile Vikings's own fanatical members, who can also build apps. They do this absolutely for free. There are now peaks of 300 API (application programming interface) calls per minute, which means that the other members also use their applications. Even the website on which the apps are available was made by a Viking: http://www.vikingapps.be/.

In September 2011 they launched VikingTalk (voice-over IP): this makes it possible via wifi and 3G for iPhone and Android users to call each other cheaply or even free of charge. It's a kind of Skype on your mobile. This time the application was developed by Mobile Vikings itself, but in close consultation with a number of Vikings members. Hundreds more tested the app and gave it the thumbs up before it finally went online. Once again, the members had proved their great added value for the company.

I sometimes get the feeling with Mobile Vikings that they have modelled themselves closely on Apple. You often hear the same talk about 'social engagement' and the members claim that they belong to a 'human' company. It is certainly true that the vast majority of members feel comfortable and appreciated by their favourite brand. Some new members even replace their own photograph on Facebook with a direct reference to their new Mobile Vikings membership.

Does any of this have a familiar ring to it? They are the kind of story you often hear about Apple, and perhaps to a lesser degree about Zappos and Trader Joe's in the US. These companies all have the highest NPS score in their category. They are all not satisfied with just being a 'good' company. They have to be the best. They search endlessly for pain points to eliminate, so that the experience of their customers can become even more unforgettable. They want to achieve ultimate customer satisfaction, as reflected in an NPS score of 66, which is exceptionally high. This same thinking dominates their staff recruitment policy. When seeking new colleagues, the engaged team at Mobile Vikings looks first for Male/Female's with the same soul. Stories are already beginning to circulate about super-talented engineers who are giving up fancy jobs with huge salaries just for the chance of working in the warm and caring environment of Mobile Vikings. And the company's founders did not discover this wisdom in any management books. It was already in their blood. Built into their DNA.

I think that the corporate dinosaurs would be well advised to take a leaf or two out of the Mobile Vikings manual, but I have a funny feeling it's not going to happen.

In essence, we are talking here about the difference between 'being different' and 'doing different'. A good example of this is the counterattack launched by Proximus at the end of 2011, which the business press labelled as being blatantly anti-Mobile Vikings. The group of extreme mobile internet-data users – the fans of smartphones and tablets – has become a key target for Proximus. With Proximus they now get 2 Gb of data for €20 euros and 10 Mb in 28 European lands for €10 euro. When the analysts worked out the figures, it turned out that Mobile Vikings were still €5 euros cheaper for each recharge. Consumers must also take account of the fact that with Proximus they are delivering themselves into the hands of the largest stock-quoted triple player in Belgium. It remains to be seen how the market will respond to this situation. But even the price-hoppers have no real incentive to switch to Proximus, since it isn't actually any cheaper. And it seems very unlikely that many of the fanatical Vikings will make the move. Why should they?

I sincerely hope that this type of Vikings company, which leans heavily on its customers/members, will gradually evolve towards a kind of cooperative, in which the members will also get their fair share from the founders and the current shareholders. Moreover, it seems likely that the current generation will start demanding this in the not-too-distant future. And they will be perfectly justified. They not only create a priceless added value for the Mobile Vikings brand, but they also ensure a much better-looking bottom line, since they are often prepared through their voluntary work to participate in the company's costs. Hopefully, this will create a new and more sustainable manner for the company to go public. In short, a PIPO – a people's IPO (initial public offering, a term coined by me). Built not with the money of gamblers and celebrities, but with the sweat of thousands of active members who are rewarded for their efforts.

This immediately reminded me of another story. 'My' Facebook story. When Microsoft announced on 24 September 2007 that they were going to buy 5% of Facebook for an amount between $300 and $500 million dollars (which placed a value of $10 billion dollars on Facebook at a time when they only had 40 million users), I launched on that same Facebook a group under the name of 'Who wants to become a Facebook shareholder?' At that time, I was a fanatical Facebook recommender. In no time at all, we had a couple of hundred members, but after being given the cold shoulder by Zuckerberg, who refused to reply to all our public posts, the group quietly faded away. A year later, during one of their frequent migrations, Facebook actually removed all the members of the group from their site.

My positioning message for the group read as follows: 'Today it was announced that Microsoft is trying to get hold of 5% of Facebook for USD $300-500 million. I think all the united individual Facebook lovers can do the same. Or even better. I guess the majority of us (the users) agree that this network is gonna be great. This group wants to become the place where the fanatics who want to become a shareholder (sooner or later) can register their explicit will to also be financially part of it. That way Facebook will be partially owned by its most addicted users: the diehards can be part of the financial game too. A REAL social network. Maybe the 'promise' everyone should make is to buy/invest $1,000 of value in Facebook. If 10% of the 40 million Facebook users do this by the end of this year, all of us together can become a solid pre-ipo partner. We 'own' a value of 4 billion US$. That's probably 25-30% of Mark's company. The VC's in Facebook only invested $40 million altogether. We can get 100 times more on board in this scheme. And have a seat in the board of directors next to them. And next to Microsoft.'

In the meantime, Facebook has gone public without us – and bombed (I'm not gloating, honestly!). But it will be interesting to see how Mobile Vikings tackles the same situation. They are already launching some interesting new initiatives (which were too fresh to be included in this book, but you might like to take a look for yourself on https://vikingspots.com).

To round off this section, I would like to close with the opinion of a true Viking: *Klein is fijn - §1 Adieu Proximus*. Read along and you will discover how a Viking – and recommenders in general – think, make decisions and help others.

At the beginning of October 2011 I started my operation 'klein is fijn' (small is beautiful). My mission? To replace all large, cumbersome, expensive suppliers with small, flexible, cheaper players, and this without any loss of quality. Less is more. This first post deals with mobile telecom and the internet.

(http://reinfecta.wordpress.com/2011/11/05/klein-is-fijn-1-adieu-proximus)

§ I Adieu Proximus, Welcome Mobile Vikings

A quick calculation of my costs with Proximus during the past 12 months shows that I paid a total amount of €50 euros x 12 months = €600 euros. The classic pre-paid formula with Mobile Vikings costs exactly €15 euros. For this you can call people for an hour (I mean telephone them – you remember?), which in my case is more than adequate, and you get 1,000 SMS's. And a very interesting 2 Gb of data. With Proximus I had a separate and expensive option for just 450 Mb, a very restrictive limit that I frequently exceeded – which was no laughing matter when the additional bill came in. A year with Mobile Vikings, with in my case virtually unlimited availability of data, will normally only cost me €15 euros x 12 months = €180 euros.

In other words, a saving of no less than 70% or 420 euros per year. I was already a Mobile Vikings customer (for a data-card for my iPad) and consequently I was able to register myself when I applied for a new simcard with number transfer. Registering someone as an existing customer entitles you to 150 so-called Vikings points, which you can use to claim a free recharge worth €15 euros. Thanks to a special action I have already won 300 Vikings points – in other words, two free recharges. This means that in the year ahead I will only pay €150 euros de facto, and even less if I can register other people as new members.

*Bearing in mind the price tag, the need to occasionally fall back on EDGE
and the loss of all that Proximus Business Club nonsense are things I can
probably live with. What's more, 3G is being squeezed by BASE (a daughter of KPN, whose network Mobile Vikings uses as virtual operator), but
for e-mail and Twitter 1Mbit/second is enough.*

*So far, I am very satisfied with Mobile Vikings, but should that ever change,
no problem. There is no contract, so you can change operator whenever
you like, with no delay. If you are considering a switch to Mobile Vikings,
all I would say is: do it! And use this referral when you do. The author of
this post will be eternally grateful – and €15 euros better off.*[13]

PEOPLE WHO RECOMMEND APPLE SHOULD ALSO CRITICISE IT EVERY ONCE IN A WHILE

- 'Occupy Apple' is being launched by a group of consumers who are deeply attached to the brand and who believe that the time has come for Apple to no longer think exclusively of Apple.
- All review sites should be 'good guides', but at the moment there is only one Good Guide that is really worth that name. Apart (of course!) from the worldwide association of consumers united through the internet.
- The purifying role of recommenders as we have described it (the 15% of hyperactive consumers who dare to open their mouth) has already made good progress, but still has a very long way to go. Even so, it is going to happen – and it won't just be restricted to product and service-related issues.
- It will cover everything that a brand stands for or should stand for.

As an example of things to come – an example that other companies would be wise to bear in mind – I am now going to put Apple through the wringer. An Apple that you don't see in the dashboard list on the following page (Facebook neither, for that matter). The list, drawn up by Greenpeace, compares the efforts made by IT companies in respect of

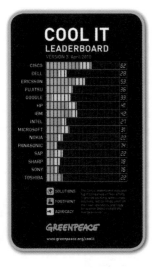

climate improvement. Sadly, there seems in general to be a lack of effective and determined leadership in these companies. Google leads the way with 53 points, and gets qualified praise from Greenpeace. 'Google has carefully charted its energy footprint and has drawn up an exceptionally detailed plan to reduce its emission of greenhouse gases. Moreover, Google talks openly in favour of ambitious climate laws in both the U.S. and the EU.' Bravo Google! And Apple and Facebook? Nowhere to be seen. They simply fail to meet the criteria for inclusion in the list.

Consequently, it is us, the Apple recommenders – and I number myself amongst them – who will have to take the lead with regard to this social aspect of company policy. And it looks like things have started moving already. At least, that's the way it seemed at the beginning of 2012, when a discussion was initiated about Apple and the conditions at Foxconn in China: the company that assembles Apple computers but also adopts some pretty dubious – some might say inhuman – working practices. The pressure of work often leads to employee suicides and the salaries are pitifully low.

Apple has long pushed the blame on to Foxconn, but people are starting to point the finger more directly at Apple, who are essentially responsible for imposing such tight deadlines and low margins on Foxconn. Foxconn simply transfers this near impossible burden to its workforce.

But if Foxconn has to make do with low margins, that is certainly not the case for Apple. In the fourth quarter of 2011 they booked 80% of the entire operational profit in the sector with a sale of 37 million units. During the same quarter Samsung brought 36 million units to the marketplace, but these were only good for 15% of the profits. Nokia and RIM (Blackberry) had to make do with a paltry 2%. Low margins? 44% for Apple, 1.5% for Foxconn.

It was the New York Times that finally blew the whistle with a detailed exposé of the situation at Foxconn.[14] The conclusions of journalists Duhigg and Barboza were shameful and made clear that 'there are few real outside pressures for change'. By this they meant the ostrich-like Apple users, who were content to play with their computers and mobiles – and otherwise buried their heads in the sand.

Apple is a celebrated brand with an exceptionally strong group of fanatical and loyal customers. Apple also has a high NPS in all the countries where is has been measured and enjoys an unassailable position in China (a Holaba score of 39.9). In the meantime, they have also become the largest company in the world (in terms of stock capital), with a share that broke its own record price repeatedly during this same period. In short, Apple is a money-making machine. That is what the New York Times said as well: 'Apple is one of the most admired brands. In a national survey conducted by the New York Times in November, 56% of respondents said they couldn't think of anything negative about Apple. 14% said the worst thing about the company was that its products were too expensive. *Just 2 percent mentioned overseas labour practices.*'

Just 2%. That is the precisely the problem – and a very shameful one, too. As long as we – the Apple consumers – fail to demand better working conditions, nothing is going to change. Fortunately, however, the New York Times article seems to have shaken thousands of Apple fans out of their torpor. And once awakened in this manner, they are finding it hard to get back to sleep with a clear conscience. Perhaps as a result, they responded more quickly than expected to the call to launch and sign petitions.

The press headlines screamed: '*Occupy Apple Protests Follow Foxconn Revelations*'[115] and they referred specifically to '*Apple lovers*' and not the bleeding hearts who are always protesting about something or other: '*Apple lovers* want the company to take a more ethical path when manufacturing its iPhone and iPad devices (…) *Apple's biggest fans are calling for change.*' The dissatisfied 2% were starting to make their voices heard.

A petition on Change.org soon collected more than 200,000 signatures. Another on SumofUs.org gathered another 60,000. I signed both of them. As an Apple lover.

On Twitter people hash-tagged on #OccupyApple. And what were they telling the company? 'Your own ads say that "the people who are crazy enough to think that they can change the world are the ones who do".'[116]

In his petition, Mark Shields asked explicitly for immediate action. As an Apple recommender, he felt the shame deeply. 'Please make these changes immediately, so that each of us can once again hold our heads high and say that "I am a Mac person".'

Taren Stinebrickner-Kauffman, the CEO of SumofUs.org was perhaps the critic who took the most politically-coloured standpoint, when she talked explicitly about ethical consumerism. She argued in favour of a higher margin for the Chinese subsidiary, even if this meant that Apple users would have to pay more: 'I think there are lots of people who love Apple products, but are unhappy about the labour conditions. We believe there are many ethical consumers out there who identify with these brands and want that part of their life to be equally as ethical. If you wouldn't have a slave in your home, you also wouldn't want to have one making your iPhone.'[117] In a follow-up mail that was sent after the petition had been running for some time, she emphasised that the ball had been set rolling by the fanatical Apple recommenders: 'Like many of you, at the beginning of this year we had only a vague idea that there might be something rotten in Apple's supply chain. As Apple consumers ourselves (most of our staff own at least one Apple product), we wanted to act.'

It was also striking that the petition explicitly asked about your relationship with Apple. In my case, I had to tick nearly all the boxes. I am Apple through and through – and am also a shareholder.

The beginnings of an Apple response came quickly. Shortly after the petition actions started, Foxconn (actually a Taiwanese-owned company, i.e. Taiwanese ownership, as opposed to the Chinese stake) increased the wages of its workforce by between 16 and 25%, adding in the press release that this was actually the third increase since 2010. After this pay rise, a junior worker in Shenzhen now earned ¥1,800 yuan ($290 dollars), with the possibility to progress to $2,200 yuan. In 2009 his salary would have been just ¥900 yuan.

In the meantime, Apple had also contacted the Fair Labour Association (FLA), requesting them to monitor the working conditions on site at Foxconn. 'As an Apple consumer, I am relieved to hear that Tim Cook is taking this seriously and is breaking ground in the industry with Fair Labour Association auditing,' said Mark Shields, the consumer who had mobilised the Change.org petition. The FLA interviewed thousands of workers and made the results public.[118]

Taren Stinebrickner-Kauffman commented: 'We are hopeful that this is a step towards a solution, but it's not even close to the solution itself. The FLA does not have a great track record of conducting effective investigations.'[119] She might have a point. Since 2006 Apple has carried out 40 similar audits at the disputed Foxconn plant (and 500 in total at all its factory sites). Little has changed since.

And indeed, not everyone has confidence in the effectiveness and objectivity of the FLA. It has been the subject of often furious debate in the past. Some claim that it is nothing but a PR bureau for the clothing sector. It was actually co-founded by Nike and its activities have not always achieved change for the better. 'Reading that Apple has been auditing their vendors since 2006 does not mean anything. Audits are truly a tool used by retailers in the US to make themselves seem to be socially compliant, but in fact does nothing to ensure factories are acting appropriately.' In other words, the FLA can report but it cannot enforce change.[120]

So is Apple fairly in the dock? Or not?

In view of the above uproar, it is perhaps surprising that during this same period Apple was chosen as 'the most respected company in the United States'. And it had (and continues to have) high scores for 'social responsibility' and 'workplace environment'. I fear that the American voters in this poll only looked at Apple-USA and failed to take account of the less reputable people and organisations that sometimes represent the company abroad. In December 2011 Harris[121] questioned 12,961 people online, so that each of the 74 screened companies had 300 scores. It is interesting to note that in 2011 Facebook occupied 31st place in the list. In 2012 it didn't even make the top 50. Not an encouraging sign for the future.

Leaving aside the specifics of the Apple case (and there will be many other similar issues in many other companies in the years ahead), it is my firm conviction that 'our' recommender group will extend its recommendations to more and more different elements of company operations that are not only product and/or service-related. Harris gives a good indication of these elements in the following graphic.[122]

Sign the petition to Apple

The quality of working conditions matters as much as the quality of your products. Make the iPhone 5 and your other products ethically.

FULL NAME

EMAIL ADDRESS

COUNTRY
— Select —

POSTAL / ZIP CODE

☐ I am an Apple customer
☐ I am an iPhone user
☐ I am an iPad user
☐ I am an iPod user
☐ I live near an Apple Store
☐ I own Apple Stock

⊕ ADD MY NAME

Apple dominates on Vision and Leadership; Amazon, despite lacking a clear human connection to consumers, wins Emotional Appeal

Corporate Leaders on the Six Reputation Dimensions

Social Responsibility		Emotional Appeal		Products & Services	
1. Whole Foods Market	83.35	1. amazon.com	82.90	1. Apple	87.33
2. Apple	81.56	2. Kraft Foods	82.33	2. Google	84.55
3. The Coca-Cola Company	81.22	3. UPS	82.14	3. Kraft Foods	83.73
4. Johnson & Johnson	79.42	4. Apple	81.60	4. Sony	83.51
5. The Walt Disney Company	79.39	5. The Coca-Cola Company	81.38	5. amazon.com	83.27

Vision & Leadership		Financial Performance		Workplace Environment	
1. Apple	88.38	1. Apple	87.93	1. Apple	86.39
2. The Coca-Cola Company	84.17	2. Google	84.56	2. Google	85.32
3. amazon.com	83.85	3. The Coca-Cola Company	83.86	3. The Coca-Cola Company	82.90
4. Google	83.85	4. The Walt Disney Company	83.78	4. Microsoft	82.59
5. The Walt Disney Company	82.84	5. amazon.com	82.98	5. Kraft Foods	81.33

At the present time, a recommender gives his recommendation on the basis of his real experience as a consumer of a particular product or service. To offer equally meaningful opinions about these other elements, he will need first to tap in to new sources of information. This will not make his role any simpler or easier. Making a valid analysis of social responsibility and workplace environment is by no means straightforward. But if they look hard enough, they will find out what they need to know.

Finally, in this chapter, a word about the Good Guide. As far as I know, the Good Guide is the only guide of its kind that goes beyond the personal experience of the consumer. In a valid scientific manner they analyse products on the axes of 'healthy, green and socially responsible'. The Good Guide is the brainchild of Dara O'Rourke, Professor of Environmental and Labour Policy at the University of California in Berkeley.

O'Rourke created the Good Guide when he realised how little we actually know about the daily products we bring into our homes. To give us all a better picture, he pulled together a team of scientists and technologists, with the purpose of gathering, collating and organising product information over a wide range of sectors, before presenting it to the consumer in easily digestible bites that everyone can understand. It is a brilliant initiative. Take a look at the site for yourself.

Is the Good Guide good news for Apple? Not really. The iPhone only occupies 70th place amongst the 500 mobile phones surveyed. Top spot goes to the Nokia C6, although this scores less well on 'social aspects'. Nobody's perfect – or so it seems.

A FINAL
COMMENT, A
FINAL THOUGHT
AND A FINAL
RECOMMENDER
TIP

Consumers who are more concerned than most about trying to make the world a better place are also more inclined than others to take account of what the recommenders have to say. They also use social media more frequently than others when seeking guidance about purchases (59% as opposed to just 46% of all respondents).[123]

Dave Meyer (founder of Value Stream Performance Advisors): 'Consumers have an unprecedented opportunity to be active shapers of the products and services they buy and use, rather than passive receivers, taking whatever companies provide. Apple's most recent litmus test on corporate social responsibility with its key Chinese supply chain manufacturing partner, Foxconn, and the resulting consumer outcry is but just one example of the power that consumers have to sway products manufacturers to alter their business patterns.'[124]

Good Guide also launched a 'transparency toolbar' that you can add to your browser. I used it to look up Ortiz anchovies and was given a result for them on the right, just above the ads. Try it for yourself with other products. But how they actually decide the way they screen the advertisements is a complete mystery to me!

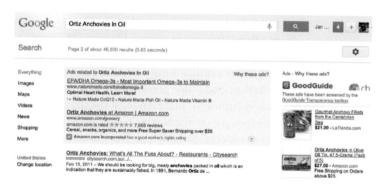

9 Some basic principles for effective recommender marketing (although there is much more to it than just marketing!)

The key to recommender marketing can be summed up in just a single sentence: *always ask everyone whether or not they will consider recommending your brand to their family, friends, colleagues, etc.* You can ask this formally or informally. At the beginning, in the middle or at the end of a conversation about your brand. You can do it online or offline. By telephone or face-to-face in a shop. By ordinary mail or by e-mail. It doesn't matter how you do it – as long as you do it!

If you are still not convinced about the value of this question or the growing importance of the recommender collective, you might as well not bother. For the time being, just limit yourself to the re-reading of this book. Or you can always phone me with a question, or send a mail with your thoughts (jevedebe@gmail.com). Or even invite me around for a chat.

Only begin with the One Question when you are well and truly ready. Because once you start, you will never stop again.

The secret of a successful approach is to continually go in search of data that you probably do not have at the moment or, if you do, only partially. This search includes looking for relevant recommenders, being found by recommenders and collecting data about them. This gradual accumulation and processing of knowledge must be a continuous process. Without a growing network of consumers who dare to open their mouths in favour of your brand and without the relevant data about these consumers, you will not travel very far, because you will be travelling in the dark. And it is, of course, your intention to travel with your eyes wide open towards a very specific destination that each company must decide for itself. Because one thing is certain: a company that travels around in circles is going nowhere very fast – except perhaps to the bankruptcy courts.

WHAT YOU NEED TO KNOW

> You must be aware of the balance of power between the different recommenders in your market. They will decide your share in that market, which in turn will be a reflection of the up-and-down turbulence operating within the group of recommenders.
> You must find out who are the recommenders of your brand and who are not, both at group level and individual level.
> You need to know which recommenders are content-makers and which recommenders are networkers, who spread that content. Remember: they are both recommenders in their different ways!
> You need to know why they recommend your brand – or why not. And what brands are they recommending, if they are not recommending yours.
> Only when you collect and continually update all this data will you be able to understand the individual actors and the relationships within the recommender group.
> Continually enrich your data with data from other non-competing brands, so that you can build up a comprehensive brand profile of the different recommender segments and the individual recommenders.

YOU MUST ALWAYS KNOW WHERE YOUR BRAND
STANDS IN RELATION TO COMPETING BRANDS

With the isolated measurement of the performance of your own brand with your own customers you will not get very far. If your measuring exercise reveals that you have a score of, say, +27, you can be at the top of your branch if all your competitors have a lower score or at the bottom of your branch if they all have a higher score. This is something you have to know!

> The measuring process must be continuous, in much the same way that a barometer continuously predicts the weather.
> Waiting for your sales figures before assessing whether you are doing well or poorly is too slow in this day and age; while you are waiting, opportunities are slipping by.
> Traditional research and reporting is also cumbersome and expensive. You need to be able to act online and in more or less real time.
> The measuring exercise must have a high level of predictive reliability with regard to your future market share. Your data must not only tell you what is happening and why, but must also be actionable. If you just collect data and then do nothing with it, you might as well not have bothered.
> Compare your previously recorded brand and product scores each month and each quarter with your actual sales figures; use relevant correlations to improve the predictive accuracy of your model.

THE STRENGTH (OR WEAKNESS) OF YOUR BRAND MUST BE EXPRESSED IN CLEAR FIGURES THAT ARE ACTIONABLE

Because these figures are the result of the relative balance of market power within the recommender group, you must get to know that group and its individual members as well as you can. This is the only way to understand why the figures are high, low, average, up, down, etc.

> You can already gain considerable insights from published scores and reviews.
> It is also necessary to identify the recommenders individually, so that you can better understand them: age, gender, place of residence, education, job, interests, brand preferences, etc.
> You cannot identify them and understand them unless you talk to them: communicate, converse and engage wherever possible (although you must remember that engagement is a step too far for many consumers).
> Permanently enrich your data with additional information from SMMMMS, which measure online influence (Klout, Kred, Peerreach, Peerindex, etc.)
> Ultimately, you also want to know why they give a high or low score and, above all, what are the weak points that you need to improve. Use intermediary SWOT analyses to define KPIs (Key Performance Indicators) for individuals and departments.

For example:

1. What product improvements are necessary?
2. How and where can you improve the service component?
3. How can you correct the things that are going wrong at the sales points?
4. What approach should you take to service delivery and after sales?
5. How can you introduce new marketing emphases or work more creatively?
6. Can your media investments be better targeted for greater effect?
7. What extra training can you give to underperforming individuals and departments?
8. What additional cross-marketing activities can you plan in relation to your acquired profile knowledge?

To achieve all this, it will be necessary to use a mixture of external and internal tools. Each of these tools must initially focus on the One Question. Once you have the answer to this initial question, you can investigate with further questions – either immediately or gradually – the reasons why people gave you the scores they did. Ultimately, this will allow you to start looking for solutions. Each of these tools has a research and conversation function. These functions are not separate from each other, but overlap. Sometime you will do a multi-brand survey, sometimes for your brand alone and sometimes for a rival brand. Once you start to fit together the various pieces of this puzzle, the overall picture will gradually become clearer.

EXTERNAL TOOLS

Online

> Identify the recommenders. They are active on blogs, review sites, social networks and in fora. It is like asking someone for a dance in a discotheque. Sometimes you will get the brush-off, but sometimes it might be the start of a beautiful friendship. Be friendly and keep on trying – that is the message.
> Invite them to take part in a third-party multi-brand survey. This is more or less what we do with Holaba in China (and has already been described in some detail earlier in the book).

Offline

> Identify the recommenders. Use all the different communication media at your disposal and ask openly and directly to receive people's opinions.

INTERNAL TOOLS

Customers

> Only 15% of your customers will belong to the recommender group. They are not always the customers who spend most money or buy your products most frequently. It is important to know who they are and you will find them in your database if you look hard enough.
> It can certainly help to build up a broader and more complete profile of the recommenders by asking third parties about them. Someone who only gives a score for one brand is probably not a recommender. Third party platforms are also ideal for investigating this aspect.

Interested parties and prospects

> It is useful to learn about other potentially interested parties. In particular, what stage of the purchasing process are they currently in and on what will they base their decision to become a customer – or not.

Ex-customers

> If they are willing, these are the people that you can probably learn most from. They will be able to tell you – from their point of view – precisely where you went wrong. And sometimes you might even be able to win them back.

Your own staff

> You cannot achieve a high score on the external market if your own staff are not giving you a high score internally. Reichheld, Bain and Satmetrix are all evolving towards a more HR-based approach to give greater empowerment to employees, which is certainly a positive step in service and retail companies, where the human factor is crucial in determining the final score.
> It is also interesting to extend your in-house survey to cover suppliers and resellers. They can often have a very different angle of approach, which can sometimes lead them to become recommenders or non-recommenders.

LOOKING FOR A CONSULTANT? For all specific consultancy work in Belgium and the Netherlands relating to NPS you can try Futurelab: http://www.futurelab.net. Their consultants have worked on many NPS projects in Europe, Asia and North America. Many of them also have the official NPS certificate.

Other names that you might like to consider are:
Bing Research: http://www.bing-research.com/
CustomerGauge: http://customergauge.com/
Altuition: http://www.altuition.nl/
Blauw Research: http://www.blauw.com/
Insites: http://www.insites.eu/

BOOK LIST The book list is relatively short. Primarily because relatively little has so far been published on this key subject. But that seems likely to change in the near future. Enjoy your reading.

Brian Solis
The End of Business As Usual: Rewire the Way You Work to Succeed in the Consumer Revolution

Charles Duhigg
The Power of Habit

Dan Ariely
Predictably Irrational, Revised and Expanded Edition: The Hidden Forces That Shape Our Decisions

Dan Ariely
The Upside of Irrationality: The Unexpected Benefits of Defying Logic at Work and at Home

Daniel Kahneman
Thinking, Fast and Slow

10 No more war? Or if that's not possible, at least less rattling of sabres. My end approaches.

P&G's marketing costs have risen by 24% during the past two years. They now amount to $10 billion dollars. During the same period sales have risen by just 6%. Is it the same where you work? We simply cannot carry on like this.

'The overall picture is of a company that is out of control, addicted to advertising budget increases, that lacks discipline and is kidding itself it is healthy because it is getting higher prices for its brands. Success that only comes after heaping increasing amounts of cash into the maw of the marketing beast isn't really "success". It's brute force. At some point, even McDonald (P&G's CEO) will have to admit this is unsustainable and a pullback will be warranted.'[125]

I began in marketing back in 1978. For this reason, I have set three crucial U.S. statistics for that year at a level of 100: advertising expenditure, gross national product and average salary. Thirty years later the average American earns 4.1 times more, GDP has grown 6.8 times and the advertising budget 7.5 times. In other words, advertising has grown (and is still growing) faster than the wealth we create and faster than the wages we pay.

It is primarily the major corporations that are responsible for turning advertising into a giant monster that will soon consume $500 billion

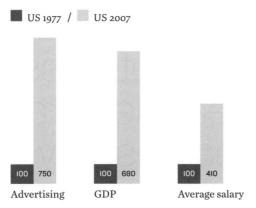

| 100 | 750 | | 100 | 680 | | 100 | 410 |
| Advertising | | | GDP | | | Average salary | |

dollars each year worldwide. And there is seemingly no end in sight, notwithstanding the global economic crisis that threatens to turn into a recession in Europe.

At least the advertising monster is growing more slowly in the U.S. at the moment. 'Just' 2.7%. Lower than the world average.

In contrast, the online share of this colossal budget is rising steadily, currently at a rate of 12.8% per annum. Online advertising now accounts for 18% of all advertising expenditure. Fifteen years ago it was nothing. Now it is worth $83.2 billion dollars. Worldwide.

The argument of the advertising apostle – an argument they never tire of telling – is very similar to the argument put forward by those who defend high levels of expenditure on defence (or aggression, if you look at it from a different perspective). The argument runs as follows: 'To defend my share of market against new threats I need money. To win market share against these others I need even more money.'

Surprisingly enough (or possibly not), the two nations with the highest levels of defence expenditure are also the two nations that spend most on advertising. At the end of 2011, China surpassed Japan and moved into the number 2 spot. Japan's advertising budget fell to $32.7 billion dollars, a consequence of the country's continuing economic malaise and the terrible tsunami of spring 2011.

In the same year, advertising in China continued to leap forward, this time by 14%, good for a total (according to international figures) of $38 billion dollars – and second place on the big spenders list, behind the United States.

THE
FASCINATING
– AND OFTEN
AMAZING –
WORLD OF
CHINESE
STATISTICS

According to Charm Communications (Nasdaq: CHRM) in 2011 advertising expenditure in China grew to ¥669.3 billion RMB. That in not $38 billion dollars but more than $100 billion dollars! Whoever has followed developments in China in recent years knows that Chinese figures and statistics are not to be trusted. So is it $38 billion or $100 billion? Who will tell us the truth? Or can you discover the truth for yourself? Not easy.

According to another official source, Chinese advertising expenditure amounted to ¥300 billion yuan in 2011. That is neither $38 billion nor $100 billion. It is $47.62 billion.

The official releasing these statistics (conducted by Zhou Bohua) was quick to emphasise that in 1979 there were only a handful of advertising companies, with a total turnover of just ¥10 million RMB.

The sector now employs 1.33 million people in more than 200 companies. Holaba is one of them, employing eight local people in our team.[126]

Whatever the truth of the statistics, enough is enough. Or rather, too much is too much. If all that money actually brought in a good return, then we could at least indulge ourselves in some 'on the one

Top 10 shares of world military expenditure in 2010

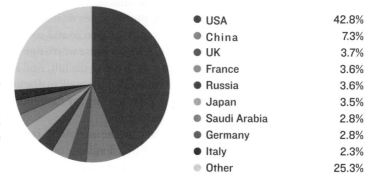

● USA	42.8%
● China	7.3%
● UK	3.7%
● France	3.6%
● Russia	3.6%
● Japan	3.5%
● Saudi Arabia	2.8%
● Germany	2.8%
● Italy	2.3%
● Other	25.3%

http://www.mrwonkish.nl/
defensie-uitgaven-
per-land-kaboem
http://www.iab.net/
insights_research/
industry_data_and_
landscape/1675/1846707

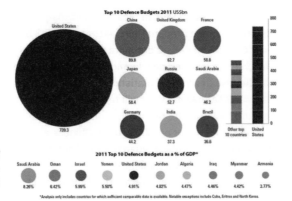

Top 10 Defence Budgets 2011 US$bn

http://motherjones.com/
mojo/2012/03/military-
spending-2011-chart

hand…on the other hand' thinking. But that is not the case. Or if there wasn't such a growing mood of anti-advertising hatred throughout the world, then perhaps we could live with the situation more easily.

In reality, however, there is now nothing that can reasonably justify this massive expenditure of € 500 billion euros each year.

Companies that use their intelligence no longer attack markets in the same way that the United States has attacked Iraq, Afghanistan and other countries in recent years. No, they now build up a secret army from the ranks of their own volunteer guerrilla troops. An army that doesn't need to be forced into action, soldiers that don't expect to be paid – but also people that they cannot ultimately control. This is the army of the recommenders. And they are directly responsible for between 20 and 50% of all the purchases we make – a huge number. If this means that we can scrap between 20 and 50% of our advertising expenditure, then that really is a cause worth fighting. A cause that I would be prepared to defend, up to the hilt. And I have high hopes.

Why have I left it to the end of the book to discuss this theme? Because I can't finish without getting my thoughts on these matters off my chest. A man's gotta do…

I have an intense dislike for the monotone, invasive, seemingly well-run super-organisms that dominate our world. They are dangerous because they only march in one direction. As dangerous as cancer. They only live to kill. A plague of locusts is less potentially destructive. At least locusts are nomadic, fading away to nothing when the cold weather comes.

Movements often begin underground, appearing from nowhere and cleverly working their way to the surface. Like moles. Some of these movements initially have a liberating effect (they see the light in the darkness and show that same light of hope to their followers), but this enlightened phase does not last long, so that they eventually come to defend what they originally opposed: the repugnance of power. A power they then assume – and misuse. Back in the dark.

It seems that during the different phases of my life I have always had to fight one or other of these demons. Movements that I cherished at first, sometimes to the extent of being a fanatical follower (often to the annoyance of those around me), but that I later cast aside. Because they were slowly strangling me.

It began with Christianity. I think that up to about my fifteenth birthday I believed that God actually did exist. I believed the people who told me the old stories. God managed to survive in my heart just ten years longer than Santa Claus. By then I had seen through the deceit of those who had created him and now preached in his name. And so I dumped him. I carried on the show for a number of years, reading out the morally improving prayers in our cosy village church, but always injecting the texts with more militant social themes. It sounds tame now, but it was fairly shocking in those early post-Vatican II years of the 1960s.

After God had left, Marx, Engels, Lenin, Stalin and Mao entered my life, albeit via the back door. They were (understandably) more earthly role models than the Divine Creator and in that worldly phase of my rebellious young life they offered something more concrete and more attractive than the promise of eternal bliss in an unreachable heaven. The Red Top Five had at least written and developed their own philosophy for themselves. Without apostles. And they were real people, not an imaginary being. Marx had even lived in Brussels for a time. They had all been men who spent a large part of their life opposing what they saw as the forces of evil. But with the exception of Marx and Engels, they went on to become the very incarnation of that evil. As soon as the old reactionary guard had been eliminated, they simply became a new and even more terrible form of precisely the same thing. And so once again I moved into the opposition camp. It was 1976 – a month before Mao died.

Unfortunately, 'being in opposition' is not a very good basis for a professional career or a career of any kind (the pay is lousy). Between dreams and reality money always intrudes. If you want to make your dreams come true, you need the cash to do it. Simple as that. And so it was that in 1977 I found myself working (more or less by chance) in advertising. My first job! As a copywriter. Because even back in those days I could write. Fairly well, in fact. At last I was earning the money that would allow me to live my dreams. And that earning gradually went better and better. So good, in fact, that I decided to start my own advertising agency. With a group of friends and a whole lot of hubris. The year was 1991.

Yet all the time I was troubled by a kind of ambivalent (almost schizophrenic) feeling towards the things I had to do to earn my living. People who knew me could see that something was not quite right; that things were not exactly as they should be. For many years I regarded – and sometimes still regard – advertising as a 'fine' profession, but I was always aware that we were nothing more than the necessary lubricant for market penetration and profit maximisation. The cheerleaders of Capitalism. We had fun, of course, lots of fun. And as long as the lubricant is stimulating and exciting, it is great to be paid large sums of money to find new ways to amuse bored consumers. But... There was always a but.

After a while, the lubricant was no longer able to stimulate the way it once had (a mental form of erectile dysfunction) and suddenly you find yourself confronted with the growing irrelevance of your once-so-promising professional activity. By now we were in 1994. I had been in advertising for 17 years and the first mentions of something new called 'the internet' were starting to appear in the press. It seemed to arrive from nowhere. From the underworld. From the opposition. (In fact, it came from the United States army, but we overlooked that at the time). I was hooked immediately. In that single year, 1994, it became clear to me that this new phenomenon would one day turn the advertising industry, my industry, on its head. And so I decided to embrace the internet as the 'Great Liberator'. I gave lectures about it to empty halls. At a time when most people in Belgium had never even heard of the worldwide web, I was already active on it. I pioneered the country's very first interactive advertising agency, Boondoggle. (It was only in 2011 that I finally sold my shares.)

A few years earlier a new man had come into my life. A certain Reichheld. I knew of him from his other books about loyalty. But I was not a great loyalty fan. However, in 2003 he wrote an article in the *Harvard Business Review* under the title 'The one number you need to grow'. Unintentionally, it was a plea for the manner in which we had already been doing business in our interactive agency for some time: focusing all attention on a small group of fanatical consumers, who regularly visited the sites of our customers, asking for samples, inviting friends, playing games, taking part in communities... In short, the recommenders.

I can hear you thinking: 'How long is he going to remain a Reichheldian?' I have no idea. At the beginning of 2012 I attended the first large meeting of NPS advocates in San Francisco, and it felt good. Yet perhaps that can be dangerous as well. There was almost a religious zeal in the conference hall. Not only from the early adopters, like me, but also from the newcomers.

The recommender movement has scarcely begun. It still has much to learn... whereas I am very clearly coming towards the end of my professional career. This book is therefore a closing of accounts. A swan-song. An epitaph. A first and last venture into the world of literature. Writing is too difficult for me. When I write, I get cold feet and red cheeks. I used to pen headliners of 17 words and body copy of 100 words. That was a piece of cake. I have now written a work of more than 65,000 words. Yet even now I have the feeling that it is still very much a 'work in progress'; that there are still too many things about which there is too much uncertainty. In this sense, the book has come too early. But it is too late to worry about that now. It is finished and will have to stand as it is. I hope that you will recommend it.

Footnotes

Are you a recommender?

1 http://commons.wikimedia.org/wiki/File:Michelangelo_Caravaggio_021.jpg

2 My personal calculation of the Share of Voice (SOV) of the recommenders is an estimate of what it could/should be, based on a mixture of common sense, expereince, literature and empirical research.

3 According to Dunbar, most of us have, on average, about 3-5 intimate friends whom we speak to at least weekly, and about 10-15 more friends whose deaths would greatly distress us (http://mentalmultivitamin. blogspot.com/2011/06/in-short-while-friendships-decay-if-not.html).

Chapter 1

4 http://www.standaard.be/artikel/detail.aspx?artikelid=3D3KDGGS

5 The Reichheld Question: How likely is it that you will recommend this brand to your family, friends and neighbours? You can answer this question with a score between 0 (very unlikely) and 10 (very likely).

6 Chapter 2 deals with this question in detail. If you want to know more, you can read that chapter first.

7 Lesbian, Gay, Bisexual, Trans-sexual.

8 http://www.tripadvisor.com/members/jevedebe

9 http://amazonfiretablet.us/usaa-jetblue-airways-symantec-trader-joes-vanguard-amazon-com-among-the-highest-in-customer-loyalty-in-satmetrix-2011-net-promoter-benchmarks.

10 Memetics is a controversial theory of mental content based on an analogy with Darwinian evolution, originating from the popularisation of Richard Dawkins' 1976 book The Selfish Gene. (It purports to be an approach to evolutionary models of cultural information transfer.) (http://en.wikipedia.org/wiki/Memetics).

11 http://www.martinlindstrom.com/fast-company-we-know-what-you-want-and-when-you-will-buy-it/

252

12 http://experiencematters.wordpress.com/2011/11/23/cx-insights-from-marriott-and-jetblue/

13 http://articles.businessinsider.com/2012-02-01/strategy/31011905_1_employee-unions-pension-benefit-guaranty-corporation-amr#ixzz1lnze6YDD

14 http://www.netpromoter.com/resources/benchmarks.jsp

15 http://www.yelp.com/biz/trader-joes-wayne-2

16 http://www.boostctr.com/blog/facebook-ad-tips/cialdini-consistency-and-facebook-likes/

17 http://www.brainjuicer.com/ BrainJuicer is the only agency to have won ESOMAR's Best Methodology award twice in the last 23 years, along with a number of other awards for innovation and entrepreneurship.

18 http://media.brainjuicer.com/media/files/Super_Bowl-Orlando_Wood-Contagious-March_2012.pdf

19 McKinsey Quarterly, April 2010.

20 Keller Fay has long tracked that about 90% of brand-related word of mouth conversations take place offline, which is face-to-face and voice-to-voice. Less than 10% of word of mouth conversations happen online through social media, email, and text (http://www.kellerfay.com/insights/importance-of-technology-conversation-catalysts153/).

21 http://www.psychologicalscience.org/index.php/news/releases/why-do-we-share-our-feelings-with-others.html

Chapter 2

22 If all the brands in a particular branch together spend 100% on all forms of advertising and a single brand accounts for 8% of this expenditure, that brand will acquire an 8% share of voice

23 Ina Garnefeld, Sabrina Helm and Andreas Eggert: Walk Your Talk: An Experimental Investigation of the Relationship Between Word of Mouth and Communicators' Loyalty (http://jsr.sagepub.com/content/14/1/93.refs.html).

24 http://www.marketingtribune.nl/nieuws/nps-je-raadt-het-je-klanten-niet-aan

25 Why did you give the score you gave (high, neutral or low)? What do we have to improve to get a higher score?

26 http://www.amazon.com/Ultimate-Question-Revised-Expanded-Edition/dp/1422173356

27 The study showed that 20% of the 'satisfied' customers intended to

leave the company in question, whilst 28% of the 'dissatisfied' cus-   **253**
tomers intended to stay (http://www.mycustomer.com/topic/market-
ing/customer-effort-score-worth-effort/140474).

28 http://www.marketingcharts.com/direct/company-executives-struggle-
with-customer-intelligence-21608/?utm_campaign=newsletter&utm_
source=mc&utm_medium=textlink

29 http:/www.managementthinking.eiu.com/sites/default/files/
downloads/Oracle_SalesandMarketing_120207r1.pdf

30 http://www.afaqs.com/news/story/26844_The-Chinese-are-a-
pragmatic-lot:-Tom-Doctoroff-JWT-China

31 http://www.business-standard.com/india/news/the-consumer-
isqueen/465884/

Chapter 3

32 http://www.vn.nl/Archief/Wetenschapmilieu/Artikel-Wetenschap-
milieu/Het-web-rond-Diederik-Stapel.htm

33 Less than a third of young Americans agreed with the statement
'I feel free to do and say things (online) I wouldn't do or say offline,'
and 41% disagreed. Among Chinese respondents, 73% agreed and just
9% disagreed (http://online.wsj.com/article/SB10001424052702303360
504577408493723814210.html?mod=WSJAsia_hpp_LEFTTopStories).

34 Roger Dooley, 'Money, Social Status Similar in Brain' (http://www.
neurosciencemarketing.com/blog/articles/money-status-brain.htm)

35 http://www.business-standard.com/india/news/the-consumer-
isqueen/465884/

36 http://www.sfgate.com/cgi-bin/article.cgi?f=/g/a/2012/03/06/
prweb9249647.DTL#ixz z10T2ucw6

37 http://www.sfgate.com/cgi-bin/article.cgi?f=/g/a/2012/03/06/
prweb9249647.DTL#ixz z10T2ucw6

38 Starting in 2006, Wave 6 is the world's largest and longest-running
study of the impact of social media on today's global marketplace –
making UM the most authoritative agency voice in the social media space.

39 http://www.warc.com/LatestNews/News/Brand_website_visits_
decline.news?ID=2950

40 SMMMMS = Social Media Monitoring, Measuring and Management
Systems

41 http://www.pewinternet.org/Reports/2011/Technology-and-social-
networks/Part-3/SNS-users.aspx

42 http://www.sfgate.com/cgi-bin/article.cgi?f=/g/a/2012/03/06/
    prweb9249647.DTL#ixzz10T36B2er

Chapter 4

43 http://www.thecomputerboy.com/2012/02/03/how-many-friends-of-
    friends-do-you-have/

44 http://www.gtellis.net/Publications.aspx

45 I make a distinction between a 'recommender' and an 'influencer'.
    The former talks more freely and with less obligation than the latter.
    The recommender gives his opinion. The influencer too, but he is
    more insistant, pushy even. Forrester uses the word 'influencer',
    whereas the person he describes strikes me a being much closer
    to what I call a recommender.

46 Forrester. 27 April, 2010. Select group of consumers drive word-
    of-mouth.

47 The act of disclosing information about oneself activates the same
    sensation of pleasure in the brain that we get from eating food,
    getting money or having sex.
    http://www.latimes.com/business/technology/la-fi-tn-self-disclosure-
    study-20120508,0,7870124.story

48 http://www.marbridgeconsulting.com/marbridgedaily/2012-02-09/ar-
    ticle/53487/rumor_chinas_app_boosting_service_firms_reach_300

49 http://www.emarketer.com/Article.aspx?R=1008865&ecid=a65060336
    75d47f881651943c21c5ed4

50 http://www.tnooz.com/2012/02/28/news/tripadvisor-dips-toe-into-
    world-of-verified-reviews-via-collection-service-for-partners/

51 http://www.internetreputation.com/testimonials
    http://www.internetreputation.com/information/how-to-remove-
    bad-yelp-reviews
    http://www.bosshi.com/why-yelp-sucks/

52 http://www.investmentu.com/2012/March/yelp-ipo-tech-bubble.html

53 http://www.cluetrain.com/ The Cluetrain Manifesto is a set of 95 the-
    ses organised and put forward as a manifesto, or call to action, for all
    businesses operating within what is suggested to be a newly-connect-
    ed marketplace. The ideas put forward within the manifesto aim to
    examine the impact of the internet on both markets (consumers) and
    organisations. In addition, since both consumers and organisations
    are able to utilise the internet and intranets to establish a previously

unavailable level of communication both within and between these two groups, the manifesto suggests that changes will be required from organisations as they respond to the new marketplace environment.

54 http://www.flowresulting.nl/knowhow/carglass-loyale-klanten-door-klantfocus-in-de-hele-organisatie/

55 http://www.frankwatching.com/archive/2012/05/07/top-100-neder-landse-merken-op-social-media-sentiment-bereik/

56 http://www.marketingonline.nl/nieuws/bericht/de-impact-van-sociale-media-op-grote-merken/
http://www.slideshare.net/Greenberrynl/top100merken-whitepaper-greenberry
http://www.frankwatching.com/archive/2012/05/07/top-100-neder-landse-merken-op-social-media-sentiment-bereik/

57 http://en.wikipedia.org/wiki/Social_grooming. In social animals, including humans, social grooming or allogrooming is an activity in which individuals in a group clean or maintain one another's body or appearance. It is a major social activity, and a means by which animals which live in proximity may bond and reinforce social structures, family links, and build relationships. Social grooming also is used as a form of reconciliation and a means of conflict resolution in some species.

58 http://psychcentral.com/news/2012/03/21/does-facebook-launch-a-thousand-narcissists/36307.html

59 Saturday, 17 March 2012. https://apps.facebook.com/theguardian/technology/2012/mar/17/facebook-dark-side-study-aggressive-narcissism.

60 Online Display Advertising: Targeting and Obtrusiveness, Avi Goldfarb and Catherine Tucker, February 2010.

Chapter 5

61 http://zuberance.com/ powers millions of Social Recommendations for leading brands on Facebook, Twitter, Yelp, Amazon and more.

62 http://en.wikipedia.org/wiki/Duncan_J._Watts

63 http://www.clickorlando.com/news/Arrest-made-in-The-Senator-tree-fire/-/1637132/9146402/-/v3we2h/-/index.html

64 http://en.wikipedia.org/wiki/Two-step_flow_of_communication

65 http://www.bbc.co.uk/news/technology-15844230

66 http://www.amazon.com/The-Influentials-American-Tells-Other/dp/0743227298

256

67 Experimental Study of Inequality and Unpredictability in an Artificial Cultural Market (http://www.princeton.edu/~mjs3/salganik_dodds_watts06_full.pdf).

68 'How Content Is Really Shared: Close Friends, Not 'Influencers' The Best Way to 'Go Viral' Is Engage Millions Who Share In Small Networks. Jack Krawczyk, Jon Steinberg Published: 7 March 2012 (http://adage.com/article/digitalnext/content-shared-close-friends-influencers/233147/)

69 http://www.tripadvisor.com/ShowUserReviews-g190454-d482579-r130947034-Hollmann_Beletage-Vienna.html

Chapter 6

70 https://loyalty360.org/resources/research/making-every-interaction-count-how-customer-intelligence-drives-customer-lo

71 In addition to information access, two heavily-used areas of eWorld were the eMail Centre and Community Centre. The Community Centre offered chat rooms and an online BBS where thousands of ePeople (eWorld users) congregated to chat about various subjects. The eMail Centre was a virtual post office. The service also housed support and Apple technical documents.

72 Philip Sheldrake is the author of The Business of Influence, Wiley, 2011. He is a founding partner of Meanwhile, the venture marketers, and chairs the CIPR's social media measurement group. He blogs at philipsheldrake.com. http://www.guardian.co.uk/media-network/media-network-blog/2012/feb/15/complexity-influence-challenge-opportunity

73 http://thenextweb.com/facebook/2012/03/29/instagram-photos-are-the-most-annoying-facebook-photo-trend-and-could-get-you-unfriended/?awesm=tnw.to_1DqPg

74 http://en.wiktionary.org/wiki/cipher

75 https://plus.google.com/116416314233992548280/posts/4WonVFkQUk1

76 http://www.bizreport.com/2012/01/31-of-display-ads-go-unseen.html

77 http://www.theatlantic.com/technology/archive/2012/05/people-click-on-about-one-of-every-2000-facebook-ads-they-see/257229/

78 http://public.dhe.ibm.com/common/ssi/ecm/en/gbe03391usen/GBE03391USEN.PDF

79 http://www.forbes.com/sites/ciocentral/2011/08/14/how-valuable-are-heavy-social-media-users-anyway/

80 http://www.businessinsider.com/facebook-commerce-2012-2?nr_

email_referer=1&utm_source=Triggermail&utm_medium=email&utm_term=SAI%20Select&utm_campaign=SAI%20Select%20Mondays%20 2012-02-20#ixzz1mxJhsTZK

81 http://www.marketingonline.nl/nieuws/bericht/facebook-veel-fans-betekent-meer-investeren/

82 Click Through Rates (CTRs): the relationship between the number of times that a banner is shown and the number of times that someone clicks on it. Not all banners that are shown are actaully seen. And not all banners that are seen are actually clicked on.

83 Carrie-Ann Skinner. http://www.pcadvisor.co.uk/news/internet/3338348/41-of-brits-getting-bored-of-social-networks/

84 http://www.fool.com/investing/general/2012/05/11/why-linkedin-is-so-much-more-than-a-social-network.aspx

85 'How likely is it that you will recommend this brand to you friends, colleagues, neighbours, family, etc.?'

86 Are brands measuring social media marketing incorrectly? Opinion, Marketing Week

87 Are brands measuring social media marketing wrong? Friday, 17 February 2012, by Sebastian Joseph

88 Data sourced from JD Power; additional content by Warc staff, 19 March 2012 (http://www.warc.com/LatestNews/News/EmailNews.news?ID=29590&Origin=WARCNewsEmail)

89 Data sourced from Marketing Week; additional content by Warc staff, 2 April 2012 (http://www.warc.com/LatestNews/News/EmailNews.news?ID=29650 &Origin=WARCNewsEmail). Brands fail to engage social media users.

90 http://www.telegraph.co.uk/technology/facebook/9175756/Women-ditching-TV-guide-for-Facebook.html

Chapter 7

91 http://www.briansolis.com/2012/03/report-the-rise-of-digital-influence/

92 http://www.goldbachinteractive.com/current-news/technical-papers/social-media-monitoring-report-2011

93 The practice of publishing APIs has allowed web communities to create an open architecture for sharing content and data between communities and applications. In this way, content that is created in one place can be dynamically posted and updated in multiple locations on the web (http://en.wikipedia.org/wiki/Application_programming_interface).

94 http://www.brandrepublic.com/news/1079339/the-br-200-july-2011-
webs-influential-bloggers-151-200/

95 http://www.constructionmarketinguk.co.uk/2011/11/07/klout-gate-
kontd-krazy-klout-and-other-cartoons/

96 http://www.fastcompany.com/most-innovative-companies/2012/in-
dustry/advertising#klout

97 http://mashable.com/2011/11/04/klout-twitter-half-life-study/

98 http://www.jeffbullas.com/2009/10/02/twitter-power-poll-what-
makes-a-brand-or-person-influential-on-twitter/

99 www.peerperks.com en http://www.wired.co.uk/news/ar-
chive/2012-02/24/peerperks

100 http://www.cmswire.com/cms/social-business/social-sentiment-
plugin-analyzes-twitter-facebook-in-real-time-013153.php

101 http://siliconangle.com/blog/2011/10/19/consumer-revolution-the-
power-is-now-in-our-hands/MELLISA TOLENTINO | OCTOBER 19TH

102 http://researchaccess.com/2012/02/exclusive-dr-minh-duong-van-
applies-physics-principles-to-text-analytics/

103 http://blog.questionpro.com/2011/11/17/pay-attention-to-sentiment-
analysis-its-where-social-media-chatter-is-going/

104 http://www.brandrepublic.com/bulletin/digitalambulletin/article/
1125378/dell-pay-customers-promote-products-social-media/
?DCMP=EMC-CONDigitalAM

Chapter 8

105 http://en.wikipedia.org/wiki/Striatum

106 http://blog.futurelab.net/2008/04/money_social_status_similar_in.ht ml.

107 http://www.kurkdroog.be/

108 http://www.slideshare.net/CM1234/microinteractions-presentation

109 http://www.bizreport.com/2012/02/study-mobile-banner-ads-very-
unpopular.html

110 http://www.digitaltrends.com/web/amazon-reviews-have-as-much-
weight-as-professional-critics-says-new-study/#ixzz1uzUFp0RF

111 A Mobile Virtual Private Network – like Mobile Vikings – operates on
an existing telecom network, but builds up its own mix of products
and services on that network. Mobile Vikings works from the platform
of KPN, the largest telecom distibutor in the Netherlands.

112 A knarr is a type of Viking cargo ship, which was 16 metres long and
capable of carrying 24 tons of cargo (http://en.wikipedia.org/wiki/Knarr).

113 http://reinfecta.wordpress.com/2011/11/05/klein-is-fijn-1-adieu-proximus/

114 http://www.nytimes.com/2012/01/26/business/ieconomy-apples-ipad-and-the-human-costs-for-workers-in-china.html?pagewanted=all

115 http://www.eweek.com/c/a/Mobile-and-Wireless/Occupy-Apple-Protests-Follow-Foxconn-Revelations-595871/

116 http://www.change.org/petitions/apple-protect-workers-making-iphones-in-chinese-factories-3

117 http://www.washingtonpost.com/business/economy/petition-calls-for-ethical-iphone-5/2012/01/31/gIQAegnvfQ_story.html

118 http://www.triplepundit.com/2012/02/pressed-protestors-apple-agrees-external-audit-supply-chain/

119 http://www.wired.com/gadgetlab/2012/02/apple-foxconn-investigations/

120 http://www.wired.com/gadgetlab/2012/02/apple-foxconn-investigations/

121 http://www.harrispollonline.com/

122 2012_Harris_Poll_RQ_Summary_Report

123 http://www.marketwatch.com/story/nielsen-identifies-attributes-of-the-global-socially-conscious-consumer-2012-03-27

124 http://sustainablebusinessforum.com/davemeyer01/56688/scalable-consumption-supply-chain-circular-economy-hope-sustainable-economies

Chapter 10

125 http://www.cbsnews.com/8301-505123_162-42750888/a-study-in-waste-pgs-ad-spend-bloat/

126 http://economictimes.indiatimes.com/news/news-by-industry/services/advertising/chinas-advertising-revenues-exceed-47-billion/articleshow/12067685.cms